13th Nordic Conference of Computational Linguistics (NODALIDA 2001)

Uppsala, Sweden
21 – 22 May 2001

ISBN: 978-1-5108-3517-7

TABLE OF CONTENTS

From Word Alignment to Machine Translation via Superlinks

Lars Ahrenberg
Department of Computer and Information Science
Linköpings universitet
S-58183 Linköping
lah@ida.liu.se

Håkan Jonsson
Nordisk Språkteknologie A/S
P.O. Box 93
N-5701 Voss
Hakan.Jonsson@gri.no

Abstract

This paper presents a data-driven lexicalist framework for machine translation based on alignment. In addition to word alignment that provides the word correspondences of source and target language, the system uses classifications of the correspondences based on supertags. We first give an overview of the framework, pointing out its fundamental concepts and then report some results from a pilot implementation and evaluation on the ATIS domain.

1. Introduction

Automatic word alignment systems have reached a level of performance that make them useful for a number of applications including machine translation.

A problem with many current systems, though, especially when applied in the construction of machine translation systems, is that they align surface strings with no information on properties such as part-of-speech or sense. Moreover, they do not provide information on the context of a word correspondence. Unless this information is provided somehow, it is impossible to select the correct alternative translation(s) for a given context. To illustrate, consider the following extract from a (constructed) parallel text:

(a) They will win.   *De kommer att vinna.*
(b) Did they win?   *Vann de?*
(c) They did win.   *De vann faktiskt.*
(d) They never win. *De vinner aldrig.*

Given more data of this kind a word alignment system would be able to find the lexical correspondences *win:vinna*, *win:vann*, and *win:vinner*. Moreover, it would also find correspondences such as *they:de* and *will:kommer_att*. These correspondences do not suffice, however, to determine the proper translation of *win* for any of the English sentences above, as there is no information at hand to guide the choice.

Methods for statistical machine translation such as Brown et al. (1990, 1993) have some measures at their disposal to handle alternatives in translation. First, the dictionary is probabilistic so that every alternative translation is assigned a probability. But consistent selection of one alternative will obviously give the wrong alternative in many cases, so these probabilities would have to be conditioned by contextual factors. One possibility is a bigram language model for the target language. Another possibility employed by these early approaches were to make translation contingent on alignment of word positions. However, none of these methods is sufficient to differentiate the translations in pairs (b) and (c) above.

In this paper we present a way of representing and processing word correspondences with their local context that enables their immediate use in a system for automatic translation. We refer to this representation as a *superlink* (cf. Ahrenberg, 2000) and the method of translation as *Superlink Constrained Lexical Transfer (SCLT)*. The paper is organised as follows: Sections 2 and 3 provide an overview of the framework. Section 4 presents an initial experiment of constructing a translation system from a translation corpus of the ATIS-domain (Jonsson, 2000).

2. Supertags and superlinks

A superlink is, basically, a pair of supertags, where one element of the pair refers to the source language and the other element refers to the target language. A supertag is "a rich description of a lexical item that impose complex constraints in a local context" (Bangalore and Joshi, 1999 : 237).

While Bangalore and Joshi use the LTAG formalism in their work, the formalism of the supertags as well as their scope can be chosen in different ways. The tags used in our work so far have a more limited power of expression.

We make a general distinction between *inherent* tags and *relational* tags. A relational tag includes an argument, while an inherent tag does not. The inherent tags used here bear strong resemblance to traditional POS-tags, but have in some of our experiments been augmented with semantic properties.

TABLE 1.　　**Some inherent tags from the English ATIS tagset**

Tag	Meaning	Examples
DIS	Det, indefinite, singular	"a"
NAS	Common noun, singular	"flight"
PMS	Proper noun, city	"Boston"
PSS	Pronoun, subject, singular	"I", "he"
SS	Preposition, spatial	"from"
VIB	Verb, indefinite base form	"need"

TABLE 2.　　**Possible relational tags in the SCOTS notation**

Tag	Meaning
LeftOf(X)	item is to the left of argument X.
LeftAdj(X)	item is left-adjacent to argument X.
RightOf(X)	item is to the right of argument X.
RightAdj(X)	item is right-adjacent to argument X.
First	item is first in the sentence.
Last	item is last in the sentence.

A few examples of inherent tags are given in Table 1, while the full set of relational tags used in the evaluation are given in Table 2. Note that relational tags are restricted to a few linear relations between words in a string. The argument X of the relational tags can be of three kinds: a token, an inherent tag or a disjunctive set of inherent tags. A supertag in our framework, then, is a conjunctive set of inherent and relational tags. An example of a superlink fitting the word correspondence *win:vinna* in sentence (a) is <VIB&RightAdj(VR) :: VIB&RightOf(VFR)>.

3. A translation model based on superlinks

Now, given the notion of a superlink we can give a characterization of the translation relation between the sentences of two languages for a given text type:

A sentence T is a translation of a (well-formed) sentence S iff

- There is a set of token alignments $<s_i, t_i>$ such that S' = s_1 s_2 ... s_n is a proper tokenization of S and T is a well-formed permutation of T' = t_1 t_2 ... t_n, where some of the t_i may be null tokens.
- For every pair $<s_i, t_i>$ there exists a superlink $<ST_i, TT_i>$ such that (i) ST_i is a proper supertag for s_i, and (ii) TT_i is a proper supertag for t_i.

This definition of the translation relation decomposes it into three relations: Thus, S is related to S' via tokenization, S' to T' via transfer, and T' to T via transposition (or permutation). However, as the transfer phase is based on the superlinks we must introduce the supertags in the processing somehow; this is done in a separate monolingual tagging phase. Finally, the transposition phase was extended with a phase of output formating to simplify the treatment of compounds, altogether giving a translation process in five stages: tokenization, tagging, transfer, transposition and output formatting.

The superlinks employed in the transfer stage act as filters on the set of translations for a given word. Probabilities may also be used at this stage. The transposition stage reorders target language words so as to satisfy constraints associated with target language supertags. Finally, output formatting performs tasks such as capitalization and compounding.

The framework can be described as lexicalist and data-driven. It is lexicalist in the sense that all processing operates on strings of lexical items (tokens). It is data-driven since a large part of the knowledge is supposed to be derived from translation corpora.

The most important knowledge sources in the system are the following:

- A source dictionary SDIC associating source tokens with supertags for the source language,
- A target dictionary TDIC associating target tokens with supertags for the target language,
- A transfer dictionary WLINKS associating source tokens with target tokens,

- A superlink dictionary SLINKS associating souce language supertags with target language supertags.

Every dictionary in this list may be obtained automatically from a translation corpus, or by generalizing results obtained from such a corpus. The source and target dictionaries are obtained from tagged versions of the translation corpus. The transfer dictionary WLINKS is obtained from (possibly corrected) links generated by a word alignment program. The superlink dictionary can be obtained in the same way as the transfer dictionary by looking at the tags rather than the words.

The central idea for transfer in this model is that the set of potential translations of a source token is filtered by the superlinks that are compatible with the actual local context. Hence the name Superlink-Constrained Lexical Transfer (SCLT).

The result of lexical transfer is a bag of pairs <token, supertag> for the target language. When several source tokens have alternative translations that are jointly allowed by WLINKS, TDIC and SLINKS, the number of bags can become quite large. In the prototype system all bags were in fact multiplied out and the set was pruned when a certain threshold had been reached.

The rules concerned with target language word order can take on a variety of forms. The general idea is to find those sequences that satisfy the constraints given by the target language supertags.

4. Evaluation

The purpose of the evaluation was to create a prototype system that could serve as a proof-of-concept for the proposed method. This prototype we refer to as SCOTS, Superlink COnstraint Transfer lexicalist translation System.

Some specific questions were:

- What could be achieved by creating all necessary translation data automatically? In particular, how would this system compare with a baseline system doing word-for-word translation based on most frequent alignments for tokens of the English source file?
- What would be the difference in performance between automatic versions and versions where translation data are improved manually?

- Would the system, in any version, be able to reproduce the corpus, or produce translations of the same standard as those in the corpus?

The overall strategy was to run and test SCOTS in a variety of different conditions. Many potential variables could be manipulated to create different testing conditions but full and systematic variation of these variables is not possible. A selection of test cases had to be made, where some of these variables were explored. In order to do this, three test series were devised.

In the first test series tag sets were varied on both the English and the Swedish side. Here though, we only report results for the most elaborated tag set. Automatic alignment was also contrasted with manual alignment. All supertags were trigram tags, i.e. every word is given information about its inherent tag and the inherent tags of its two nearest neighbours. For instance, the word *Boston* occuring in the context '*from Boston to*' would be assigned the trigram tag (PMS, RightAdj(SS), LeftAdj(SS)).

In the second test series the knowledge sources were improved manually after inspection of system errors. The third test series was performed to investigate some issues that had arised during the first two series. For lack of space, we cannot report all of the evaluation here, but give only a brief summary.

The corpus chosen for the experiment was a small English-Swedish corpus of machine-translated sentences from the ATIS domain, where the translations were produced by the SLT system (Agnäs et al., 1995). This corpus was chosen partly because we wanted to see whether the SCLT method could produce results similar to a knowledge-based MT system. A few sample translations from the corpus are given in Figure 1.

The corpus was divided into a training set consisting of 232 sentence pairs and a test set comprising 30 pairs.

In all test cases translation was performed in the direction from English to Swedish.

does continental fly from denver to san francisco
flyger continental airlines från denver till san francisco

what ground transportation is available in boston.
vad finns det för marktransport i boston.

i would like a flight from philadelphia to dallas.
jag skulle vilja ha en flygning från philadelphia till dallas.

Figure 1. Example translations in the ATIS corpus.

4.1 Extraction and construction of translation data

The process of extracting translation information was divided into three stages. The stages are ordered in such a way that the actions in each stage are prerequisite to carry out the next.

In stage 1, the preprocessing stage, tokens are created. A phrase extraction tool (Merkel & Andersson, 2000) was used to retrieve recurrent multi-word units (MWUs) automatically from both the English and the Swedish halves of the ATIS corpus.

Then the tokenized English and Swedish input files were tagged using a Brill tagger with the different tag sets. From this output each token was assigned a trigram tag.

In stage 2, required files were automatically generated using different combinations of tokens and tagged language files. All such generations were only done using the training corpus. Several different versions of each of the four required domain files, TDIC, SDIC, SLINKS and WLINKS were produced. The SDIC and TDIC files are created from the tagged texts. The automatic WLINKS file is created with the use of of a word alignment system (Ahrenberg et al, 2000). This program does not only generate a lexicon but also link instances which are used in combination with the tagged files to create different SLINKS files. A sample entry from the SDIC files is the following:

```
<boston,
        ((PMS, RightAdj(SS), Last)[0.35],
        (PMS, RightAdj(SS) LeftAdj(S))[0.04],
        (PMS, RightAdj(SS), LeftAdj(SS))[0.54],
        (PMS, RightAdj(SS), LeftAdj(ST))[0.08]])>
```

The figures associated with the trigram tags reflect are probabilities estimated by Maximum Likelihood Estimation from the corpus. They are primarily used for rating and filtering the word bags that result from transfer.

In stage 3, the best automatically extracted files were improved manually, e.g. by restructuring compounds, generalizing tags across natural word classes, introducing relational tags that refer to tokens rather than tags, and more.

4.2 Evaluation criteria and measures

The following criteria were chosen as a basis for evaluation of performance:

- *Word Selection Criteria.* Ability to select the correct TL tokens. Measured as recall and precision.
- *Word Order.* Ability to order the target language tokens correctly. Measured for correct target tokens only.
- *Identity.* Identical reproduction of the reference translations
- *Translation* quality, subjectively experienced. Two measures were used: accuracy and grammaticality.

4.3 Results and discussion

A sample of the measures obtained are given below. In Table 3 the different test cases are explained, while Table 4 provides the figures. The baseline case (Bl) means word-for-word translation based on most frequent translation for any given word.

TABLE 3. **Test Cases Shown**

Test case	SL inh. tagset	TL inh. tagset.	Word Al-ignment	Super-links
1:3	ATIS	ATIS	Auto	Auto
1:6	ATIS	ATIS	Manual	Auto
2:4	ATIS	ATIS	Manual	Refined
3:1	As 2:4 + lexical coverage of test corpus			
Bl	-	-	Manual	-

TABLE 4. **A sample of results (Tr means training corpus, Tst test corpus)**

Case	Pcn	Rcl	Ord	% Id	% Gr	Acc
1:3 Tr	.809	.855	.740	30.6	45.0	.700
1:3 Tst	.687	.739	.679	0.0	20.0	.463
1:6 Tr	.935	.950	.953	66.8	95.0	.950
1:6 Tst	.802	.825	.789	16.7	65.0	.788
2:4 Tr	.995	.992	.998	95.3	90.0	1.00
2:4 Tst	.791	.811	.796	16.7	60.0	.663
3:1 Tst	.855	.855	.822	33.3	50.0	.700
Bl Tr	.813	.846	.748	13.8	-	-
Bl Tst	.791	.817	.761	10.0	-	-

These measures warrant the following conclusions:

- There is clear evidence (1.6 vs. 1.3) that performance improves as word alignment gets more accurate. The quality of the word alignment is, not surprisingly, very important for the quality of the output.
- Word-by-word translations achieve rather high evaluation scores. However, translation using

automatically extracted superlinks performs better than manually refined word-by-word translation. There is a marked difference for the training corpus, but only a slight difference for the test corpus.

- With manual refinements, the ceiling of all measures are approached on the training corpus. It is quite possible on this domain to make SCOTS memorize the whole training corpus.
- On the other hand, results on the test corpus are markedly lower than on the training corpus. These results must be seen against the background of the sparse training corpus causing the test corpus not to be well covered by the superlinks generated from the training corpus.
- The performance on the training corpus increases from case 1:6 to case 2:4. Further results shows that this increase was largely due to the addition of proper handling of compounds. This increase in performance is not visible on Accuracy, however.
- The scores of case 3:1 are a marked improvement to those of 2:4 on the test corpus. Still, the scores are lower than what is achieved on the training corpus.

As the corpus used has been small and the ATIS domain is simple and restricted, we are not in a position to draw definite conclusions as to the performance of the method. However, we regard these results as encouraging.

There are obviously a number of ways in which to extend and improve this work. First of all, the SCOTS prototype should be tested on a larger and more complex corpus. Second, it would be interesting to study the effects of using more informative supertags, e.g. syntactic information in the form of dependency relations between words.

References

Agnäs, M-S., Alshawi, H., Bretan, I., Carter, D., Ceder, K., Collins, M., Crouch, R., Digalakis, V., Ekholm, B., Gambäck, B., Kaja, J., Karlgren, J., Lyberg, B., Price, P., Pulman, S., Rayner, M., Samuelsson, C., & Svensson, T. (1994). *Spoken Language Translator: First-Year Report. 1994.* Swedish Institute of Computer Science, SICS. SICS research report R94:03. ISRN: SICS-R-94/03-SE.

Ahrenberg, L, Andersson, M. and M. Merkel (2000). A knowledge-lite approach to word alignment. In J. Veronis (ed.) Parallel Text Processing : Alignment and Use of Translation Corpora, pp. 97-116. Kluwer Academic Press.

Bangalore, S. And A. K. Joshi, 1999. Supertagging: An Approach to Almost Parsing. *Computational Linguistics* 25(2): 237-265.

Brown, Peter, John Cocke, Stephen Della Pietra, Vincent J. Della Pietra, Fredrick Jelinek, John D. Lafferty, Robert L. Mercer and Paul S. Roossin, 1990. A Statistical Approach to Machine Translation. *Computational Linguistics*, 16(2): 79-85.

Brown, Peter F., S. A. Della Pietra, V. J. Della Pietra and R. L. Mercer, 1993. The mathematics of statistical machine translation: Parameter estimation. *Computational Linguistics*, 19(2): 263-311.

Jonsson, Håkan (2000). Exploring Superlink Constrained Lexicalist Transfer in Machine Translation. Master's thesis, Department of Computer and Information Science, Linköpings universitet.

Merkel, M., & Andersson, M. (2000). Knowledge-lite extraction of multi-word units with language filters and entropy thresholds. *Proceedings of the 6th Conference on Content-Based Multimedia Information Access, RIAO-2000,* Paris, France.

The VISL System:
Research and applicative aspects of IT-based learing

Eckhard Bick

e-mail: lineb@hum.au.dk

web: http://visl.sdu.dk

1. Abstract

The paper presents an integrated inter active user interface for teaching grammatical analysis through the Internet medium (Visual Interactive Syntax Learning), developed at Southern Denmark University, covering 14 different languages , half of which are supported by live grammatical analysis of running text. For reasons of robustness, efficiency and correctness, the system's internal tools are based on the Constraint Grammar formalism (Karlsson, 1990, 1995), but users are free to choose from a variety of notational filters, supporting different descriptional paradigms , with a current teaching focus on syntactic tree structures and the form -function dichotomy. The original kernel of programs was built around a multi -level parser for Portuguese (Bick, 1996, 2000) developed in a dissertation framework at Århus University and used as a point of departure for similar systems in other languages . Over the past 5 years, VISL has grown from a teaching initiative into a full blown research and development project with a wide range of secondary projects, activities and language technology products. Examples of application oriented research are NLP -based teaching games, machine translation and grammatical spell checking. The VISL group has repeatedly attracted outside funding for the development of grammar teaching tools, semantics based Constraint Grammars and the construction of annotated corpora.

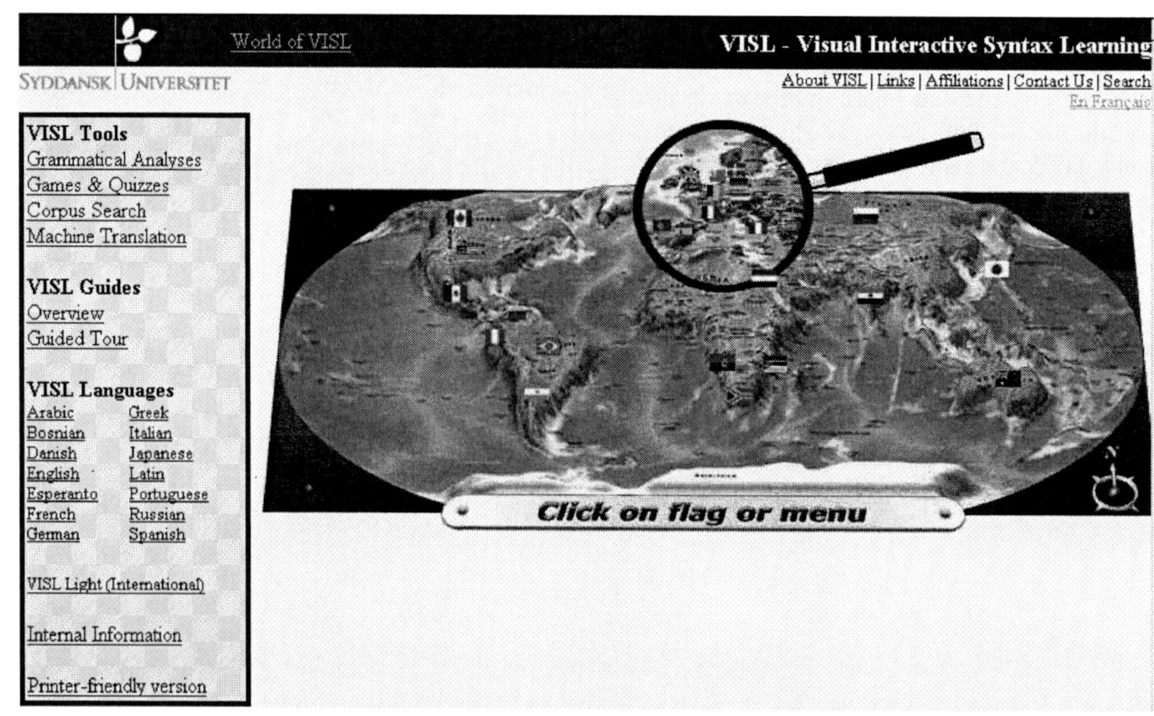

1. Background

When the VISL project started in 1996, its primary goal was to further the integration of IT tools and IT based communication routines into the university language teaching milieu at Odense University (Denmark), and more specifically, to develop tools for Visual Interactive Syntax Learning. The initiative was funded jointly by CTU (Center for Teknologi-Støttet Uddannelse) and Odense University for 3 years, and the languages involved were English, German, French and Portuguese.

Already in the early stages of the project it became clear that a distinction would have to be made as to whether the   language data to be used in the teaching interface would be limited text book examples or unlimited natural language text. We decided to develop both a "closed" and an "open" system, and to design the teaching applications for maximal synergy, such that t   hey would be able to take input from both the closed and open language data sources,   - and do so in a largely language independent way.

For the closed system a notational formalism was developed that allowed the textual expression of graphical syntactic t ree structures, and data bases of manually analysed sentences were built for all participating languages, the original target being 500 text book sentences and 500 running text sentences. With the help of enthusiastic students and teachers, these "closed c orpus" data bases are constantly being enlarged, and today VISL covers 14 languages, among them the basic Romance and Germanic languages as well as a number of more exotic specimen, like Arabic, Japanese and Esperanto.

The open system is research based an   d centered around the Constraint Grammar paradigm, introduced by Fred Karlsson at Helsinki University in the early 1990ies (Karlsson, 1991, 1995). The 1996 role model for the syntactic VISL system was my Portuguese CG parsing system (Bick 1996, 2000), whic   h featured a full dependency analysis of subclause structure and a prototype CG   -to-tree syntax transformation grammar. I have since developed similar CG based systems for Danish, Spanish and Esperanto. For English and German, VISL has   corrected a nd amplified licensed commercial CG systems from the Finnish software firm Lingsoft.

2. A unified approach to grammar

The central principle of VISL's language analysis is   its focus on surface structure (expressed as either dependency relations or syntactic tree s   tructures) and the form - function dichotomy. Following Bache et.al. (1993, 1999), function symbols start with upper case letters, form symbols with lower case letters, and both   are combined in a combined colon -separated symbol (text) or function   -over-form sy mbol (graphics). For the dependency notation, international CG conventions are followed, with upper case letters for all primary tags, using the @ -symbol to introduce function tags, and arrow heads (>,<) for head oriented dependency markers.

VISL light vertical tree (non-graphical notation)	VISL vertical tree (non-graphical notation)
UTT:cl(fcl)	STA:fcl
S:prop VISL	S:prop VISL
P:v(v-pr) er	P:v-fin(v-pr) er
Cs:g(np)	Cs:np
=D:art et	=DN:art et
=H:n forskningsprojekt	=H:n forskningsprojekt
=D:cl(fcl)	=DN:fcl
==S:pron(pron-rel) der	==S:pron-rel der
==P:v(v-pr) involverer	==P:v-fin(v-pr) involverer
==Od:g(np)	==Od:np
===D:pron(pron-indef) mange	===DN:pron-indef mange
===D:adj forskellige	===DN:adj forskellige
===H:n sprog	===H:n sprog

VISL	[VISL]	<heur> <*>	**PROP** NOM	@SUBJ>
er	[være]	<vk>	**V** PR AKT	@FMV
et	[en]		**ART** NEU S IDF	@>N
forskningsprojekt	[forskningsprojekt]		**N** NEU S IDF NOM	@<SC
,				
der	[der]	<rel>	**INDP** nG nN NOM	@SUBJ>
involverer	[involvere]	<vt>	**V** PR AKT &MV	@FS-N<
mange	[mange]	<quant>	**DET** nG P NOM	@>N
forskellige	[forskellig]		**ADJ** nG P nD NOM	@>N
sprog	[sprog]		**N** NEU P IDF NOM	@<ACC
.				

Meeting regularly over 4 years, the VISL group of university teachers has invested considerable effort in discussing the compatibilies, incompatibilies and blind spots of different national and linguistic grammar traditions, and agreed on a common superset of symbols. Recently, a reduced symbol set for propedeutic use and schools, "VISL light", was agreed upon, and the Danish X-and-O-system adapted to match the function categories used in VISL light. At the lowe st level, 11 word classes and 14 primary functions are used.

- ● Predicator (P), Verbal (V)
  - ○ Auxiliary (Vaux), also as <> (D)
  - ✪ Main verb (V*, Vm), also as ★ (H, K)
  - ⊙ Verb chain particle (Vp), also as <> (D), simplified as ⋎ (A)
  - ↻ Infinitive marker (Vi, INFM), also as <> (D)
- ✕ Subject (S)
  - (✕) Formal or provisional subject (Sf), possibly with the subclass of situative subject (Ss)
- ▲ Direct (accusative) object (Od)
  - (▲) Formal or provisional object (Of)
- ■ Indirect (dative) object (Oi)
- ◆ Prepositional object (Op), emneled, evt. forenklet som ⋎ (A)
- ⊗ Subject complement (Cs), Subject predicative (Ps)
  - [⊗] Free subject predicative (fPs, fCs), simplified as ⋎ (A)

⊕   Object complement (Co), Object predicative (Po)
[⊕]   Free object predicative (fPo, fCo), simplified as ⅋(A)
⅋   Adverbial (A), with possible subdivision of free (⅋ fA) or bound (⋀ bA, bAs, bAo)
★   Head (H), Kernel (K)
◇   Dependents (D)
↘   Subordinator (SUB)
↔   Co-ordinator (CO)
Conjunct (CJT)
《》   Underspecified constituent at clause level (e.g. clause body)

3. Internet based teaching tools

One lesson to be learned from the VISL project, is that it is not at all easy to introduce IT-based tools into an existing teaching environment. Ap art from hardware problems (there never being enough - compatible and updated - machines in the right room at the right time), there is the very central problem of psychological resistance against the new medium, simply because it may feel too "technical".   All things technical have a very low acceptance rate in the Humanities, and teachers often resent the personal investment in time and effort necessary to acquire the necessary skills   - not to mention changes in teaching material and exams. There is, of co   urse, a fundamental difference in terms of "technicality" between a human teacher and a computer terminal, - the latter lacks the teacher's *naturalness, interactivity, flexibility* and *tutoring* capacities. On the other hand, computers do have evident teachin   g advantages - they can integrate the senses, making use of colours, pictures and sounds in a more flexible and impressive manner than paper can. Also, a computer program can "know" more - in terms of facts and examples, and within a well -defined subject matter - than a human teacher. And last, but not least, a computer system, especially if accessible through the internet, can teach an unlimited number of students at the same time in what optimally still amounts to an individual manner.

Given these advant ages, it makes sense to invest some effort in addressing the four main disadvantages, as listed above. The VISL grammar teaching interface tries to make advances with regard to the following four principles:

(i) Flexibility
The VISL interface is notationally f   lexible, i.e. th e user can choose between several notational conventions (e.g. flat dependency grammar, enriched text, meta text notation, tree structures), and move back and forth between different levels of complexity. For instance, depending on the exer cise chosen, the type and number of grammatical categories used (e.g. word classes) may be changed. In order to make work more colourful, it is also possible to move between text book material, copied "live" texts, randomized test sentences and one's own creative idiolect.

In the tree structure example below, the user can switch back and forth between letter symbols and graphical symbols, more than double the number of categories, or reduce the tree to a pure function tree (green only).

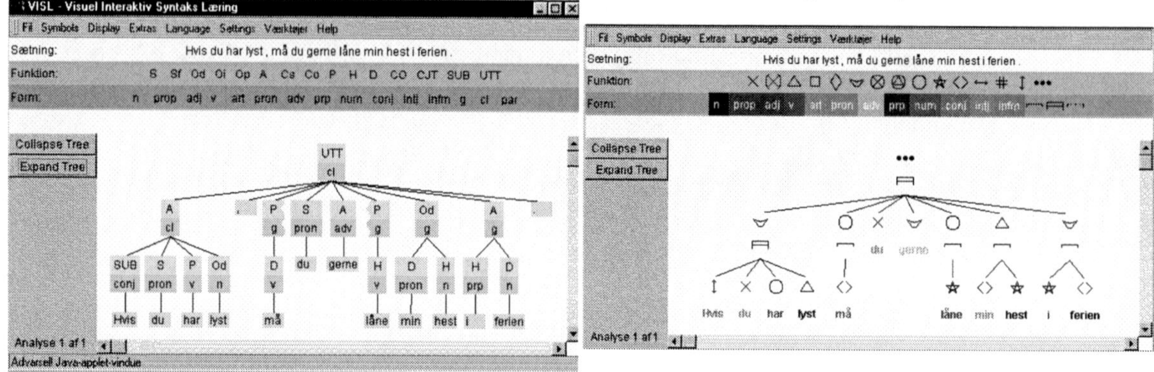

VISL's unique integration of teaching and research tools would even allow the user to experiment with different kinds of subjects or add a couple of place and time adverbials and rerun the sentence in free-text mode – with exactly the same graphical setup and paedagogical functionality.

(ii) Interactivity

VISL's java -tree interface for grammatical analysis allows the step -by-step interactive inspection, construction and labelling of syntactic trees using menus, mouse clicks and drag -and-drop movements, all known from b asic text processor functionality.

In the first example below, a student has recognized the np *"min hest"*, but has yet to assemble *"lyst"* onto the predicator *("har")* of the adverbial subclause to the left.

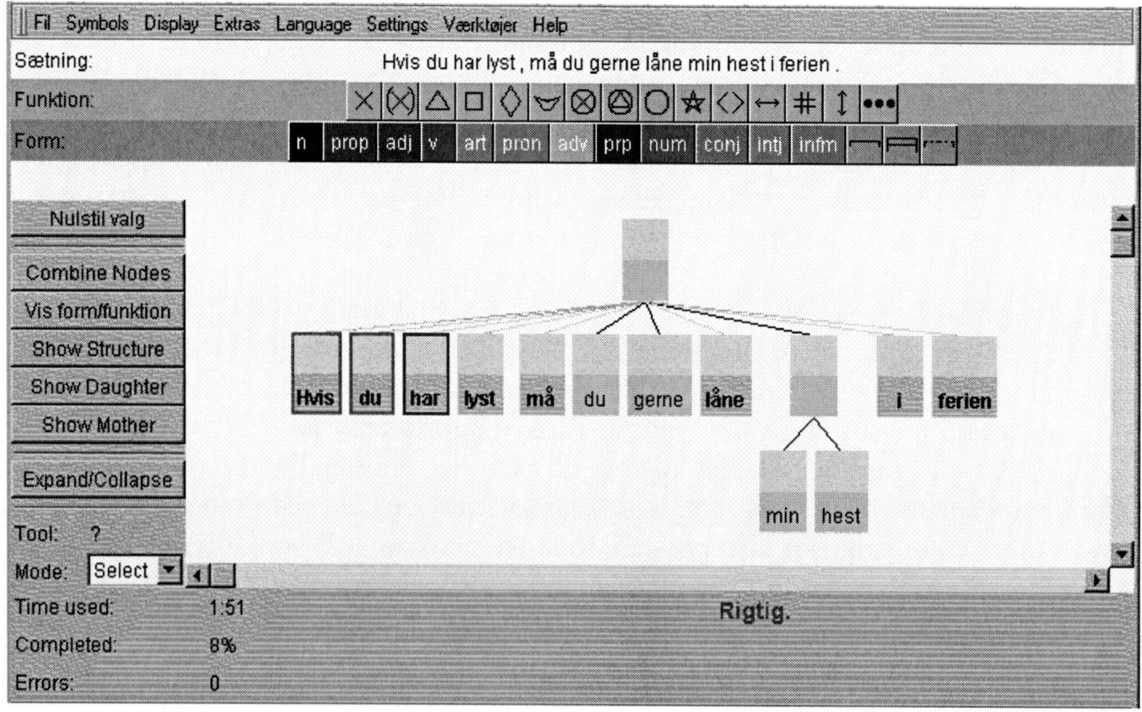

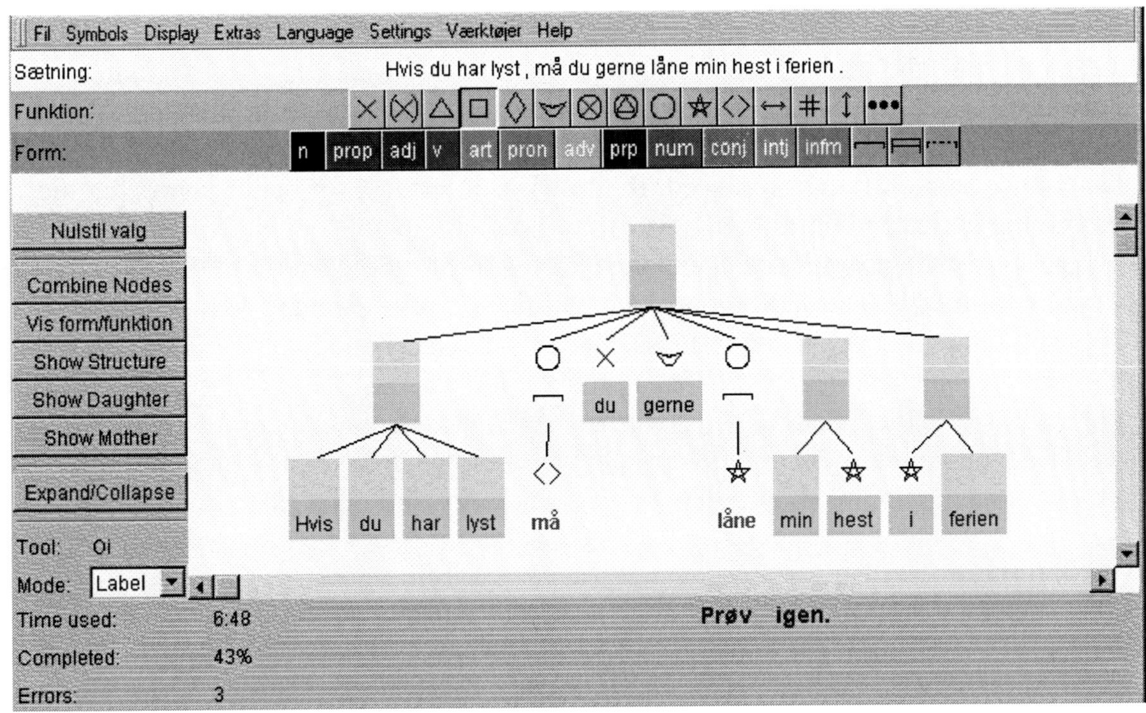

When a sentence proves problematic or incomprehensible, the user can modify it, or ask for the computer 's opinion (show -me option). In grammar games like *Paintbox, Post Office* or *Shoot-the-Verb,* interactivity inegrates a c ertain element of competition, and is further enhanced by sound effects, timers and high-scores.

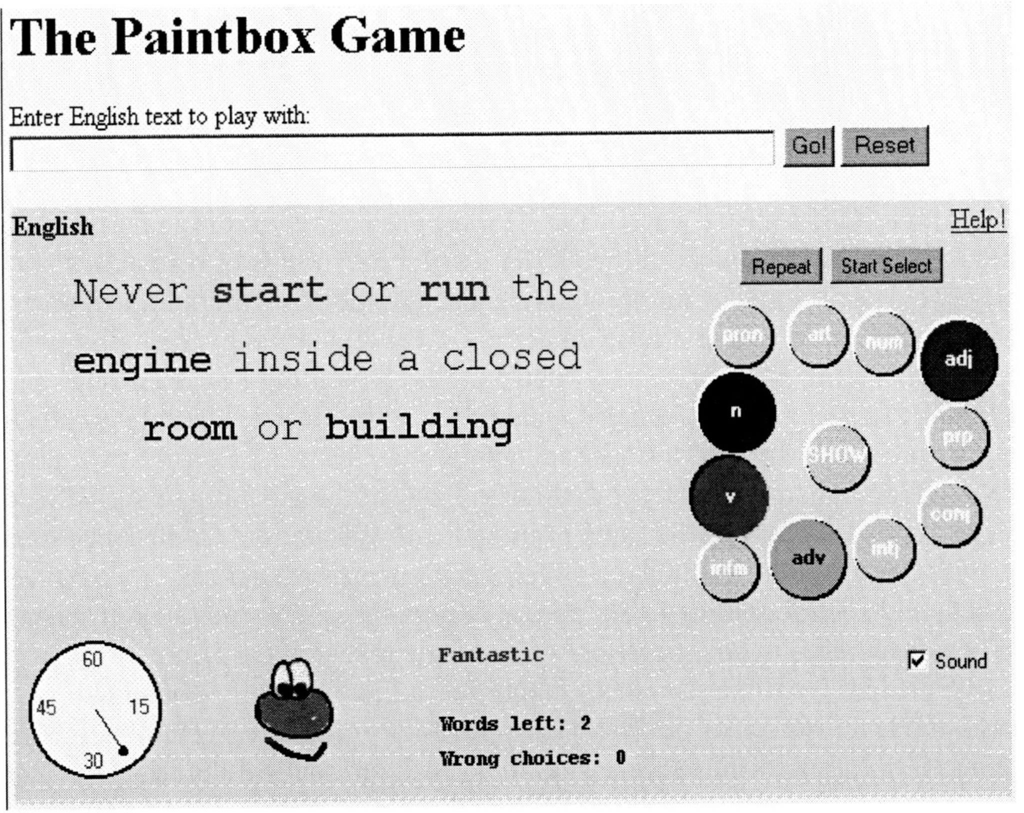

(iii) Naturalness

A major draw back of most language teaching software (or, for that matter, language analysis software) is that they do not run on free, na tural language, but only on a small set of predefined sentences or structures ("toy lexica" or "toy grammars"), that cannot be modified or replaced. In the VISL interface, for better or worse, the underlying lexica and grammars cover the whole language,   supporting gradual and comparative changes in a given sentence, or confronting the user with the stimulating lexical freshness and structural unpredictability of running natural text.

The second aspect of naturalness concerns, as mentioned above, "untech   nical" ergonomics, and as much keyboard   -interaction as possible has therefore been replaced by graphical and mouse governed tools, like menu choices and help windows. Being internet based, the system automatically takes advantage of a browser's navigation tools, scroll bars, page memory and cut'n'paste functionality.

(iv) Tutoring

Tutoring is traditionally a human task, and difficult to simulate in a computer interface. Therefore, it has been one of the last features to be broadly implemented on the VISL site. A certain minimum of tutoring can be achieved simply by providing guided tours, help windows, clickable definitions of grammatical terms, show   -me-buttons, and ready access to topic conditioned corpus examples (throug   h VISL's corpus search site). Howev   er, real tutoring asks for more specific and individual comments. Therefore, to help students with the tree -building and -labelling task, we have implemented so -called error -comment files , where pedagogic remarks (and suggested reading -links) are stored for all common and some rarer combinations of "correct label expected" and "wrong label chosen", as well as for different types of wrong attachment (phrase and clause grouping).

4. A methodological research paradigm

An important difference between   the VISL approach and traditional schools of grammar is the fact that what unifies VISL's different strands of research is not primarily a descriptive or interpretative paradigm, but a methodological one. Constraint Grammar with its focus on corpus data , lexicography, disambiguation and word based tagging is simply a very robust method, yielding low error rates and information-rich output easy to handle and filter with relatively simple text based computer programs. In descriptive and applicative terms   , Constraint Grammar is more a tool grammar than a target grammar. Thus, at the teaching level, VISL uses different represantations of the same grammatical information, for instance graphical trees with form   -function nodes, word class colouring or head bas   ed function indexing, and a number of different corpus annotation and corpus search schemes have been supported in collaboration with outside research partners.

Constraint Grammar can be thought of as a hierarchically organized progressive level system of lexical data bases and grammars, dynamically adaptable to different tasks and different levels or angles of grammatical description.   In the table below , a hierarchy of "pure" and "applicational" modules are shown for the present VISL languages, half of which incorporate CG modules at different levels.

Modules Languages	Po	En	Da	Sp	Ge	Es	Fr	It	Ar	Ja	Gr	Ru	La	Bo
Morphological parsing lexica	+	(+)	+	+	(+)	(+)	*	*						
Valency lexica	+	(+)	+	+										
Semantic lexica	+		+											
Morphological CG	+	x	+	≈+	x	≈	*+	*						
Syntactic CG	+	x+	+	≈+		≈	≈							
CG-to-tree PSG or equivalent	+	+	+	+			?							
Polysemi CG (partial)	?													
Bilingual electronic lexica (into TL)	Da En	Da	Es En											
Machine translation to TL or from SL: (with translation mapping CG)	Da		Es Po		Da									
Spelling/grammar checker CG		?	?											
CG-to-tree compatible teaching corpora	+	+	+	+	+		+	+	+	+	+	+	+	+
CG tagged corpora	+	+	+											
CG based tree corpora	+													

+	VISL-built module
(+)	Lexicon as part of a closed CG system, licensed form Lingsoft, Helsinki
x	Closed CG, licensed from Lingsoft, Helsinki
x+	Closed commercial CG with VISL add-ons (correction module, subclause function etc.)
≈	"Cloned" from the Portuguese PALAVRAS system
*	Probabilistic Tree Decision Tagger (Helmut Schmid & Achim Stein, Stuttgart)
*+	Probabilistic Tagger with correction CG
?	Partial pilot project

5. Spin-off results

Transcending its original target area, internet based grammar teaching tools, VISL has generated a number of collateral spin-off results both technological and linguistic. Thus, a number of comprehensive bilingual lexica, valency -lexica and semantic prototype lexica are under development for several languages, and GNU -licence compilers for CG and PSG are being made available to the public. VISL's corpus site offers a search interface handling regular expressions and CG tags, and text corpora are accessible in both raw and tagged for m for VISL's core languages. S eparate sub-projects are the construction of a large freely accessi ble Danish corpus (now 10 million words, in cooperation with DSL, Denmark) and a 2 million word tree bank for Portuguese (in cooperation with the AC/DC-project, Oslo).

    VISL's corpus material is partly integrated into the main site, part ly accessible through a separate search interface (http://corp.hum.sdu.dk), which allows the use of regular expressions for running text, and the combination and chaining of word forms, base forms, word class, inflexion and syntactic tags for CG-tagged text.

The table gives an overview of VISL-products within different core areas:

	Teaching	Corpus and general linguistics	Constraint Grammar
Programs	**Java-trees:** Interactive inspection, construction and labelling og syntactic trees **Paintbox:** Word class colouring game **Post office:** Syntactic function stamping game **Shooting gallery:** Selection of grammatical categories in moving sentences	**Search engine** for raw text and CG-tagged corpora **Filters** for a number of different notational conventions	flexible **CG-compiler** for Constraint Grammars **PSG-compiler** for CG-to-tree-grammars
Linguistic data	**Text book sentences:** Hand-analysed or machine analysed and proof-read "closed corpora" for 14 languages	Collection of **raw-text corpora** for 6 languages **CG-tagged corpora** for En, Po, Da New **Danish free corpus** Portuguese **treebank**	English **benchmark** text Port. **benchmark** text
Grammars	**Unified approach** to grammatical analysis and common category inventory across languages Danish **X-and-O-symbols**	Corpus driven grammar development **PSG-grammars** for CG-to-tree-conversion, for En, Da, (Po, Sp)	Port. CG (ca. 5000 rules) Dan. CG (ca. 3000 rules) Spa. CG (ca. 3000 rules) Esp. CG (port. clone) Eng. add-on CG Ger. add-on CG
Lexica	**Term bank** with definitions of grammatical categories etc. **Online dictionaries:** Po-Da, Da-Po, Da-Es, Es-Da	**Bilingual MT-lexica** for running text translation: Po-Da, Po-En, Da-En, En-Da	**Valency lexica:** Po, Da, Sp **Semantic class lexica:** Po, Da, En
Texts & documents	Online grammar **manuals**, guided tours and **tutorials** *EB: Grammy i Klostermølle-skoven (Da-En-Ge-Fr), Portuguese Syntax Manual*	Manuals, e.g. on **regular expression** in corpus searches (JMD & HK) Articles, reports and evaluations	Scientific **articles**, BA- and Ph.D.-**projects** *EB: The Parsing System "Palavras"*

Among VISL's non -teaching applications, machine translation is the most controversial one, while the tiny Danish spell-checker module is the one that even at the idea level generates most commercial interest.

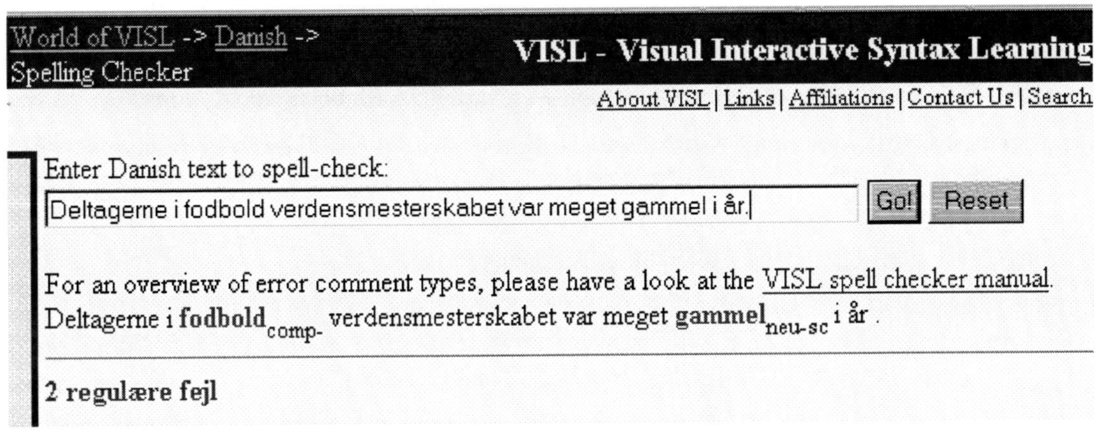

A kind of "dictionary" translation service can easily be incorporated as polysemy disambiguated base form translations added onto CG tag lines, but MT proper asks for a number of additional modules, such as target language inflexion generation, syntactic transformations, instantiation of complex tenses and so on. Constraint Grammar functions here as a context sensitive mapping device fo r structural markers or special translation equivalents.

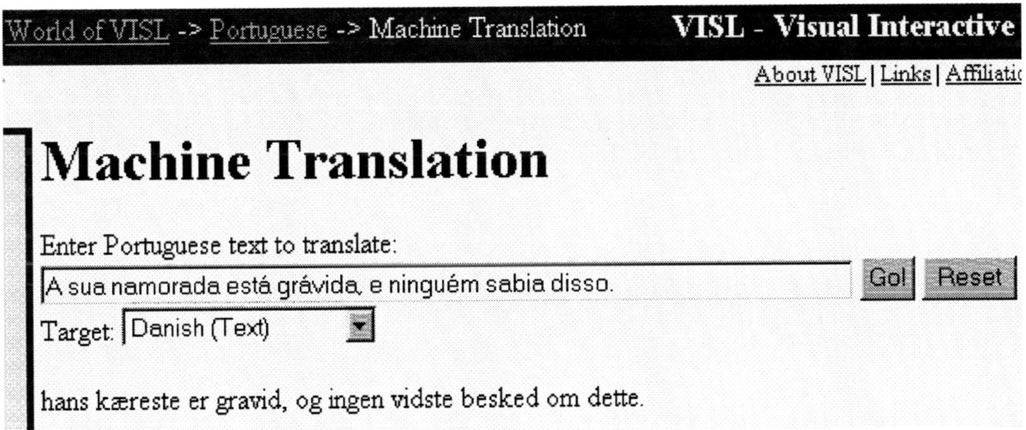

Bibliography:

Bache, Carl et. al. (1999). *English Sentence Analysis,* København: Gyldendal

Bick, Eckhard (1996). *Automatic Parsing of Portuguese.* In García, Laura Sánchez (ed.), *Anais / II Encontro para o Processamento Computacional de Português Escrito e Falado.* Curitiba: CEFET-PR.

Bick, Eckhard (1997) *Internet Based Grammar Teaching*, in: Christoffersen, Ellen & Music, Bradley (eds.), *Datalingvistisk Forenings Årsmøde 1997 i Kolding, Proceedings,* pp. 86 -106. Kolding: Institut for Erhvervssprog og Sproglig Informatik, Handelshøjskole Syd

Bick, Eck hard (2000 -1), *Portuguese Syntax* (Teaching Manual), http://www.portugues.mct.pt/Repositorio/Bick_Portuguese_Syntax3.doc and http://visl.sdu.dk/visl/pt

Bick, Eckhard (2000 -2), *The Parsing System "Palavras" – Automatic Grammatical Analysis of Portuguese in a Constraint Grammar Famework,* Aarhus: Aarhus University Press

Bick, Eckhard (2001), *Grammy i Klostermølleskoven - "VISL light": Tværsproglig sætningsanalyse for begyndere* (Teaching Manual), http://visl.sdu.dk/visl/light

Dienhart, John (2000), *VISL-projektet: Om anvendelse af IT i sprogundervisning og -forskning.* In: *At undervise med IKT,* pp. 51-70. Gylling: Narayana Press

Karlsson, Fred (1990) . *Constraint Grammar as a Framework for Parsing Running Text.* In Karlgren, Hans (ed.), *COLING-90: Papers presented to the 13* [th] *International Conference on Computational Linguistics,* Vol. 3, pp. 168-173. Helsinki: RUCL

Karlsson, Fred, et. al. (1995). *Constraint Grammar, A Language -Independent System for Parsing Unrestricted Text.* Berlin: Mouton de Gruyter.

Santos, Diana & Eckhard Bick (2000). *Providing Internet access to Portuguese corpora: the AC/DC project* , in Maria Gavrilidou et al. (eds.), *Proceedings of the Second International Conference on Language Resources and Evaluation*, LREC 2000 (Athens, 31 May-2 June 2000), pp.205-210.

Tapanainen, Pasi (1996). *The Constraint Grammar Parser CG -2.* Publication No. 27. Helsinki: Department of General Linguistics, University of Helsinki

Voutilainen, Atro & Heikkilä, Juka & Anttila, Arto (1992). *Constraint Grammar of English, A Performance-Oriented Introduction,* Publication No. 21. Helsinki: Department of General Linguistics, University of Helsinki

Voutilainen, Atro (1 994). *Designing a Parsing Grammar.* Publications No. 22. Helsinki: Department of General Linguistics, Helsinki University

Improving Precision in Information Retrieval for Swedish using Stemming

Johan Carlberger, Hercules Dalianis, Martin Hassel, Ola Knutsson

NADA-KTH

Royal Institute of Technology

100 44 Stockholm, Sweden

ph: +46 8 790 91 05

fax: +46 8 10 24 77

email: { jfc, hercules, xmartin, knutsson}@nada.kth.se

ABSTRACT

We will in this paper present an evaluation[1] of how much stemming improves precision in information retrieval for Swedish texts. To perform this, we built an information retrieval tool with optional stemming and created a tagged corpus in Swedish.

We know that stemming in information retrieval for English, Dutch and Slovenian gives better precision the more inflecting the language is, but precision depends also on query length and document length. Our final results were that stemming improved both precision and recall with 15 respectively 18 percent for Swedish texts having an average length of 181 words.

Keywords

Stemming, Swedish, Information Retrieval, Evaluation

1. INTRODUCTION

Stemming is a technique to transform different inflections and derivations of the same word to one common "stem". Stemming can mean both prefix and suffix removal. Stemming can, for example, be used to ensure that the greatest number of relevant matches is included in search results. A word's stem is its most basic form: for example, the stem of a plural noun is the singular; the stem of a past-tense verb is the present tense. The stem is, however, not to be confused with a word lemma, the stem does not have to be an actual word itself. Instead the stem can be said to be the least common denominator for the morphological variants. The motivation for using stemming instead of lemmatization, or indeed tagging of the text, is mainly a question of cost. It is considerably more expensive, in terms of time and effort, to develop a well performing lemmatizer than to develop a well performing stemmer. It is also more expensive in terms of computational power and run time to use a lemmatizer than to use a stemmer. The reason for this is that the stemmer can use ad-hoc suffix and prefix stripping rules and exception lists while the lemmatizer must do a complete morphological analysis (based on a actual grammatical rules and a dictionary). Another point of motivation is that a stemmer can deliberately "bring together" semantically related words belonging to different word classes to the same stem, which a lemmatizer cannot.

A problem concerning stemming is the issue of overstemming. If the stemmer removes too much in its quest for the stem the result is that, morphologically or semantically, unrelated words are conjoined under the same stem. For example, if both the words *tiden* ("time") and *tidning* ("newspaper") are stemmed to *tid*, a search for *tidning* also would return documents containing *tiden*. The graveness of this problem depends on both the set of stemming rules and the document collection

---

[1] This project is supported by NUTEK (Swedish board for Industrial and Technical Development) FavorIT programme in cooperation with Euroseek AB.

(more precisely; the index terms used to index the document collection). This is due to the fact that both the set of rules and the set of index terms used influence the amount of index terms conjoined under the same stem.

Here follows a number of algorithms previously used to find the stem of a word, (these are not using static lexicons which also can be used but are not so general).

The so-called Porter stemmer (Porter, 1980) for English, which removes around 60 different suffixes, uses rewriting rules in two steps. The Porter stemmer is quite aggressive when creating stems and does overstemming, but still the Porter stemmer performs well in precision/recall evaluations. KSTEM is another stemmer described in (Krovetz, 1993). KSTEM is not as aggressive as the Porter stemmer, and it does not create as many equivalence classes as the Porter stemmer does. KSTEM is also considered more accurate, but does not produce better results in evaluation experiments. A stemmer for Slovene is described in Popovic & Wilett (1992). Since Slovene is morphologically more complicated than English, the Slovene stemmer removes around 5 200 different suffixes. A Porter stemmer for Dutch is described in Kraaij and Pohlman (1994).

Based on the work in constructing a Swedish tagger (Carlberger & Kann 1999) we developed techniques to find the stems of Swedish words and we have used these techniques in our information retrieval work. Our stemming algorithm for Swedish uses about 150 stemming rules. We use a technique where we, with a small set of suffix rules, in a number of steps modify the original word into an appropriate stem. The stemming is done in (up to) four steps and in each step no more than one rule from a set of rules is applied. This means that 0-4 rules are applied to each word passing through the stemmer. Each rule consists of a lexical pattern to match with the suffix of the word being stemmed and a set of modifiers, or commands, see Figure 1.

The technique is quite general and can easily be adapted to inflectional languages other than Swedish.

<pre>
*   Don't remove or replace anything
–   Remove matched if a preceeding vowel is found
+   Remove matched
=   Remove matched if matching the whole word
.   Stop matching (break)
abc   Replace with abc
</pre>

Figure 1. The set of commands applicable to words being stemmed.

In step 0 genitive-s and active-s are handled; these are basically –s stripping rules. Definite forms of nouns and adjectivies are handled in step 1, as well are preterite tense and past participle.

<pre>
hals *.   Don't remove or replace anything and stop matching. ("neck")
abel –   Remove matched if a preceding vowel is found
sköt +.skjut   Remove sköt, insert skjut ("shoot" or "push") and break
</pre>

Figure 2. Example of exception rules.

In step 2 mainly plural forms of nouns and adjectives are handled. Noun forms of verbs are handled in step 3. In step 3 there are also some fixes to cover exceptions to the above rules, see Figure 2.

A word's stem does not have to be of the same part of speech as the word; in whatever sense you can talk about part of speech for the stem. The rules are designed so that word classes can be 'merged'. This means that, for example, **cykel** ("bicycle") and **cyklade** ("rode a bicycle") are both stemmed to **cykl**.

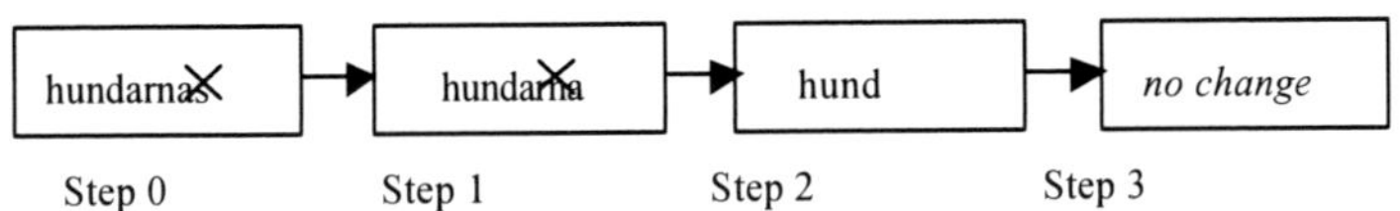

Figure 3. Example of stemming of the word *hundarnas* **(the dogs' (genitive form)) to** *hund* **(dog).**

This technique, see Figure 3, works well when the stem is to be used as a internal representation for a set of morphological variants and semantically related words. The stems themselves are, however, too cryptic to be presented to the user as bearing any information.

2. PRECISION AND RECALL[1] IN INFORMATION RETRIEVAL

Regarding information retrieval, there have been experiments using stemming of texts before indexing, or query expansion of the query before retrieving the text collections to investigate the improvement on precision. These experiments have been made for English but also for Slovene and Dutch.

Xu & Croft (1998) describe that stemming at document indexing time is more computational efficient than at query time (query expansion). Query expansion and stemming in information retrieval are regarded as equivalent, but most experiments have been carried out with stemming both on the document collection and on the query, i.e. normalization of both the query and text. (One can also just use query expansion on the query and no stemming on the document collection. Query expansion means that all possible inflections of a word are generated)

Popovic & Wilett (1992) found that there is no difference in precision using manual truncation of the query and automatic stemming; both methods gave the same results, at least for Slovene texts.

The first investigations by Harman (1991) indicated that there were no significant improvement in the retrieval using stemming, but in a later study by Krovetz (1993), an improvement of the retrieval (around 40 percent increase in precision) was proven specifically for shorter documents (average 45 words) with short queries (average 7 words). Longer texts (average 581 words) and with short queries (average 9 words) gave only 2 percent increase in precision.

According to Hull (1996), stemming is always beneficial in retrieving documents, around 1-3 percent improvement from no stemming, except on very small document collections.

Popovic & Wilett (1992) showed that stemming on a small collection of 400 abstracts in Slovene and queries of average length of 7 words increased precision in information retrieval with 40 percent.

In the above experiments the relation between the number of documents (500 to 180 000 documents) in the document collection and the number of unique questions range between 0.1 percent and 10 percent of the document collection.

3. THE KTH NEWS CORPUS

From the KTH News Corpus, described in detail in Hassel (2001), we selected 54 487 news articles from the period May 25, 2000 to November 4, 2000. From this sub-corpus we randomly selected 100 texts and manually tagged a question and answer pair central to each text; see Figure 4, for an example.

Question

<top>

<num> Number: 35

<desc> Description: (Natural Language question)

---

[1] Precision = number of found relevant documents / total number of found documents

Recall = number of found relevant documents / total number of relevant documents

Vem är koncernchef på Telenor? (Who is CEO at Telenor?)

</top>

Answer

<top>

<num> Number: 35

<answer> Answer: Tormod Hermansen

<file> File: KTH NewsCorpus/Aftonbladet/Ekonomi/0108238621340_EKO__00.html

<person> Person: Tormod Hermansen

<location> Location: Norden

<organization> Organization: Telenor

<time> Time: onsdagen

<keywords> Keywords: Telenor; koncernchef; teleföretag; mobilmarknaden; uppköp

</top>

Figure 4. Questioning and answering tagging scheme

4. EVALUATION

Our information retrieval system uses traditional information retrieval techniques extended with stemming techniques and normalization of both the query and text. (The system can also be executed without using the stemming module).

We used a rotating questioning-answering evaluation schema to avoid training effects of running the information retrieval system. Each of three users answered 33, 33 and 34 questions respectively with and without stemming functionality. The three users were not allowed to do more than five trials on each question to find the answer and were not allowed to use longer queries than five words. No background knowledge was allowed, which means that only the words used in the natural language question were allowed. Boolean expressions and phrase searches were allowed but rarely used.

After going through all of the 100 questions and finding answers to these, that is 33 questions each, we rotated the work and we became evaluators of the previous persons' answers assessing how many of the found top ten answers were correct and how many were wrong.

Of the 100 questions, the test persons found 96 answers, 2 questions did not give any answers at all and 2 other questions gave unreadable files. Each of the asked queries had an average length of 2.7 words. The texts containing the answer had an average length of 181 words.

We found a 15 percent increase on precision on the first 10 hits for stemming compared to no stemming (see Table 1). We also compared with weighting the first hits higher than the last ones and we found no significant difference: 14 percent better with stemming and weighting. (We gave the first hit a weighting factor of 10 and the second hit a weighting factor of 9, decreasing the weighting factor until the last tenth hit giving it 1 and then we normalized everything to 1).

Table 1. No stemming versus stemming

Precision/Recall at 10 first	Wordform	Stemming	Weighted Wordform	Weighted Stemming
Number of questions	96	96	96	96
Average precision	0.255	0.294	0.312	0.353
Increase of precision %		15.2%		13.1%
Average relative recall	0.665	0.784		
Increase of relative recall %		18.0%		

Regarding the recall, we calculated the relative recall. Maximum number of recalled texts per question is 21 (=10+10+1). This is calculated using the found unique or disjunctive texts when retrieving using both no stemming and stemming and also adding the tagged correct answer. We calculated the increase in recall taking the difference of the average relative recall, and we found an improvement of 18 percent on relative recall using stemming.

5. CONCLUSIONS

Stemming (and/or manual truncation) can give better precision (4-40 percent) in information retrieval for short queries (7-9 words) on short documents (500 words) than no stemming at all for languages as English, Dutch and Slovenian. Our experiments show that stemming for Swedish can give at least 15 percent increase in precision and 18 percent increase on relative recall depending on the set of rules and the document collection. We are convinced that the cost in creating a stemmer is proportional to the gain when using the stemmer. This indicates that using stemming on morphologically complicated languages will give great gain in precision.

ACKNOWLEDGMENTS

We would like to thank the search engine team and specifically Jesper Ekhall at Euroseek AB for their support with the integration of our stemming algorithms in their search engine and allowing us to use their search engine in our experiments.

6. REFERENCES

J. Carlberger and V. Kann. 1999. *Implementing an efficient part-of-speech tagger*, Software Practice and Experience, 29, 815-832, 1999. ftp://ftp.nada.kth.se/pub/documents/Theory/Viggo-Kann/tagger.pdf

D. Harman. 1991. *How effective is suffixing?* Journal of the American Society for Information Science, 42(1): 7-15.

M. Hassel. 2001. *Internet as Corpus – Automatic Construction of a Swedish News Corpus.* NODALIDA '01 - 13th Nordic Conference on Computational Linguistics, May 21-22 2001, Uppsala, Sweden.

D.A. Hull. 1996. *Stemming Algorithms - A Case Study for Detailed Evaluation.* Journal of the American Society for Information Science, 47(1): 70-84

W. Kraaij and R.Pohlmann. 1994. *Porter's stemming algorithm for Dutch.* In L.G.M. Noordman and W.A.M. de Vroomen, editors, Informatie wetenschap 1994: Wetenschappelijke bijdragen aan de derde STINFON Conferentie, pp. 167-180.

R. Krovetz. 1993. *Viewing Morphology as an Inference Process.* In Proceedings of the 16th Annual International ACM SIGIR Conference on Research and Development in Information Retrieval, ACM, New York, pp 191-202.

M. Popovic and P. Willett. 1992. *The effectiveness of stemming for natural-language access to Slovene textual data.* Journal of the American Society for Information Science, 43(5): 384-390.

M.F. Porter. 1980. *An algorithm for suffix stripping.* Program, vol 14, no 3, pp 130-130. (Se also http://open.muscat.com/developer/docs/porterstem.html)

J. Xu and W. B. Croft. 1998. *Corpus-based Stemming using Co-occurrence of Word Variants.* ACM Transactions on Information Systems, Volume 16, Number 1, pp 61-81, January 1998.

The interaction between local focusing structure and global intentions in spoken discourse

Sofia Gustafson-Capková
Department of Linguistics, Computational Linguistics
Stockholm University
S-109 61, Stockholm
Sweden
sofia@ling.su.se

ABSTRACT

The purpose of the study reported in this paper is to investigate how local focusing structure, analysed in terms of Centering Theory (Grosz, Joshi & Weinstein, 1995), and global d iscourse structure, analysed in terms of discourse segments and discourse segment purposes (Grosz & Sidner, 1986), interact. Swedish dialogue was analysed according to Centering Theory and Grosz and Sidners (1986) discourse theory. The results indicate an interaction between locally implicit elements and global intentions. Also indications concerning discourse markers varying intonation were found.

Introduction

Discourse can be described as built up from discourse building blocks called discourse segments   (hereafter DS). These DS are the units for forming a hierarchical discourse structure. They are described in e.g. Grosz & Sidner (1986, hereafter G&S) where claims are made about the use of the DS in the global discourse structure as well as their connect ion to the coherence of the discourse, and in Centering Theory (Grosz, Joshi & Weinstein, 1995, hereafter CT), where claims are made about the internal structure and coherence of the DS:s.

Grosz & Sidner (1986) have applied their discourse theory to both   argumentative text and task oriented dialogue, while CT traditionally has been applied to narrative text. In recent times, however, an interest for applying CT to dialogue has arisen, and some attempts to do that has been carried out (e.g. Brennan, 1998, B   yron & Stent, 1998, Eckert & Strube, 1999).

In applying G&S theory, a problematic point is the importance of speaker intention, which governs both the discourse segmenting and the discourse structure. It is unclear whose perspective, that should be taken; the speakers original intention, the listeners understanding of the intention or the analysers interpretation of the intention. However, one thing that is for sure is that the analyser will certainly face a challenge if attempting to find out original speaker/listener intentions.

The major problematic issues in applying CT the issue of both utterance segmenting and discourse segmenting effects almost all other aspects of the analysis. Another problem with CT is to decide what concepts that are accessible, or *realised*, in an utterance.

The pilot study presented in this paper is of explorative character, and addresses a range of problems encountered in a combined G&S-type analysis and CT analysis of task oriented dialogue, i.e.:

- Utterance segmenting, i.e. the units between which local coherence is computed
- Discourse segmenting, i.e. larger constituents affecting the global discourse structure. These segments correlates with what Carletta et al. (1997) calls "game".
- What items that are possible centers
- The CT notion of a *realised* item

The aim of this paper is to give a picture of how those problems are connected to each other, and to outline how to refine a multiple -level analysis. It is also an attempt to apply a global and local analysis to spok   en language data, and to give account for specific problems that arises by such an analysis. It is the hope of the author that results from investigations like this should help to develop e.g. instructions for more extensive investigations in the field.

1   Background

G&S and CT are two theories that give account for discourse structure and coherence, but a t different levels of the discourse. G&S mainly addresses the global discourse structure, while CT gives account for the local coherence. I will here give a short description of both theories.

G&S (1986) describe discourse as consisting of three structures   : i) the linguistic structure, ii) the intentional structure and iii) the attentional state. These three structures interact, but they are still to be considered as separate structures. The interaction between them works roughly as follow: The linguistic s tructure, i.e. the string of words, is divided into discourse segments. Each segment has a Discourse Segment Purpose (DSP) which is part of the intentional structure. According to how the DSP:s are satisfied, different relations hold between the discourse segments and the attentional state is modelled out of these relations.

Thus, in G&S, disourse segments are intentionally delimited, i.e. a discourse segment is governed by a main intention, the DSP. The range of DSP:s is unlimited. DS may be nested, an   d the relations that hold between discourse segments are limited to two: i) dominance and ii) satisfaction -precedence. Dominance means in short that a discourse segment B which is part of the satisfaction of the intention governing the discourse segment A   is dominated by A, i.e. A dominates B. Satisfaction   -precedence on the other hand holds in the cases where the intention of a discourse segment C has to be fulfilled before the intention of the discourse segment D appears, i.e. C satisfaction-precedes D.

The relations dominance and satisfaction precedence contributes incrementally to the discourse structure and model the global coherence. This is done by stack manipulations, which could be described as modelling a temporal sequence of intentions in attention al focus in the discourse. This process will however not be closely described here.

Centering Theory is a theory, which gives account for the degree of local coherence between utterances within a discourse segment. This is made by segmenting the linguistic   string into utterances and classify the transitions between them. The transitions are computed on basis of two factors: backward   -looking center Cb and forward -looking center(s) Cf. Sometimes the preferred center, i.e. the highest ranked member of the Cf -list is singled out as Cp. The choice of centers is in standard CT (Grosz, Joshi & Weinstein) based on grammatical roles: subject>object>other roles. It is important to note, that the centers does not have to be explicitly present in the linguistic string (directly realized), but may also be implicitly present in the conceptual representation (realized). This means, that centers are not linguistic units, but concepts.

The four transitions are computed on basis of the C:s, as shown in Table 1.

Table 1 Table over the transitions in Centering Theory.

	$Cb(U_i) = Cb(U_{i-1})$ *or* $Cb(U_{i-1}) = [?]$	$Cb(U_i) \neq Cb(U_{i-1})$
$Cb(U_i) = Cp(U_i)$	CONTINUE	SMOOTH-SHIFT
$Cb(U_i) \neq Cp(U_i)$	RETAIN	ROUGH-SHIFT

In addition two rules are used in CT. The first is "The pronoun constraint". This rule state that if something in U_i is realized as a pronoun in U_{i+1} the Cb of U_{i+1} must also be realised with a pronoun.

The second rule states that sequences of continuation   are preferred over sequences of retain. The shift transitions put generally a higer inference load upon the hearer.

The segmenting issue is certainly important also in CT, but it is not closer addressed by Grosz, Joshi & Weinstein (1995), i.e. no explicit base for the discourse segments is given here. It is however a good guess that they should be of the same nature as by Grosz & Sidner, who mentions centering as possible additional mechanism (Grosz & Sidner, 1986, p. 91).

A modified version of CT is made by Walker (1997). She has replaced the DS by something that could be described as a moving window. This means that the CT -analysis is done continually through the whole discourse, and it does not start and stop over and over again by the initiation or endi ng of a DS. The elements from the Cf-list are saved in a cache, which is incrementally updated in the way that new items are added and old items are erased. Walker suggests that the size of the moving window should consist of two or three sentences, or seven propositions.

Both utterance boundaries and discourse segment boundaries are difficult to delimit in spoken language. Utterances are difficult because there is often no formally correctly completed sentence structure in spontaneous speech.

General strategies for segmentation of spoken discourse are prosodic phrasing, cue -words, and the use of form for referring expressions (e.g. Passonneau & Litman, 1997, Grosz & Sidner, 1986, Walker, 1997).

An additional problem in analysing dialogue is that it is no   t quite clear how to apply a theory like CT, mainly developed with work on narrative text, for a multi -party discourse. E.g. is the previous utterance for X the linearly previous utterance, or the previous utterance uttered by X? One has to work with at le ast two persons interpretations of the discourse, interpretations which do not have to be overlapping, in terms of both DS and focus of attention, i.e. one should try to keep track on whose center that is analysed.

2   Method

In order to give spoken language a discourse analysis in terms of both G&S and CT, elicited spoken dialogue was analysed. The spoken language material was from one Map Task dialogue in Swedish (Helgason). In all 60 turns from one dialogue with two speakers were analysed.

The dialogue was segmented with a pause -detecting tool, which detected silent pauses longer than 100 ms. After examination of the segmented data the analyser decided that pauses 300 ms or longer should be used as utterance boundaries. This pause length is roughly correlating with clause boundaries according to Garman (1990), who sets clause boundaries to 400 ms. The segmentation based on 300 ms or longer pauses resulted in 100 utterances. The decision was also made that change of speaker also indicated new utterance.

All linguistic units were regarded as valid, i.e. no filtering out of utterances consisting only of e.g. humming (mmm…) was done, as done by e.g. Byron & Stent (1998).

The transitions between the utterances were computed accordi ng to CT, but the ranking of centers were limited to linear appearance. When it comes to items possible carry center, 1 and 2 sg. pronouns were filtered out. After this the material was examined according to intentional content. Boundaries between DS, whic   h correlated to certain intentions, were annotated and also the intentions were described. This resulted in 36 labelled discourse segments, which were analysed in terms of relations between different DS (dominance and satisfaction -precedence). Change of speaker was not taken to imply new DS.

3   Results and discussion

One of the main problems in discourse analysis is choosing an interpretation that is as general as possible, i.e. to try to minimise the subjectivity in the interpreta tion. The reason for this is the need for a possible replication of the analysis of the interpretation, i.e. the analysis should not be too bounded to the analysers subjectively based interpretation. The analyser is thus forced to keep language interpretat ion and discourse analysis strictly separated. This is in itself a paradox, because to analyse a stretch of discourse means to analyse an interpretation of the stretch of discourse. However, human natural language is never impersonally interpreted, it is a lways interpreted through the filter of a subjective human thinking, so the interpretation and the analysis blend. In fields as e.g. computational linguistics, one tries to model a pure and objective interpretation, which in fact is the most unlikely inter pretation in its pureness. The question is, how is it possible to keep on searching for the most general interpretation but still avoid both subjectivity and artificiality in the interpretation, i.e. to make the claim of the analysis part of the interpretation, as objective as possible, so that it is scientifically valid, but still keep as much subjectivity as possible in the interpretation so that the outcome mimics language users as much as possible. In the subjectivity of human language understanding lies also the robustness and the generality of human language use.

To use dialogue is one way to try to delimit the degree of subjectivity in the analysis, but still allow subjectivity in the interpretation. The reason for this is that the primary task for the analyser is not to interpret the text/speech, but to understand how the current speaker interpreted what the former speaker said. This means that the analyser has a reference point for the interpre tation outside herself. In following the dialogue it is also possible to follow how a person actually interprets the current speaker. The analyser is not completely alone with her own interpretation, but is able to get a glimpse of how another person interprets the utterances.

To use the pause -tool for detecting utterance boundaries was another way to try to limit the influence of subjective interpretation. The interpreter was not determining the segmentation herself, but used a kind of bootstrapping in deciding the utterance units.

The results showed that the utterance segmentation in many cases was quite good, but still, in many cases the granularity was finer than preferred. The discourse segmenting on intentional basis did not pose great problems, but perhaps that just indicates the readiness by the analyser to assign explicit intentions to certain segments. Below an overview of the segmented material is shown.

- Turns: 60
- Utterances: 100
- Discourse segments: 36

3.1   Segmenting the utterances

Cases where the pause -based utterance segmentation was not optimal could sometimes have been avoided if the intonation contour had been taken into consideration. In Example 1, given below, the speech signal was segmented at the point Utt 2. (the pause preceding that position is longer than 300 ms), but this break could have been avoided if the fact, that the intonation contour is stable (i.e. neither rising nor falling) had been taken into consideration.

Example 1

Utt. 1. .då ska vi se då har vi. .en. .en s!0 .;*karta* här framför oss. .och jag har. .;. *landstigit* på en *plats*, →
Utt. 2. .på den här ön.

In the analysis cases like Example 1 were however regarded as two utterances.

3.2   The CT analysis

After the segmentation into utterances, the 100 utterances were analysed in terms of CT. At this poi   nt in the investigation no attempt to divide the discourse into DS was made. Following Walker (1997) a continual examination of the centers and the transitions was done throughout the whole discourse.

3.2.1   Analysing the centers

Concerning the analysis of the centers the ranking based on grammatical role did not turn out to be suitable for the analysed dialogue, partly due to the fact that 1 and 2 sg. pronouns were filtered out. Instead the analyser followed three simple statements:

- All kinds of elements (e.g. complex phrases as well as single words) were ranked after the linear occurrence in the speech signal.
- Phonetic prominence was taken into account. A phonetically prominent element was given a higher rank than a phonetically non-prominent element (the pronoun constraint was however always kept).
- Coordinate and subordinate clauses were specially handled. A con -/subjunction inside an utterance started a new Cf-list, which was given higher prominence than the first list.

An example of the ranking of elements in an utterance is given in
Example 2, where the underlined "men" initiates the second Cf   -list (also underlined), from where the preferred center is chosen.

Example 2

.ja. .det är ett *aningers.* *.när när*mare floden än ;. .;. .kust!0. .!0kanten där <u>men</u> det är *nästan mitt* emellan.

Cb = ja<du snuddar nästan vid en flod när du är där (preceding utterance)>
Cf = 1. [närmare floden, kustkanten] 2. <u>[mittemellan <floden & kustkanten>]</u>
Cp = mittemellan <floden & kustkanten>

As earlier noted, Cb:s could be directly realised or realised. In Example 1 for instance some elements are present in the analysis, but not present in the utterance or in the appropriate place in the utterance. Such instances are marked out with <> in the analysis. In Example 1 there are t wo instances of such partly implicit elements: 1. <du snuddar nästan vid en flod när du är där> and 2. <floden & kustkanten>. In the first case, "ja" does not only seem to be a way to signal that the listener have understand, but also a way to signal that   the representation of the concepts is still relevant and active, i.e. "ja" functions as a short "keep active -signal". This is found in all ja -instances. Similar findings are reported by Eckert & Strube (1999), who claim that those utterances have high rel evance for grounding in dialogue. In the second case both the river (flod) and the shore (kustkanten) are introduced, but in the later part of the utterance (after "men") the focus is on the point between the both elements. However, the elements are still highly active in defining the point in between that is why the conjunction of the both concepts is analysed as present. Such partly implicit elements are frequent in the material, but also completely implicit elements. Interesting is, that in the case of a complete implicit element in an utterance as: ".och *fortsätter* <vägen> norrut", the Cp in the utterance, the concept "road" (<vägen>) is a crucial concept in the formulation of the DSP (the discourse segment purposes, the intentions motivating a discours e segment). Thus, the concept could be said to be contextually highly activated, i.e. activated by the task and the situation itself, or activated on the global level. As well as we can talk about local and global focus, we can also be able to distinguish   between a local and a global level of activation.

To get a view over the proportions of implicit vs. explicit reference in discourse all the Cb:s were counted and sorted as directly realised (explicitly present) or realised (implicit or partly implicit pre sent). The result is shown in Table 2.

Table 2

	Explicitly present	partly implicitly present	fully implicitly present
N = 100	19	71	10

The above figures indicate that 81% of back reference in a discourse is implicit, which makes human communication seem like an iceberg.

The proportion of transitions between utterances was computed, and the results are given in Table 3.

Table 3 Transitions between the 100 utterances in the material

Continue	Retain	Smooth-shift	Rough-shift
47	36	10	5

Please not that one instance of Rough -shift is clearly discourse initial, so it is left out in the table above. These results will be closer discussed under the heading 3.3.

3.3 *The global structure of the discourse*

The global structure of the discourse was analysed in terms of the relations dominance and satisfaction -precedence between discourse segments. In making this analysis the analyser experienced a need to make a more fine   -grained distinction between different instances of the relation satisfaction-precedence. Thus, the relations used were:

- Dominance, corresponds to the dominance relation between two segments (mother-daughter).
- Single pop, corresponds to two adjacent segments on the same level both without daughters (sisters without daughters). This is the same as the relation satisfaction-precedence between two sisters without daughters.
- Multiple pop, corresponds to two segments, textually adjacent but on different levels in the hierarchical analysis, i.e. the youngest daughter in one branch and a potential mother for another branch. This is the same as satisfaction-precedence between two nodes on different hierarchical levels.

As noted in Table 3 above there was an overwhelming number of the relations Continue and Retain. Both shift   -transitions were quite rare, and it is worth noting that all Rough -shifts appeared either i) inside a discourse segment (4) ii) between two discourse segments related to each other by the relation dominance (1) iii) after a very clear indication that the discourse topic will change ("då så, då   ska vi se". This is the one left out in   Table 3). The last alternative is possible to exclude on the basis that it is better to consider this as a new discourse and not a shift inside the same discourse. The two fi rst alternatives however indicate, that rough -shift appears only inside a tightly defined intentional space, in the data it never appears together with a shift of the intention. It never appeared between DS:s related with Single pop or Multiple pop. A mech   anism as rough -shift seems thus not to be the

appropriate way to make such a change of direction in the discourse, rather it indicates misunderstanding or a "jumping" inside one isolated intentional space.
The transitions between discourse segments is shown in Table 4 below.

Table 4 CT-Transitions at different kinds of DS boundaries.

	Continue	Retain	Smooth-shift	Rough-shift
Multiple pop	0	9	0	0
Single pop	0	6	2	1
Dominance	6	6	0	4

In investigating what could be characteristic for discourse segment boundaries with different relations all discourse segment boundaries were investigated. The results are given below.

- Multiple pop: Indicates in seven cases of nine with a combination of pause, cue   -words and phonetic prominence (***och sen/och fortsätter***).
- Single pop: Indicates in five cases of nine with a combination of pause and cue-words (och sen / då)
- Dominance: No special preferences found.

4   Summary and further work

This investigation reported in this paper is certainly suffering from a range of weak points; for instance a larger set of data and an evaluation of inter coder reliability would be highly desirable. The analysis is now very dependent on one analysers own interpretation. The results however give quite interesting indications concerning the interaction between local focus and global intentions, e.g. the connection between the implicit centers and the intentions behind the discourse segments.

The use of pauses for utterance segmentation would certainly be better if the intonation contour could be integrated in the analysis. In the data it also seems to be a regularity in the use   of intonation by the use of cue -words, i.e. the alternation between phonetically prominent and phonetically non   -prominent correlates with the different relations Multiple pop and Single pop, it is however difficult to say anything for sure without analys   ing a larger amount of data.

Further work in this direction would, except more data, include a more thorough investigation of the ranking order. To isolate what concepts that are present, or rather accessible, in an utterance in a certain context is also   indeed an important, but difficult task to attack. It would also be of interest to connect findings from analyses like this to dialogue coding, as described by e.g. Carletta et al.

5   Acknowledgments

Many thanks to Harald Berthelsen, who made the pause detecting tool, and to Petur Helgason who made the Swedish Map Task dialogues available.

6   Literature

Carletta et al. (1997): *The Reliability of a Dialogue Coding Structure Scheme*. Computational Linguistics, vol. 23 no. 1.

Berthelsen, H.: Pause detecting tool.

Brennan, S (1998): *Centering as a psychological resource for achieving joint reference in spontaneous discourse*. In Walker et al. 1998, Centering Theory in discourse.

Byron, D. & Stent, A. (1998): *A Preliminary Model of Centering in Dialog.* In the Proceedings of the 36th Annual Meeting of the Association for Computational Linguistics (ACL'98) student session.

Eckert, M. & Strube, M (1999): *Resolving Discourse Deictic Anaphora in Dialogues*. In EACL '99.

Garman, M. (1990): *Psycholinguistics.* Cambridge University Press.

Grosz, B. & Sidner, C. (1986): *Attention, Intentions and the Structure of Discourse*. Computational Linguistics, vol 12, no 3.

Grosz, B., Joshi, A. & Weinstein, S. (1995): *Centering: A Framework for Modelling the Local Coherence of Discourse*. Computational Linguistics, vol. 21, no. 2.

Helgason, P. : *The Stockholm Corpus of Spontaneous Swedish.* Map Task corpus, Department of linguistics, Stockholm University.

Passonneau, R. & Litman, D. (1997): *Discourse Segmentation by Human and Automated Means*. Computational Linguistics, vol 23, no 1.

Some problems related to the development of a grammar checker

Kristin Hagen, Janne Bondi Johannessen and Pia Lane
University of Oslo

{kristiha, jannebj, pial}@mail.hf.uio.no

1. Introduction

Developing a grammar checker presents problems to the linguist and to linguistic software that are far from trivial. In this paper we will discuss various kinds of problems that we have encountered during our work with developing a grammar checker for Norwegian (Bokmål). The grammar checker in question, developed in cooperation with Lingsoft OY and to be used in Microsoft Word from the summer 2001, will be applied on text that has been grammatically tagged and disambiguated by the Constraint Grammar method (Karlsson et al 1995, Hagen and Johannessen 1998, and Hagen, Johannessen and Nøklestad 2000a, 2000b). The fact that the input text has been multi-tagged and disambiguated before grammar checking has certain advantages, but also presents certain problems, as we shall see.

Below, we shall give a brief review of statistical measures and an outline of the structure of the grammar checker, and then give an overview of the error types that our grammar checker is meant to cover. Many people find it hard to believe that grammar errors occur to any large extent. We shall therefore show some authentic examples from manually proofread tests. The errors can be categorised in two main groups: 1) Errors caused by a sloppy use of the "cut and paste" options of modern text editors, and 2) errors due to people's mistaken beliefs about the written language norms.

We shall then focus on problems that present a challenge in more ways than the obvious ones that deal with recognising mistakes and suggesting improvements. First, we shall focus on mistakes that have caused us having to rewrite the tagger that is used for the input text (undo disambiguation and redo it differently). Second, we shall look at mistakes that are caused by the fact that certain non-standard inflectional forms are homographous with other words found in the lexicon, and suggest a way of dealing with those. Third, we shall see what kinds of problems occur when words are missing, and hence not tagged at all. Finally, we shall show briefly why it is important for a grammar checker to include a component of grammatical analysis.

2. Statistical measures and other grammar checkers

The Norwegian grammar checker has been developed using Constraint Grammar rules. This method has previously been used to develop a Swedish grammar checker (see Birn 2000, Arppe 2000). The resulting precision for this grammar checker is reported to be 70% (according to Birn 2000:38), counted as good alarms divided by the sum of good alarms and false alarms. The resulting precision for the Norwegian grammar checker is 75 % from a test corpus of 890 000 words from the newspapers *Nordlys* and Sarbsborg Blad. However, depending on what kind of text that is used as a test corpus and what kind of rules that are included, these numbers can vary a great deal. For example, if we include a rule that tests whether there are any finite verbs in a sentence, and apply the grammar checker on newspaper text with a lot of verb-less headlines, the precision rises to approximately 91 % (and the same goes for the Swedish grammar checker).

3. The structure of the grammar checker

The grammar checker is composed of two main components: a tagger (consisting of three subparts) and an error detector:

(1)   *The main structure of the grammar checker:*

I Tagger
•<u>A preprocessor</u> that among other things splits the text into sentences, identifies abbreviations and fixed expressions and marks capitalised unknown words in non-sentence initial position as proper nouns.
•<u>A multi-tagger</u> that uses NORTWOL (Karlsson et al 1995) to give a morphological analysis. Each word form is given all the possible tags that are appropriate for it.
•<u>A morphological disambiguator</u>, which is a modified version of the disambiguator made by *Taggerprosjektet* (Hagen and Johannessen 1998, and Hagen, Johannessen and Nøklestad 2000a, 2000b).

II Error detector that identifies different kinds of grammatical errors (see below).
•For each error that is identified, the user gets a short error message and if possible a suggestion of how to correct the error. The user is also given the possibility of reading a longer help text.

4 Error types

The Norwegian grammar checker is designed to detect the following main error types:
- Noun phrase internal agreement:
  - Definiteness
    (*et huset --> et hus*)
  - Gender agreement
    (*en nytt hus --> et nytt hus*)
  - Number agreement
    (*et grønt epler --> et grønt eple*)

- Two adjacent adjectives without a comma or conjunction
    en rød rask bil --> en rød, rask bil/en rød og rask bil
- Subject complement agreement
    Bilen er rødt --> Bilen er rød
- *Ingen* and *noen* and negation
    Jeg kjøpte ikke ingen bok i bokhandelen --> Jeg kjøpte ikke noen bok i bokhandelen
    Jeg kjøper noen bok i bokhandelen --> Jeg kjøper ei bok i bokhandelen
- *og/å* errors
    De gikk å sang --> De gikk og sang
    Hun skal å vise meg den nye kjolen --> Hun skal vise meg den nye kjolen
    Den lille gutten kan både snakke å synge --> Den lille gutten kan både snakke og synge
    Jeg trenger og sove --> Jeg trenger å sove
    Han skal prøve og skrive korrekt --> Han skal prøve å skrive korrekt
    Han orket sykle til jobben. --> Han orket å sykle til jobben.
- Too many finite verbs in a sentence or no verb in the sentence at all
    De kan forsøker å hjelpe deg --> De kan forsøke å hjelpe deg
    I Norge er var det slik --> I Norge er det slik.

Den gamle mannen syk. --> Den gamle mannen er syk
- Word order errors
    Jeg går ikke ut hvis det slutter ikke å regne --> Jeg går ikke ut hvis det ikke slutter å regne.
    Nå gutten kommer --> Nå kommer gutten.

5 Some errors from authentic texts

Below we will show a few of the errors we have found when testing the Norwegian grammar checker. They are all found in published newspaper texts from *Nordlys, Stavanger Aftenblad* and *Sarpsborg Blad.*

(2)

    (a) <u>D</u>e første <u>kampen</u> spilles torsdag.

    (b) Som leder av Kommunalstyret for kultur, idrett og kirke (kik) har han tatt initiativ til at alle kultursøknader som sendes til staten, underskrives av <u>de</u> fire <u>kommunen</u> sammen.

    (c) Det har vært en del tyverier på Sølvberget, men aldri tidligere har noen brukt skrujern for å hente en gjenstand i <u>et</u> <u>monter</u> på en utstilling. --> en monter

    (d)Vi merker oss at for eksempel Illiosfestivalen i Harstad fikk økt sitt budsjett fra 95.000 kroner i fjor til 250.000 kroner i år, at Nordland Musikkfestuke fikk <u>ei</u> <u>økning</u> på 90.000 (...) --> en økning

6. Challenging problems

6.1 Errors that have caused us to rewrite the tagger

Usually, a disambiguating tagger can assume that the text to be disambiguated is correct with respect to spelling and grammar. A tagger that is to be used with a grammar checker, however, has to assume that the text may contain errors. Therefore, a lot of rules in the disambiguating part of our original tagger had to be rewritten or discarded. Let us take one example:

In Norwegian, *den* can both be a determiner, as in (3), or a pronoun, as in (4):

(3) *Den* bilen likte han godt
(4) *Den* likte han godt

In the original disambiguator there are CG rules based on the knowledge that a Norwegian determiner agrees in gender and number with the rest of the noun phrase of which it is a part. These rules state that *den* is a pronoun if

- there is no masculine determiner immediately to the right (*den neste bilen*)
- there is no masculine adjective immediately to the right (*den røde bilen*)
- there is no masculine noun immediately to the right (*den bilen*)

In all other cases the word *den* would be a pronoun since the above rules have made it clear that it is not part of a noun phrase. I.e., if there is no agreement, the pronoun reading is chosen.

But when we want the grammar checker to find errors like *den eplet* or *den bilene*, i.e., possible noun phrases with erroneous gender and number agreement, we cannot discard the determiner reading. We therefore had to remove the original pronoun rules from the disambiguator, leading to the resulting text being more ambiguous than before.

6.2 Errors due to non-standard inflections and spellings being homographous with other words found in the lexicon

The spell checker handles ordinary misspellings and is run before the grammar checker. But what happens if a word is wrongly spelled or inflected and at the same time homographous with other words or inflections found in the lexicon?

The word *seire* is a good illustration of this. According to the official norm, this word is the infinitive form of the infinitive *seire* 'win', as in (5). However, it turns out that many people also use this word as a plural indefinite form of the noun *seier* 'victory' instead of the correct form *seirer*, as in (6).

(5) Folket vil *seire*
(6) a. Laget vant to viktige *seirer*   (Correct plural form of *seier*)
    b. Laget vant to viktige *seire*   (Incorrect plural form of *seier*)

The spell checker cannot reveal the error since *seire* is a correctly spelt word in the lexicon. The result of the multi-tagging and disambiguation is therefore that *seire* is analysed as an infinitive, and the grammar checker has no chance of discovering the fact that *seire* is a wrongly inflected noun. A solution would be to expand the lexicon, so that it would contain commonly misspelled words like these:

> *(7) Lexicon entries for misspelled words:*
>   seire N MASC PL INDEF NOM <Incorr>

6.3 Errors because of missing words

Finding that a word is missing can be a real problem for the grammar checker. The reason is simple: The grammar checker has no semantic knowledge - it does not understand the meaning of words. Determining whether there is a word missing, and what it might be, is almost impossible. Still, we have included CG rules for one seemingly simple case: that of a missing infinitive marker *å*.

Simplifying somewhat, infinitives generally cannot occur on their own without a modal verb or an infinitive marker:

    (8) Han kan sykle   (with a modal verb)
    (9) Han har lært å sykle   (with an infinitive marker)
    (10)* Han har lært sykle   (missing infinitive marker)

It is easy to make the grammar checker find errors like the one in (10): If there is no infinitive marker or modal verb in front of the infinitive, then notify the user that there is something missing. Below is an authentic example:

(11) Hun bruker _ låne deres fres fordi hennes egen står der med brukket splint, sår bihule og tett snabel (...)

However, there is still an overall problem: How does the grammar checker actually know that a given word is an infinitive? Infinitives are frequently ambiguous with other words.

7. Advantages of a system based on a morpho-syntactic analyser

We have seen above that the grammar checker is applied on text that has been grammatically tagged and disambiguated by a Constraint Grammar component. The fact that the input text has been morphologically analysed before grammar checking is an important feature of the system: It is often the case that a sequence of words may be grammatical in one larger context, and ungrammatical in another. Let us take as an example the sequence below:

(12)   de situasjonen

In (13a), this sequence is grammatically incorrect, and in (24b), correct:

(13)   a. * Vi liker ikke de situasjonen
            b. I dag forstår de situasjonene

In (13a), *de* is a determiner with the wrong number agreement features with respect to the following noun; in (13b), *de* is a pronoun. With no morphosyntactic analysis, the difference between these two sentences would be impossible to detect.

References

Arppe, A. 2000. Developing a grammar checker for Swedish. In Nordgård, T. (ed.) *Nodalida '99 Proceedings from the 12th Nordiske datalingvistikkdager*, Department of Linguistics, University of Trondheim, p. 13-27.

Birn, J. 2000. Detecting grammar errors with Lingsoft's Swedish grammar checker. In Nordgård, T. (ed.) *Nodalida '99 Proceedings from the 12th Nordiske datalingvistikkdager*, Department of Linguistics, University of Trondheim, p. 28-40.

De Smedt, K. and V. Rosén. 2000. Automatic proof reading for Norwegian: The challenges of lexical and grammatical variation. In Nordgård, T (red.) *Nodalida '99 Proceedings form the 12th "Nordiske datalingvistikkdagar"*, Department of Linguistics, University of Trondheim, p. 206-215.

Hagen, K., and J.B. Johannessen. 1998. *Disambiguering uten syntaks.* In Faarlund, J.T., Mæhlum, B. og T. Nordgård (eds.) MONS 7, p. 68-79,Novus forlag, Oslo.

Hagen, K., J.B. Johannessen and A. Nøklestad. 2000a. The shortcomings of a tagger. In Nordgård, T (red.) *Nodalida '99 Proceedings form the 12th "Nordiske datalingvistikkdagar"*, Department of Linguistics, University of Trondheim, p. 66-75.

Hagen, K., J.B. Johannessen and A. Nøklestad. 2000b. A Constraint-based Tagger for Norwegian. I Lindberg, Carl-Erik og Steffen Nordahl Lund (red.): *17th Scandinavian Conference of Linguistics. Odense Working Papers in Language   and Communication 19*, 31-48, University of Southern Denmark, Odense.

Karlsson, F., A. Voutilainen, J. Heikkilä og A. Anttila. 1995. *Constraint Grammar.* A Language-Independent System for Parsing Unrestricted Text. Mouton de Gruyter, Berlin.

Internet as Corpus

Automatic Construction of a Swedish News Corpus

Martin Hassel

NADA-KTH

Royal Institute of Technology

100 44 Stockholm, Sweden

ph: +46 8 790 66 34

fax: +46 8 10 24 77

email: xmartin@nada.kth.se

Abstract

This paper describes the automatic building of a corpus of short Swedish news texts from the Internet, its application and possible future use. The corpus is aimed at research on Information Retrieval, Information Extraction, Named Entity Recognition and Multi Text Summarization. The corpus has been constructed by using an Internet agent, the so called newsAgent, downloading Swedish news text from various sources. A small part of this corpus has then been manually tagged with keywords and named entities. The newsAgent is also used as a workbench for processing the abundant flows of news texts for various users in a customized format in the application Nyhetsguiden.

Keywords

News text, Corpus, Swedish, Internet

Introduction

Two years ago we built an automatic text summarizer called SweSum (Dalianis, 2000) for Swedish text. We wanted to evaluate SweSum but there were no tagged Swedish corpus available to evaluate text summarizers or information retrieval tools processing Swedish as it is for the English speaking community, mainly through the TREC, (Vorhees & Tice 2000), MUC and TIPSTER-SUMMAC evaluation conferences (Mani et al. 1998, Krenn & Samuelsson 1997). The purpose of this project[1] was to construct test bed for new natural language technology tools, i.e. *automatic text summarization, named entity tagging, stemming, information retrieval/extraction*, etc. In the process of building this system, Nyhetsguiden (Hassel 2001), we also made it capable of gathering the news texts into a corpus, a corpus we have used to train and evaluate such tools as mentioned above. As this corpus is aimed at research on information and language technology applied on redundant text, the system does not, contrary to (Hofland 2000), remove duplicated concordance lines

1. Nyhetsguiden – A user centred news delivery system

The system has a modular design and consists of three parts, the user interface, the user database and the main application, newsAgent. Being modular, the system can be run as a distributed system or on a single web server. When run as a distributed system, at least newsAgent must be run on a computer with Internet access. The user interface (Nyhetsguiden) and the user database can reside on either an Internet or Intranet capable server depending on the desired public access to the system. newsAgent is the core of the system and is basically a web spider that is run in a console window. The spider is implemented in Perl, which makes it platform independent, that is, it can run on any platform running Perl (Unix/Linux, Windows, Macintosh, BeOS, Amiga, etc). On intervals of 3-5 minutes newsAgent searches the designated news sources (Appendix A) for new news texts, that is news texts not seen by the system before. When a new news text is encountered it is fetched, the actual news text and accompanying illustrations are extracted (by removing navigation panels, banners, tables of links, etc).

---

[1] This project is supported by NUTEK (Swedish board for Industrial and Technical Development) FavorIT programme in cooperation with Euroseek AB.

The resulting document is then passed through the system and, depending on configuration; stored, summarized and routed to the end recipient.

2.   Construction of a Corpus of Swedish News Texts

Traditionally it has been hard work constructing a corpus of news text. In Sweden there are no newspapers that on a yearly basis offer their paper in digital form[2], as some foreign newspapers do (for example Wall Street Journal), meaning that obtaining this material has to be done on demand. Many Swedish newspapers are, when inquired, unwilling to release texts from their archives for research purposes, and even when they do, it is often the question of a small amount of news texts with an age of several years. This may potentially lead to the exclusion of contemporary words and giving unusually high, or low, occurrence frequencies to words related to phenomena limited to a certain period of time.

In the past, the solution would be to collect newspapers in their paper form and type or scan (using a Optical Character Recognition program) them in order to convert them to a format manageable by computers.

The World Wide Web is, on the other hand, today a large collection of texts written in different languages and thus giving an abundant resource for language studies already in a format, by necessity, manageable by computers. Many of the web pages are also frequently updated and thus give us a steady access to concurrent use of language in different fields. In this situation, neglecting the usability of Internet as a corpus would be foolish. In our case we used a tool called newsAgent that is a set of Perl scripts designed for gathering news texts, news articles and press releases from the web and routing them by mail according to subscribers defined information needs.

3.   KTH News Corpus

The project with the KTH News Corpus was initiated in May 2000. We started out collecting news telegrams, articles and press releases from three sources but with the ease of adding new sources we settled for twelve steady news sources (Appendix D). The choice of these news sources was based partly on site and page layout, partly on the wish to somewhat balance the corpus over several types of news topics. Among the chosen news sources are both general news, "daily press", and specialized news sources. The reason for this is the possibility of comparing how the same event is described depending on targeted reader (wording, level of detail, etc). As of February 2001 we have gathered more than 100.000 texts amounting to over 200Mb with an increase of over 10.000 new texts each month. The increase in word forms during March was almost 230.000. The lengths of the texts vary between 5 and 500 lines with a tendency towards the shorter and an average length of 193 words per text.

The texts are stored in HTML tagged format but only the news heading and the body of the news text is preserved. All other page layout and all navigation tables and banners are removed. Each text is tagged with Meta tags storing the information on time and date of publication, source and source URL. We stored the news in different categories (Appendix A) and thus giving the possibility to study the difference in use of language in, for example, news on cultural respectively sports event. We did this using the news sources own categorization of their news texts (finance, sports, domestic, foreign, etc), instead of a reader based categorization, such as described in (Karlgren 2000). The corpus is structured into these categories by the use of catalogue structure, a Hypertext linked index and a search engine driven index thus giving several modes of orientation in the corpus.

For the purpose of evaluating a Swedish stemmer in conjunction with a search engine (Carlberger et al 2001), we manually tagged 100 texts TREC style and constructed questions and answers central to each text. We also tagged each text with named entities (names, places, organisations and date/time) and the five most significant keywords for future evaluation purposes.

---

[2] We have as yet only been able to aquire 1995 years issue of Svenska Dagbladet (SVD) and I know that the Scarrie Swedish News Corpus (Dahlqvist 1998) contains all articles published in SVD and Uppsala Nya Tidning (UNT) during the same period.

Unfortunately copyright issues remain unsolved, we have no permission from the copyright holders except fair use, and so the corpus can only be used for research within our research group. The tool for gathering the corpus, newsAgent, is on the other hand available for use outside our research group (with the exclusion of mail routing and FTP plug-ins).

4.   Areas of Use

So far the corpus has been used for evaluation and training purposes. Knutsson (2001) has employed the corpus for evaluating error detection rules for Granska (Domeij et al), a program for checking for grammatical errors in Swedish unrestricted text. The tagged texts have besides, as mentioned above, being used for evaluation of a Swedish stemmer also been utilized in the evaluation of SweSum (Dalianis & Hassel 2001), an automatic text summarizer that among other languages handles Swedish unrestricted HTML tagged or untagged ASCII text and for the training and evaluation of a Named Entity Tagger (Dalianis & Åström 2001).

In the near future parts of the corpus will be used and for expanding SweSum with Multi Text Summarization. Other possible areas of use are for producing statistics and lexicons, and for developing a Topic Detection Tracking (Wayne 2000), system for Swedish news.

5.   The Future of the Corpus

I am now on the verge of rewriting the corpus tools since we now are more fully aware of its potential uses. Among planned improvements are:

- Internal representation in XML
- Automatic tagging of:
  o Parts-of-speech
  o Clause and sentence boundaries
  o Named Entities (persons, locations, etc.)
- Automatic summarization of each text
- Automatic running statistics
  o Average increase per month/week in number of:
    - Texts
    - Sentences
    - Words
    - Word forms
  o Average:
    - Text length (in sentences, words & characters)
    - Sentence length (in words & characters)
    - Word length
  o Total number of:
    - Texts
    - Sentences
    - Words
    - Word forms
- Hopefully a solution to the current copyright issues
- A more balanced choice of channels/sources

This will hopefully result in a tool that in a short period can build a corpus of plain, tagged and summarized versions of the same news text along with appropriate statistics.

6.   Conclusions

A concluding remark is that a small piece of programming has grown to a complete system which we had great use of in training and evaluation of various natural language tools and that the newsAgent has been a incentive to push our research beyond foreseeable limits. As a part of our online service Nyhetsguiden we have also gained as much as fifty willing beta testers of our language technology tools. We are now on the verge to incorporate our new Named Entity Tagger into newsAgent. We also believe that this proves that it is feasible to acquire a substantial corpus, over a short period of time, from the Internet. One may argue that as long as copyright issues are note solved, the corpus has no legal use outside our research group. While this is true, the corpus has been of great use to us in our research and the corpus tools still remain for public use. The tools have proven to be practically service free run without major problems. Since the same news reports are, potentially, repeated over news sources and time, the resulting corpus will be of much use for research on Information Extraction/Retrieval and Topic Detection Tracking.

Acknowledgements

I would like to thank Hercules Dalianis and Ola Knutsson for comments on early versions of this paper.

7.   References

J. Carlberger, H. Dalianis, M. Hassel, O. Knutsson 2001. *Improving Precision in Information Retrieval for Swedish using Stemming.* NODALIDA '01 - 13th Nordic Conference on Computational Linguistics, May 21-22 2001, Uppsala, Sweden.

B. Dahlqvist 1998. *The SCARRIE Swedish News Corpus,* Reports from the SCARRIE project, editor A. Sågwall Hein. Uppsala University, Sweden

H.Dalianis 2000. SweSum - A Text Summarizer for Swedish, IPlab-174, Technical report, NADA, KTH October. http://www.nada.kth.se/~hercules/Textsumsummary.html

H. Dalianis and M. Hassel 2001. *Development of a Swedish Tagged Corpora for Evaluating Summarizers.* NADA-KTH. Technical report for the SeaSum project, FavorIT programme, NUTEK. http://www.nada.kth.se/~hercules/papers/TextsumDraft.pdf

H. Dalianis and E. Åström 2001. *A Swedish Named Entity Tagger – Its Construction and Evaluation.* NADA-KTH (forthcoming).

R. Domeij, O. Knutsson, J. Carlberger, V. Kann 1999. *Granska - an efficient hybrid system for Swedish grammar checking.* NODALIDA '99, 9-10 December 1999, Trondheim, Norway.

M. Hassel 2001. *newsAgent - A tool for automatic news surveillance and corpora building.* Technical report for the SeaSum project, FavorIT programme, NUTEK. http://www.nada.kth.se/~xmartin/papers/Nutek.pdf

K. Hofland 2000. *A self-expanding corpus based on newspapers on the Web.* In Proceedings of Second Internation Conference on Language Resources and Evaluation. LREC-2000 Athens, Greece, 31 May - 2 June 2000. pp 1271-1272.

J. Karlgren 2000. *Assembling a Balanced Corpus from the Internet.* In Stylistic Experiments for Information Retrieval. Dissertation for the Degree of Doctor of Philosophy, Stockholm University, Department of Linguistics. pp 99-104.

O. Knutsson 2001. *Automatisk språkgranskning av svensk text* (in Swedish). Dissertation for the Degree of Licentiate of Philosophy, Kungliga Tekniska Högskolan, NADA.

B. Krenn and C. Samuelsson 1997. The Linguist's Guide to Statistics (Chapter 3 Basic Corpus Linguistics, http://www.coli.uni-sb.de/~krenn/edu.html

I. Mani, T. Firmin, D. House, M. Chrzanowski, M. Klein. G. Hirschman, B.Sundheim and L. Obrst 1998. The TIPSTER Text Summarization Evaluation. Final Report. Mitre Technical Report MTR 98W0000138, October 1998.

E.M. Vorhees and D.M.Tice 2000. The TREC-8 Question Answering System Track, In the proceedings of Second International Conference on Language Resources and Evaluation. LREC-2000 Athens, Greece, 31 May-2 June 2000. pp. 1501-1508.

C. Wayne 2000. *Multilingual Topic Detection and Tracking: Successful Research Enabled by Corpora and Evaluation.* In Proceedings of Second Internation Conference on Language Resources and Evaluation. LREC-2000 Athens, Greece, 31 May - 2 June 2000.

Appendix A
News sources and categories used by newsAgent.

Source:	Categories:
Aftonbladet	- Economics, cultural, sports, domestic and foreign news
Amnesty International	- Press releases and news on human rights
BIT.se (Sifo Group)	- Press releases from companies
Dagens Industri	- News on the industrial market
Dagens Nyheter	- Economics, cultural, sports, domestic and foreign news
Homoplaneten (RFSL)	- News concerning rights of the homosexual community
Tidningen Mobil	- News articles on mobile communication
International Data Group	- News articles on computers
Medströms Förlag	- News articles on computers
Senaste Nytt.com	- News flashes (discontinued)
Svenska Dagbladet	- News flashes
Svenska Eko-nyheter	- News flashes
Sveriges Riksdag	- Press releases from the Swedish Parliament

On Ambiguity in Internet Searches

Gordana Ilic Holen, Janne von Koss Torkildsen and Janne Bondi Johannessen

Tekstlaboratoriet, University of Oslo
P.b. 1102 Blindern
N-0317 Oslo
Norway
jannebj@ilf.uio.no

1 Introduction

1. 1 Prospect

The aim of this project is to decide to what extent the results of Internet searches contain irrelevant information because of ambiguous search words. If the amount of irrelevant information is great, users will be discouraged from employing the Internet for information retrieval. There are several different types of ambiguity. Some of these seem easy to filter out. Above all, we are interested in finding ambiguity which coincides with membership in different
grammatical categories, because this type of ambiguity could easily be reduced by using a tagger for grammatical disambiguation.

1.2 About the project

We have studied log files containing the search words in Fast's search engine and reconstructed the searches for the most frequent words. If a search word were ambiguous, we sorted its meanings according to several different criteria. In deciding whether a word was ambiguous or not, we employed a number of different sources, among these encyclopaedias and dictionaries. The results of this inquiry show that almost one fourth of the most frequent search words were ambiguous, and in about 90% of these cases there was a correlation between meaning and grammatical category. (This number means that whenever a search word was multiply ambiguous, at least two grammatical categories could be found to match at least two of the different meanings.)

The paper is organized as follows: Section 2 explains the research methods and the material we used. Section 3 contains examples. In section 4 we systematize the results by providing some statistics, and in section 5 we present some concrete proposals which all make use of tagging. Section 6 is the conclusion.

2.0 Methods and research material

2.1 Period picture
The project took place in the summer of 2000, employed two students and lasted two months, thus constituting four months of labor.

2.2 The log files of search words
The research material consists of about 900 000 search words form Fast Search and Transfer's log files coming from several different search engines. We sorted the material by frequency, and grouped together identical word forms. From the sorted word list, we picked the 5500 most frequent words for further investigation. In this way we made sure to work on only very common search words.

Even if the material contained no less than 5500 search words, the number of lexemes is much smaller. There are two reasons for this: a) the files distinguish between capital and non-capital letters (e.g. Liv and liv), b) in several cases many different spellings are used for the same word (e.g. pokemon, Pokemon, pokèmon, pokémon, Pokèmon)

We have not gathered together all the words that belong to the same lexeme, but simply used the word forms as they appeared in the log files.

Some users have searched for more than one word at a time. We chose to split up all these complex searches. The result is that function words such as *i* 'in', *på* 'on' appear as search words in our files, even though the chances are that no one actually searched only for these words. In any case, this choice does not seem to have affected the general result.

The most frequent content words were *sex* and *chat* having 52 000 and 36 000 searches respectively. (We keep the truly most frequent function words like *i* ('in') and *på* ('on') out of the discussion.) The least frequent of the 5500 search words were *hyttetomter* and *a.s*, 275 and 210 searches respectively.

2.3 Information about the search words
A lot of the words in the Norwegian language are ambiguous, and the task of seeing all the different meanings a word can have is not an easy one. Usually the ambiguous words appear in a grammatical context which rules out most of the possible interpretations and in a pragmatic context which gives a clue as to which meanings are interesting to consider.
Take the sentence *Per var høy* 'Per was tall'. Each of the words has at least two meanings:

(1)

```
"<Per>"
        "*per" subst mask prop              (egennavn)
        "per" prep                          (= pr.)
    "<var>"
        "var" adj pos m/f ub ent            (= følsom)
        "var" subst nøyt appell ent ub      (= et putevar)
        "var" subst nøyt appell fl ub       (= flere putevar)
        "vare" verb imp                     (= ikke slutt!)
        "være" verb pret                    (= hadde egenskapen)
    "<høy>"
        "høy" adj pos m/f ub ent            (= ikke lav)
        "høy" subst nøyt appell ent ub      (= gress)
```

As language users, we are usually unaware of such ambiguities, and therefore we do not think about possible ambiguity in the search criterions we use in Internet searching. The students working on this project were more aware of such problems than the average user, and did also use dictionaries and encyclopedia.

In order to find out if certain words were ambiguous, we used the Internet edition of *Multitaggeren* (developed by Tekstlaboratoriet and Dokumentasjonsprosjektet at the University of Oslo, and which is a further development of, among others, Bokmålsordboka). The main difference between *Multitaggeren* and standard dictionaries is that it also provides information on inflected words, not only the word forms. In other words, it provides information not only on a word form such as *bilde* 'picture', but also *bilder* 'pictures'. *Multitaggeren* provides information about the grammatical properties of a certain word, but not about its meaning.

Regarding the meaning(s) of the words, we used the web edition of *Bokmålsordboka* (Landrø and Wangensteen 1986), and the encyclopedia *Store Norske Leksikon* by Kunnskapsforlaget.

2. 4. The Work Process

All together, we examined the 5500 most frequent search words in the log files. For each search word, we checked whether it was ambiguous by looking it up in *Multitaggeren*, and when ambiguity was found we investigated what kind of ambiguity was involved, and how grammatical categories and properties correlated with the different meanings. Note that we have only considered those differences in meaning that can be gathered under the term homonymy, and not those which are counted as polysemy. (We have for example considered the "putevar" and "følsom" meanings of *var* as relevant, but not the-lowest-part-of-a-leg and the-lowest-part-of-a-mountain meanings of *fot* 'foot'.)

For each word we conducted a search on the Internet using Fast's search engine Alltheweb.com. In this way we found out what kind of results the search word led to, whether the hits varied depending on the ambiguity of the words, and whether the hits was relevant according to what we considered to be the preferred meaning of these words. We only looked at the first 100 hits for each word. This number should probably have been higher, as the hits are often grouped in such a way that the hits involving the same meaning of a search word appear together. However, we had limited time available, and it was extremely time-consuming to go through the search results, since it was often impossible to see which meaning of the search word was used from the few lines that accompanied each search result. In such cases, it was necessary to check on the web-page itself, and the web-link could be broken, or the page could be under construction or simply take time to download.

For this reason, the data presented should not be regarded as conclusive. Nevertheless, the material provides a good indication of what is to be found.

We completed a little form for each search word.

(2)

```
1. Ambiguity:
        - Important for search?
2. Inflected form:
3. Name:
        - Ambiguity:
            - Person:
            - Place:
            - Firm/org:
            - Other:
4. Note
```

In the talk we will say more about how we filled in these forms, and about the results, illustrating with examples.

Using existing written language analyzers in understanding natural spoken Finnish

Tommi Jauhiainen
Department of General Linguistics
University of Helsinki

Abstract

In this paper we consider the possible use of existing linguistic (mainly morphological) analyzers for written Finnish in order to create a system that uses speech as its interface. We also present means to enhance the usability of these analyzers in this respect.

1 USIX Interact–project

In the USIX Interact project ("http://www.mlab.uiah.fi/interact/", Tekes–project 40691/00), which is mainly funded by the National Technology Agency, we are designing a general platform for systems which use a natural language interface in communicating with their users. The Interact project is a joint effort between the University of Art and Design Helsinki, the University of Helsinki, the Helsinki University of Technology and the University of Tampere. As a demonstration we are constructing a system which should be able to answer inquiries about the timetables of public transportation.

The problem that we at the University of Helsinki are solving at the moment is the mapping of the utterance of the speaker into relevant semantic units which are in turn processed by the dialogue manager. After dialogue manager has done it's processing it produces new semantic units, out of which it is our problem to generate natural language. We are also responsible for creating a dictionary for the speech recognition system.

2 Written vs. spoken Finnish

It is a widely known fact that Finnish is written so that one grapheme corresponds to one phoneme. "Spoken as it is written". Much less known is the fact that spoken Finnish differs greatly from its written form. The current written form of Finnish was established to serve a compromise between all the Finnish dialects and as such it has never really been a good transliteration of any form of spoken Finnish.

Given the current state of user independent speech recognition, we are forced to use full word lists which include all the morphological forms that we are trying to understand from the user's utterance. Because of the difference between written and spoken Finnish, existing tools cannot handle the word forms used in natural spoken Finnish.

In order to deal with the variation between the several different ways to pronounce any written word, we have to generate a list of the most probable pronunciations for each one. Then we map each one of these pronunciations to standard forms that can be found from the written language. These standard forms are then passed forward to any linguistic analyzers that are being used by the system.

To do this we need a tool which takes as its input the written forms we decide are necessary and as its output gives the forms that can actually be found from spoken language.

3 Two corpora

At the moment we have two small corpora of spoken language dialogues which deal with public transportation. The first corpus includes 32 dialogues and its transliteration was done at the University of Art and Design. The second corpus includes 24 dialogues and it was transliterated at the University of Helsinki. The quality of the first corpus was partly inadequate for the task at hand. The largest problem being the fact that most of the numbers had been transliterated as numerical characters.

The first corpus includes around 8500 words and 2000 different word forms. The morphological analyzer used (*fintwol*, TWOL 92, by K. Koskenniemi and Lingsoft, Inc) understands a little over 80% of the forms and words used.

The statistics for the second corpus are outlined in the table 1.

	# Words	# not undestood	% not undestood
Client words	2274	610	26.8
HDesk words	2515	514	20.4
All words	4789	1124	23.5
Client forms	846	261	30.9
HDesk forms	773	193	25.0
All forms	1303	378	29.0

Table 1.

37 of all the word forms are such that they do not have any substitute in the lexicon of the fintwol (they are mainly proper names). 20 word forms are actually made out of two different lexemes and should not be written together according to the current standards of the written Finnish. After removing these troublemakers the number of different forms is 1246 and out of those 321, or 25,8%, were not understood by the morphological analyzer.

4 Rules of transformation

Generally the variation between the written and the spoken forms seems to be quite regular, and we have been able to construct some rules for generating the spoken forms from the written. For this presentation we are more closely examining the five most important of those rules. When reading the examples it must be noted that several of these rules can be applied to a given word, but so that of the rules one, two and three only one is applied.

Any rule that would change the word into any other existing word with a different semantic meaning is usually not applied. But this is not always so, for example the word 'että'.

"että" (that) ––> "ett", by rule 1.
"ett" ––> "et", by rule 5.

If in the spoken language we see the form 'et', it is most propably a contracted form of the word 'että' and not the written language form 'et' (you do not). This phenomena also creates the problem that the morphological analyzer thinks that it understands the word, even if it doesn't. This percentage decreasing factor has not been considered in the values of the table 1.

4.1 Rule 1

The most common (54/321 instances) variation was the deletion of the final vowel 'a' or 'ä' when it was preceded by a consonant. This variation seems to be fully productive and all words must be thus modified.

$$/[aä]/ \rightarrow \emptyset\ /\ C\_\#$$

Examples of the rule from the corpus:
"automaatista" ––> "automaatist" (from the automat)
"kyllä" ––> "kyl" (yes)
"neljätoista" ––> "neljätoist" (fourteen)
"siinä" ––> "siin" (there)
"huopalahdessa" ––> "huopalahdes" (in huopalahti)

4.2 Rule 2

The deletion of the final consonant 'n' (44/321 instances) is fully productive in non–verbal forms.

$$/n/ \rightarrow \emptyset\ /\ \_\#$$

Examples of the rule from the corpus:
"ainakin" ––> "ainaki" (at least)
"ensimmäinen" ––> "ensimmäine" (the first)
"martinlaaksoon" ––> "martinlaaksoo" (to martinlaakso)
"kakkonen" ––> "kakkone" (number two)
"tuohon" ––> "tuoho" (over there)

4.3 Rule 3

The deletion of the final vowel 'i' if it is preceded by the consonant 's' (42/321). This rule is not fully productive and some very short words do not tend to do this, for example the word 'tosi' (true) never becomes 'tos'.

$$/i/ \rightarrow \emptyset / s\_\#$$

Examples of the rule from the corpus:
"anteeksi" ––> "anteeks" (sorry)
"kuusisataa" ––> "kuussataa" (six hundred)
"saisi" ––> "sais" (would get)
"uusi" ––> "uus" (new)
"kuukausilippu" ––> "kuukauslippu" (ticket for a month)

This rule could create problems, for it is productive also inside compound words. The lexicon of the speech recognizer is done in such a way that all compound words are divided to non compound words, which solves this problem.

4.4 Rule 4

The deletion of the phoneme 'i' in diphthongs that are further in the word than the first syllable (31/321).

$$/i/ \rightarrow \emptyset / VC^+V\_$$

Examples of the rule from the corpus:
"aikaisemmin" ––> "aikasemmin" (before)
"tarkoitan" ––> "tarkotan" (I mean)
"kysyisin" ––> "kysysin" (I would ask)
"silloin" ––> "sillo" (at that time)
"viimeinen" ––> "viimenen" (the last)

4.5 Rule 5

If after applying any of the preceding rules (mainly the rule number one) a double consonant is found from the end of the word it shortens to a single consonant (18/321).

$$/C_1C_1/ \rightarrow C_1 / \_\#$$

Examples of the rule from the corpus:
"missä" ––> "mis" (where)
"mutta" ––> "mut" (but)
"kehällä" ––> "kehäl" (at the ring)
"vaikka" ––> "vaik" (though)
"sitten" ––> "sit" (then)

5 Implementing the rules

The program that does this variation can be fairly small. Table 2 shows the simple substitutions that are needed as regular expressions in Perl.

s/([^eyuioåäöa])[aä]$/$1/;
s/n$//;
s/si$/s/;
s/([eyuioåäöa][^eyuioåäöa]+[eyuoåäöa])i/$1/g;
s/ss$/s/;
and so on in the format: s/$C_1C_1$$/C_1/;

Table 2.

It should generate the original form and all the different forms that any combinations of the above rules can generate. Out of the 321 forms that were originally not understood, these rules would touch 156 (48,6%) and would completely generate 126 (39,3%). Thus reducing the overall percent of the forms not understood to 15,0% from the initial 25,8%. Implementing additional rules will still reduce this percentage.

We have also partly implemented these rules using Xerox's tools for two−level morphology (*twolc, Two−Level Compiler 3.1.4 (7.3.8)*). It is easier to handle and to represent the order and parallelism of the rules.

The reason not to include these forms or transformations directly into the lexicon of the morphological or syntactical analyzer is that we don't want to tie our hands into using any one existing software. Also if new analyzers are developed, they will probably be designed for written language.

At the moment we are using Lauri Carlson's *C−parse* as syntactic analyzer. The *C−parse* is designed to analyze *fintwol*'s output, but for example *TextMorfo* (v.2.0, Kielikone Oy 1999) is not. If in the future we decide to use *TextMorfo*, it is important that the mapper from spoken to written language is an independent module.

The differences between the syntax of the spoken and written languages is a completely separate problem of equal or greater proportions and is not discussed here.

Table 3 shows some examples from the generated lexicon for the speech recognizer.

| MISSÄ m i s s ae / m i s s / m i s |
| SILLOIN s i l l o i n / s i l l o i / s i l l o / s i l l o n |
| TARKOITAN t a r k o i t a / t a r k o t a / t a r k o i t a n / t a r k o t a n |
| UUSI u u s i / u u s |
| VIIMEINEN v i i m e i n e n / v i i m e i n e / v i i m e n e / v i i m e n e n |

Table 3.

6 Further use for the rules

The use of these rules for other purposes such as speech generation has been contemplated. It would be a significant improvement to the quality of any speech synthesizer if it were able to generate word forms that are found in actual spoken language. Written language word forms have not been considered a real problem because of the low quality of the other more important attributes like intonation and stress in the current synthesizers. The USIX Suopuhe project is developing a synthesizer with better intonation and stress. The use of the above rules especially with numerical expressions is considered.

References

Koskenniemi, Kimmo. 1983. *Two−level morphology : a general computational model for word−form recognition and production.* Helsinki, University of Helsinki.

Lehikoinen, Laila. 1994. *Suomea ennen ja nyt : suomen kielen kehitys ja vaihtelu.* Helsinki, Finn Lectura.

Suihkonen, Pirkko. 1988. *Murteiden generointia atk:n avulla : showmur-ohjelma.* Helsinki. University of Helsinki.

Wall, Larry. 2000. *Programming Perl.* Sebastopol (CA), O'Reilly.

En automatisk navnegjenkjenner for
norsk, svensk og dansk

Janne Bondi Johannessen, Universitetet i Oslo
jannebj@mail.hf.uio.no

1. Generelt

I dette foredraget vil vi presentere et prosjekt som nettopp har kommet i gang, og som har fått NOK 1 000 000 fra NorFA til et nordisk nettverk. Prosjektet har to siktemål som henger nøye sammen. Det ene er å bygge nettverk mellom fire forsknings- og utviklingsmiljøer ved UiO (Tekstlaboratoriet), UiB (HIT-senteret), GU (Språkdata) og CST. Det andre er praktisk: å utvikle en automatisk navnegjenkjenner for norsk, svensk og dansk. (En automatisk navnegjenkjenner er et program som klarer å skille typer navn, som firmanavn, steds- og personnavn, fra hverandre). Produktet som utvikles, kan ha kommersiell interesse. Vi er samarbeider med Internett-firmaet FAST Search & Transfer, som vurderer å gå inn med studentstipendmidler.

For at det skal være mulig i et søke- eller informasjons-behandlingssystem å søke etter et navn med spesifisering av hva slags navnetype det er, må det utvikles særspråklige navnegjenkjennere. De tre deltagerspråkene har ulike navnetradisjoner, og samme navn kan gjerne være personnavn i ett land og steds- eller firmanavn i et annet. Videre vil navnenes språklige kontekst være ulik i de ulike språkene, slik at det må utvikles en separat navnegjenkjenner for hvert språk.

Vi ønsker altså å utvikle en automatisk navneentitetsgjenkjenner for norsk (bokmål og nynorsk), svensk og dansk. Mens en vanlig grammatisk tagger vanligvis vil kjenne igjen et ord som egennavn, er det en helt annen sak å kjenne igjen hva slags type egennavn det er snakk om i de enkelte tilfellene. Navnegjenkjenneren skal kunne ta en hvilken som helst ukjent tekst og bestemme for hvert egennavn hva slags navneentitet det dreier seg om: om det er et personnavn, et stedsnavn eller et firmanavn. Man skulle kanskje tro at en slik navnegjenkjenning ville være fort gjort om man bare hadde noen store navnelister, men i praksis er det ikke så lett. I Norge er det for eksempel vanlig at stedsnavn har gitt opphav til gårdsnavn, og så til etternavn: *Bondi* er både et stedsnavn og et personnavn. Og overalt i verden er det vanlig at personnavn brukes som firmanavn: Lefdal er både et firmanavn og et personnavn. Dessuten vil mange tekster, ikke minst fra aviser, ikke bare inneholde nasjonale navn, men navn fra hele verden.

De enkelte miljøene ved UiO, GU og CST kommer til å benytte ulike metoder for utvikling av navnegjenkjenneren, ikke bare fordi vi dermed kan sammenligne metodene og til slutt velge den eller de vi mener er best, men også fordi vi til dels har ulik programvare i utgangspunktet og ulik kompetanse i miljøene. I foredraget vil vi snakke om noen av metodene som er mulige å bruke, og hvilke vi vurderer eller har bestemt oss

for. Dette inkluderer f.eks. navnelister, statistiske tilnærminger, og kontekstuelle regler,
eller en blanding av disse, slik det er beskrevet i Mikheev et al. (1998, 1999).

2. Hva finnes i dag for de enkelte språkene?

Det finnes i dag ikke noen skikkelig navnetypegjenkjenner for de tre skandinaviske
språkene. For dansk og norsk finnes det ingen, mens det for svensk finnes en begrenset
utgave (se nedenfor). Derimot finnes det et minimum av språklige verktøy som er
nødvendige for å gjennomføre prosjektet.

Dansk

For dansk finnes det en Brill-tagger. Den er basert på transformasjonsregler snarere enn
rent statistiske metoder. Den gjenkjenner ca. 96, 5 % av taggene korrekt, og plukker også
ut egennavn (men over 10 % av feilene var feil ved gjenkjenning av egennavn) (Pedersen
2001). Det er denne taggeren som kommer til å bli brukt i prosjektet som et
utgangspunkt.

Videre har det blitt utviklet en navnegjenkjenner for dansk til bruk for
tekstresymeringssystemer, som spesielt legger vekt på å gjenfinne egennavn som
sådanne, og i tillegg finne nominale syntagmer som koreferer med disse i tekstene
(Nelson 2000).

Svensk

Innenfor EU-prosjektet AVENTINUS ble det utviklet en begrenset navnetypegjenkjenner
av Dimitris Kokkinakis. Denne bruker ikke navnelister, og ikke statistikk, men lingvistisk
kontekst. Mye av det som ble gjort i det prosjektet vil kunne brukes videre i det
herværende prosjektet (se Kokkinakis et al 2001).

Det finnes flere grammatiske taggere som er aktuelle å bruke i prosjektet.

Norsk

Det finnes ingen navnetypegjenkjenner for norsk. Ved Universitetet i Oslo
(Tekstlaboratoriet) finnes det en tagger som gjenkjenner egennavn (se Johannessen et al
2000). Leksikalsk funnrate (recall) er på 99,2%, mens presisjonen er på 96,8%. Denne vil
bli brukt for den norske navnetypegjenkjenneren.

Referanser

Johannessen, J.B., K. Hagen og A. Anders Nøklestad. 2000. A Constraint-Based Tagger
for Norwegian. I Lindberg, Carl-Erik og Steffen Nordahl Lund (red.): *17th
Scandinavian Conference of Linguistics. Odense Working Papers in Language
and Communication 19,* 31-48, University of Southern
Denmark, Odense.

Kokkinakis, D., M. Gellerstam, Y. Cederholm, T. Rasmark. Språkdata
    Presentation/Discussion Paper. Foredrag presentert på første
    navnegjenkjennerseminar på Fefor, januar.
Mikheev, A., C. Grover og M. Moens. 1998. Description of the LTG system used for
    MUC-7. I *Seventh Message Understanding Conference (MUC-7): Proceedings of
    a conference held in Fairfax, Virginia.*
    http://www.muc.saic.com/proceedings/muc_7_toc.html
Mikheev, A., M. Moens og C. Grover. 1999. Named Entity Recognition without
    gazetteers. I *Proceedings of EACL 99, Ninth Conference of the European Chapter
    of the Association for Computational Linguistics*, s. 1-8.
Nelson, M. Propriumsyntagmer i tekstresumeringssystemer. Ph.d.-avhandling,
    Handelshøjskolen i København.
Pedersen, B. 2001. Danish Proper Nouns in the Brill Tagger. Foredrag presentert på
    første navnegjenkjennerseminar på Fefor, januar.

Understanding Multimodal Interaction by Exploiting Unification and Integration Rules

Håkan Johansson

Department of Computer and Information Science
Linköping University
Sweden

g_hakjo@ida.liu.se

Abstract

This paper presents a model for synergistic integration of multimodal speech and pen information. The model consists of an algorithm for matching and integrating interpretations of inputs from different modalities, as well as of a grammar that constrains integration. Integration proper is achieved by unifying feature structures. The integrator is part of a general framework for multimodal information systems with dialogue capabilities. Those parts of this framework that are relevant and affects the design of the integrator are also presented.

1. Introduction

In recent years, a number of studies have shown that interfaces that allow interaction through more than a single modality (e.g., speech) can empower users in their day-to-day interaction with computers (for a good up-to-date review, consult Oviatt et al., 2000). Carefully designed multimodal interfaces promise to make human-computer interaction more flexible, efficient, habitable, and natural. This is of most importance when it comes to walk-up-and-use systems, such as information kiosks. These are systems with which users do not interact on an everyday basis and therefore need to be designed to allow an intuitive interaction. An instance of such a system is a time table information system for the local bus and train transportations in a city and its surroundings. This kind of system is currently being developed at the Natural Language Laboratory (NLPLAB) at Linköping University.

The project aims to develop a publicly available time table information system capable of synergistic multimodal speech and pen interaction. In parallel to the development of the specific application, a general framework for multimodal information systems with dialogue capabilities, called MALIN, is set up. MALIN is an elaboration of an earlier architecture for unimodal typed natural language dialogue systems, and therefore this paper describes how the interpretation module has been expanded to handle multimodal speech and pen interaction. The primary focus of this paper is on how the problem of integrating, or fusing, the information received from the speech and pen modalities has been solved. This problem has previously been addressed by a number of researchers (cf. Neal et al. 1989; Wahlster, 1991; Koons, Sparrell, and Thorisson, 1993; Nigay and Coutaz, 1995; Johnston et al., 1997; Johnston, 1998; Johnston and Bangalore, 2000), but no single technique has become standard or even widely reused. This paper presents an approach to multimodal integration that falls somewhere between two of the earlier approaches, namely that of Johnston et al. (1997) and that of Johnston (1998). The integrator proposed consists of an algorithm for matching and integrating interpretations of input from different modalities, as well as an grammar formalism that constrains integration. The integration proper is performed by unification of feature structures.

2. MALIN

MALIN is an acronym for Multimodal Application of LINLIN. LINLIN, in turn, is an acronym for Linköping Natural Language Interface and is a general architecture for natural language interfaces capable of entertaining a coherent dialogue (Jönsson, 1997). MALIN is an extension of LINLIN and presents a general framework for multimodal dialogue applications. The framework consists of modules for interpreting and generating multimodal input and output, dialogue management, domain knowledge management, and user interface management (Dahlbäck et al., 1999). In the present paper, the focus is on the multimodal interpretation module.

The interpretation module consists of five separate parts: a speech recognizer, a natural language interpreter, a gesture recognizer, a gesture interpreter, and a multimodal integrator. The composition of these parts are illustrated in figure 1 below:

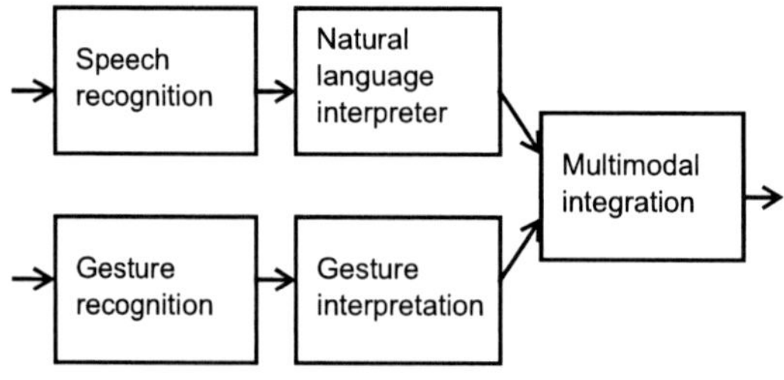

Figure 1: The interpretation module in the MALIN framework.

The architectural composition illustrated in figure 1 deviates very little from the typical multimodal interpretation architecture discussed in Oviatt et al. (2000, p. 275). The only discrepancy between the two architectures is that the one shown above does not regard the dialogue context when integrating multimodal information. More specifically, integration, as proposed in the present paper, only occurs locally within a single interactional segment. References that remain unresolved after multimodal integration (e.g., references to previous dialogue contributions) are solved by the dialogue manager in the MALIN framework.

2.1 Speech recognizer

The speech recognizer, which is currently not available, is assumed to be a standard continuous, speaker-independent recognizer for Swedish. However, it is essential that the recognizer can provide information on the temporal onset and offset of the individual tokens in a recognized string. For example, if recognition results in the string "depart from here", the recognizer must provide temporal information about when 'depart', 'from', and 'here' were uttered respectively. Currently, such speech recognizers exist for other languages than Swedish, and the lack of such a recognizer is a practical problem rather than a theoretical one.

2.2 Natural language interpreter

The natural language interpreter combines shallow and partial parsing (Strömbäck and Jönsson, 1998), which leads to a degree of flexibility suitable for spoken natural language. The interpreter is based on an extended PATR-II formalism. It has been extended to allow the occurrence of unknown words within phrases in order to avoid analysis to break down in the face of words that are not present in the lexicon. Furthermore, the parser environment has been extended to allow the application developer to specify which of the inactive edges that constitute the parse result, i.e., the result is a set of partial parses. The representational format is directed acyclic graph (DAG) representations of feature structures.

The temporal information provided by the speech recognizer is incorporated into the resulting partial parses. It is therefore required that the grammar is defined in such a way that all the information extracted from a single word or subphrase is represented within a single partial parse, rather than being distributed over several different partial parses. This is a limitation that has not been an issue in the current application, but could prove to be a problem in other applications. However, it is in many cases possible to construct the rules in the grammar such that this problem can be avoided.

2.3 Gesture recognizer

The gesture recognizer is triggered when the pen is pressed to the surface of the screen and terminates recognition when the pen is released from the screen. The recognition result is represented as a feature structure containing information on the "touched" coordinates, as well as the onset and offset of a number of consecutive pen gestures. The only task the gesture recognizer has is to convert a continuous stream of information in a symbolic, non-interpreted, representation.

2.4 Gesture interpreter

The gesture interpreter further process the feature structure received from the gesture recognizer in that it receives an interpretation according to a specification of a gesture language. Different interpretations are assigned depending on where in the interface the gesture was made. The output of the gesture interpreter is a DAG.

3. Multimodal Integrator

As can be inferred from the previous sections, the multimodal integrator receives as input two feature structures, or more specifically, two DAG:s. The integrator process the DAG:s and attempts to integrate them in order to construct a coherent interpretation of a user's actions.

3.1 Algorithm

The algorithm is quite straightforward. Informally, the algorithm maps every subDAG in one modality (i.e., the interpretation of input from one modality) to every subDAG in the other modality. In other words, the algorithm attempts to integrate every combination of subDAG:s. This means that the algorithm has to consider $S * G$ combinations, where S is the number of subDAG:s of the interpreted speech, and G is the number of subDAG:s in the interpreted gesture. In order for the combinations of subDAG:s to be integrated they have to match some rule in an ordered set of rules. These rules are ordered with regards to specificity, and therefore this is a case of conflict resolution by specificity (cf. Jackson, 1999, p. 86).

A few other points are worth noticing. First, what is considered for integration is subDAG:s along with the feature (or attribute) of which they are a value. Since we are considering only proper subDAG:s, every subDAG is the value of some feature. However, in the current natural language interpreter, cardinal numbers are used as features to iterate a number of similar structures. For instance, if the user specifies multiple locations, these are located by iteration under a feature *locations*. In the case where a subDAG is a value of a feature that is a cardinal number, the algorithm replaces this number with the feature name at the next shallower level.

Another point worth noticing is that in the current implementation, speech is considered to be the primary modality. This means that if the algorithm receives non-empty DAG:s but is unable to integrate them, the speech-DAG is returned. However, if the speech-DAG is empty and the gesture-DAG is not, the latter is returned.

3.2 Integration rules

As previously mentioned, the integration rules are an ordered set where each rule is a set of constraints on the combination of DAG:s to be integrated. For a rule to be applicable, all constraints must be satisfied. The constraints regard both the semantic and temporal information represented in the DAG:s.

3.3 Temporal constraints

When interacting with computers multimodally, users utilize a wide range of temporal integration patterns (cf. Oviatt et al., 1997). Therefore, the integration rules consists of constraints on these patterns. These constraints are placed on Δt_{onset} and Δt_{offset}. Δt_{onset} is calculated by subtracting the onset of gesture from the onset of speech. Δt_{offset} is similarly calculated by subtracting the offset of gesture form the offset of speech. The constraints are set by placing a maximum and a minimum value of Δt_{onset} and Δt_{offset} respectively, i.e., by setting an interval within which the values must range.

3.4 Semantic constraints

The semantics of a subDAG is taken to be the attribute of which it is a value (henceforth referred to as parent attribute) along with the attributes within the subDAG. The semantic constraints differs from the temporal in that they are optional. If the semantic constraints are left out, the integration process will be driven entirely by temporal information. This can work for some cases, but the risk is that absurd integrations will take place. For instance, if the user points to a location in the map while uttering a timepoint this information might be integrated.

The parent attribute is constrained by declaring which literal string it must be equal to. Constraints on the attributes contained within the subDAG on the other hand is more complex. These constraints can have the following three forms:

- *<attribute>* = *w*
- *<attribute>* = []
- *<attribute>* = ε

The symbol *w* denotes some string, [] denotes an empty dag, and ε denotes that no constraint is placed on the value (i.e., one only states that the attribute in question should be present).

3.5 Summary of constraints

The list below summarizes the different constraints that can be placed on the subDAG:s being compared:

- constraints on the intervals within which Δt_{onset} and Δt_{offset} must fall,
- constraints on the parent attributes, and
- constraints on the attributes contained within the respective subDAG:s.

4. Example Integration

It is now useful to turn to a more concrete example in order to better understand the integrator's functionality. The figures to which this section refers can be found on the last page of the paper.

The scenario is this: a user says "Jag vill åka <u>därifrån</u> till Resecentrum". The underlining means that the user simultaneously pointed somewhere in the map-part of the interface. We will now step through the different parts of the integration process.

First the gesture is recognized and represented in the form seen in the left part of figure 2. This feature structure simply contains information on when and at which coordinate in the interface the gesture was made. This structure is then passed to the gesture interpreter, which realizes that the coordinate corresponds to some location in the map-part of the interface. Based on this it assumes that the user intended to indicate some physical location. The gesture interpreter does however not interpret exactly which location the user indicated. This is later done in the domain knowledge manager in the MALIN framework. Hence, if the user utters the name of one location while pointing to another, this is not resolved until the integrated result reaches the domain knowledge manager.

On the speech side, the utterance is first passed through the speech recognizer, which passes the string representation of the recognition result to the natural language interpreter. The parser outputs the DAG seen in figure 3.

The output of the gesture interpreter and the natural language interpreter is then passed to the integrator. Since neither of the DAG:s are empty initially, the algorithm proceeds to check all combinations of subDAG:s against the integration rules. The gesture-DAG contains three subDAG:s, while the speech-DAG contains seven. All in all, 21 combinations have to be checked for integration. Assume that the grammar contains the following rule:

- $(0.0 \leq \Delta t_{onset} \leq 1.0)$ AND
- $(2.0 \leq \Delta t_{offset} \leq 5.0)$ AND
- (parent_attribute$_{speech}$ = "locations") AND
- (parent_attribute$_{gesture}$ = "locations) AND
- (<location>$_{speech}$ = [])

The first and second constraints specify the intervals for Δt_{onset} and Δt_{offset} respectively. The first constraint declares that gesture must have the same onset as, or precede speech by up to most 1.0 time unit. The second constraint declares that the pen must be lifted from the touch screen somewhere between 2.0 and 5.0 time units before speech ends. Constraints four and five declares that both speech and gesture should have received an interpretation as being some form of location. Finally, constraint five declares that the speech-subDAG should contain an attribute 'location' that has an empty DAG as value, i.e., it should *not* have been interpreted as some *specific* location.

It should be clear in this simple example which parts of the DAG:s that are integrable, simply recall that cardinal numbers can not be parent attributes. The result of the integration can be seen in figure 4. Time stamp information has been dropped at this point since no other module in the MALIN framework makes use of it.

5. Discussion

This paper has presented a mechanism for integrating, or fusing, information received through different channels (i.e., speech and pen). However, some issues remain and deserve further elaboration. To some extent the four issues raised by Johnston et al. (1997) can serve as a useful ground for discussion.

First, the multimodal integrator has initially been designed to handle only simple deictic pointing gestures. However, this is not a fundamental limitation of the integrator. The choice to limit the integrator in this sense has been made because there is currently no gesture recognizer or gesture interpreter implemented. Therefore, minimal assumptions about these modules has been made.

Second, the integrator is to some extent speech-driven, i.e., in the presence of speech it tries to find elements in speech that can be integrated with gesture. However, the integration rules can be declared in such a way that the two modalities can stand on more equal ground. Furthermore, in the absence of speech, the interpreted gesture can constitute the entire interpretation.

Third, the multimodal integrator is based on a formally well defined and understood meaning representation formalism, i.e., feature structures. This makes the integrator more readily integrable with other parsers than if it utilized some novel technique.

Finally, the integrator is semi-formally well defined even though it lacks a full formal specification.

References

Dahlbäck, N., Flycht-Eriksson, A., Jönsson, A. and Qvarfordt, P. (1999). An Architecture for Multi-Modal Natural Dialogue Systems. In *Proceedings of ESCA Tutorial and Research Workshop (ETRW) on Interactive Dialogue in Multi-Modal Systems*, Germany.

Jackson, P. (1999). *Introduction to Expert Systems*. Addison Wesley Longman Ltd.

Koons, D. B., Sparrell, C. J. and Thorisson, K. R. (1993). Integrating Simultaneous Input from Speech, Gaze, and Hand Gestures. In M. T. Maybury (Ed.) *Intelligent Multimedia Interfaces*, pp. 243-261, Menlo Park, *CA: AAAI/ MIT* Press.

Johnston, M. (1998). Unification-based Multimodal Parsing. In *Proceedings of the 36th Annual Meeting of the Association for Computational Linguistics and the 17th International Conference on Computational Linguistics*, pp. 624-630, Montreal, Quebec, Canada.

Johnston, M. and Bangalore, S. (2000). Finite-state Multimodal Parsing and Understanding. In *Proceedings of the 18th International Conference on Computational Linguistics*, Saarbrücken, Germany.

Johnston, M., Cohen, P. R., McGee, D., Oviatt, S. L., Pittman, J. A. and Smith, I. (1997). Unification-based Multimodal Integration. In *Proceedings of the 35th Annual Meeting of the Association for Computational Linguistics*, pp. 281-288, Madrid, Spain.

Jönsson, A. (1997). A Model for Habitable and Efficient Dialogue Management for Natural Language Interaction. *Natural Language Engineering*, 3(2/3), pp. 103-122.

Neal, J. G., Thielman, C. Y., Dobes, Z., Haller, S. M. and Shapiro, S. C. (1989). Natural Language with Integrated Deictic and Graphic Gestures. In *Proceedings of the 1989 DARPA Workshop on Speech and Natural Language*, pp. 410-423.

Nigay, L. and Coutaz, J. (1995). A Generic Platform for Addressing the Multimodal Challenge. In *Proceedings of Conference on Human Factors in Computing Systems (CHI '95)*, pp. 98-105, Denver, Colorado.

Oviatt, S., Cohen, P., Wu, L., Vergo, J., Duncan, L., Suhm, B., Bers, J., Holzman, T., Winograd, T., Landay, J., Larson, J., and Ferro, D. (2000). Designing the User Interface for Multimodal Speech and Pen-based Gesture Applications: State-of-the-Art Systems and Future Research Directions. *Human-Computer Interaction*, 15(4), pp. 263-322.

Oviatt, S., DeAngeli, A., and Kuhn, K. (1997). Integration and Synchronization of Input Modes during Multimodal Human-Computer Interaction. In *Proceedings of Conference on Human Factors in Computing Systems*, pp. 415-422, Atlanta, Georgia.

Strömbäck, L. and Jönsson, A. (1998). Robust Interpretation for Spoken Dialogue Systems. In *Proceedings of the International Conference on Spoken Language Processing*, pp. 491-494, Sydney, Australia.

Wahlster, W. (1991). User Discourse Models for Multimodal Communication. In J. W. Sullivan and S. W. Tyler (Eds.) *Intelligent User Interfaces*, New York, *NY: ACM* Press.

```
┌                                 ┐        ┌                                        ┐
│0: ┌ coord: ┌x:   786┐        ┐ │        │0: ┌ locations: ┌location: ┌x:   786┐ ┐┐│
│   │        │y:   256│        │ │        │   │            │          │y:   256│ ││
│   │                          │ │        │   │                                 ││
│   │ time:  ┌begin:  10┐      │ │        │   │ time:      ┌begin:  10┐          ││
│   └        └end:    13┘      ┘ │        │   └            └end:    13┘          ┘┘
└                                 ┘        └                                        ┘
```

Figure 2: To the left a DAG representing a recognized gesture, and to the right its interpretation.

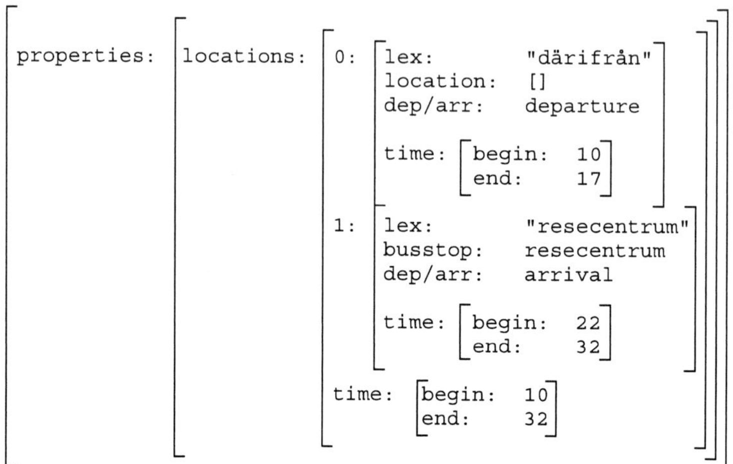

Figure 3: A DAG representing the interpretation of the spoken utterance "Jag vill åka därifrån till Resecentrum".

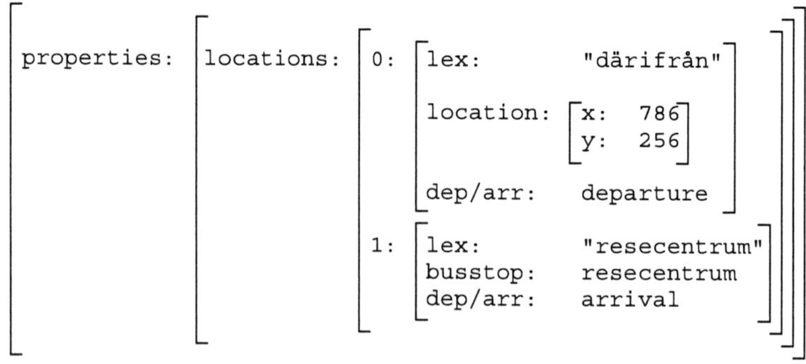

Figure 4: A DAG representing the result of integrating the DAG to the right in figure 2 and the DAG in figure 3.

Clustering dialogue knowledge with self -organizing maps

Mauri Kaipainen, Kristiina Jokinen, Timo Koskenniemi, Antti Kerminen, Kari Kanto

Media Lab, University of Art and Design Helsinki

kristiina.jokinen@uiah.fi

1. Introduction .

One of the biggest prob lems in building large dialogue systems is the need   for defining in advance the number and type of categories, necessary for the operation of the system. Apart from requiring an amount of labor, this approach requires   restrictive a priori judgments. Furthermore, this leads to data-specificity of the systems and difficulties to adapt to novel data. In this paper we report progress of an ongoing   research of how categorisation could be automated by using elementary data description and data   -driven self -organising maps as a tool. The experiments deal with deriving different types of dialogue acts using a small corpus of information-seeking dialogues. We compare clusters of dialogue acts obtained by the SOM to the manually tagged dialogue corpus.

2. Dialogue information

The Interact project aims at developing a generic interaction model that would enable users of online services to interact with various applications in a flexible and natural way.   In order to demons trate this model and to explore   the applicability of various methods in dialogue processing we are building a dialogue system that deals with public transportation timetable inquiries.

Based on the view that communication is action in context, we describe dialogues with the help of two well -known concepts: dialogue acts and topics . The former describes the act that the speaker performs by   particular utterance , and can be regarded as representing application-independent dialogue information, while the latter describe   the semantic content of the utterance and provide information related to the application   domain itself. Dialogue acts and topics seem to provide a useful first approximation of the utterance meaning by abstracting over possible linguistic realisations. Consequently, the system's internal states can be reduced to a combination of   dialogue acts and topics, both of which form an independent source of information for the system to decide on the next move.   In this pape r we focus only on dialogue acts   , although topics form an   analogous problem related to the underlying task and application domain.

The number and type of dialogue acts   is not fixed but depend   s on the theoretical premises as well as   on the type of the dialogues being studied (e.g. information-seeking, negotiation, argum entation). Although there are on -going activities for standardizing the set of dialogue acts and their definitions (e.g. the DRI   -initiative, Carletta et al. 1997), the practical dialogue systems exploit their own classifications especially designed for the application in hand. To facilitate the classification of the data into necessary and meaningful categories for the purposes of practical systems   , we explore possibilities to learn   intrinsic categories of the dialogue data   automatically. In particular, we study categorization of utterances into dialogue act classes on the basis of morph   o-syntactic features of the words that occur in the utterances, and   use the self -organising map algorithm to produce data   - driven clusterings. Using minimally analysed information as an input and a specified method for distance comparison, the SOM forms clusters of the   input in a manner which can be interpreted as a classification of dialogue acts.

3. Self-organising maps

The self -organizing map (SOM) , originally introduced by Kohonen (1982), is an unsupervised artificial neural network model. The input data for the model is described in terms of vectors, each of which consists of components representing an elementary featu re of the data item, expressed as a numeric value. The output is a similarity -based map of the data items, similarity being defined as proximity of items in the feature space. The clusters of near-similar items are fuzzy sets (Zadeh 1965) by nature. As a hint of the relation of such clusterings to the physically implemented mind, they ar   e reminiscent of electro -magnetic response fields observed   on cortex (e.g. Wall 1988). In addition, such maps can even represent hierarchical structures in terms of   mutually embedded fields , as was shown by the study of Ritter and Kohonen (1989), in which meaningful semantic relations were found from linguistic data.

The self-organizing maps differ from the supervised learning methods in that the SOM, needs no external teacher in the   learning phase. We can thus avoid   restrictive pre - categorizations of data that may hinder seeing meaningful relations among the data items that do not necessarily follow chosen guidelines. Unlike alternative statistical methods, such as multidimensional s caling and principal component analysis, the SOM approach also offers a platform for continuous upgrading of the data, a   requirement native to online services, and important to learning dialogue systems (Jokinen 2000).

4. Description of data

Our dialo gue corpus consists of spoken dialogues recorded at the Helsinki   regional transport (HKL)   service centre and contains 22 dialogues between customers and the service agent. The corpus was transcribed, manually segmented and   tagged with dialogue acts. Transcription takes into account simultaneous speaking so that different types of feedback could be distinguished.

The corpus contains 352 turns and 492 utterances. Each utterance is assigned one dialogue act. The list of dialogue acts with their frequences is given in Table 1.

acknowledgement	141
question	82
check	55
repetition	42
statement	37
thanking	26
call_to_continue	26
ending	23
opening	23
answer	21
confirmation	12
addition	2
wait	2

Table 1. Distribution of dialogue acts.

Two different types of feedback are distinguished. *Acknowledgement* is the most frequent act and represents feedback given by the speakers that they have understood and accepted what the partner said. Usually it inc   ludes turntaking, i.e. the speaker continues with a statement or a question of her own. The act   *call_to_continue* is similar but refers to back - channelling whereby the speaker gives simultaneous acknowledgment of her understanding and encourages the partner to continue without actually taking the turn. The act *addition* is a separate act representing the speaker's completion of the partner's utterance after a short pause.

5. Description of features

In our experi ment, we wanted to test how well   some simple features of the utterance.

distinguish different dialogue acts . We used the following features: the speaker, *wh*-words, the question morpheme *-kO*, the part -of-speech category of the stem of the *kO*-particle, whether the utterance contains a verb, conditional, negation, the particle *entä*, words used in greetings, words used in thankings, words used in acknowledgements and the scaled number of word forms shared with the previous utterance.

P1	speaker
P2	*Wh*-word
P3	*-kO*
P4	verb & *-kO*
P5	conditional
P6	negation
P7	*entä*
P8	greeting
P9	includes a verb
P10	thanking
p11	feedback
p12	Scaled number of shared words betw. current and previous utterance

Table 2. The set of elementary features used to describe utterances.

Preprocessing of the corpus for the SOM dealt with normalizing spoken language and slang expressions and converting inflected word forms to the base form by the Two-level morphological analyser (Koskenniemi 198 3). Ambiguous word forms were solved heuristically by favoring the shortest and simplest analysis. The normalized and morphologically analysed utterances were used as sample instances for the SOM. Each utterance was converted into a vector consisting of the twelve morpho-syntactic features as the components.

6. Results

We computed a map of 12 x 8 units [1] and the resulting map is given in Figure 1 . The light areas in the map depict data points that are close to each other, the dark areas represent distortions of the plane where data points are far apart, i.e. cluster boundaries. The dialogue acts that fall into a particular cluster are listed with the frequency at each point in the map. The labels refer to the dialogue act which has been assigned to the corresponding utterance in the manually tagged corpus.

---

[1] Using the standard algorithm as defined in SOM-PAK (http://www.cis.hut.fi/research/som_lvq_pak.shtml), 12 dimensions, bubble neighborhood

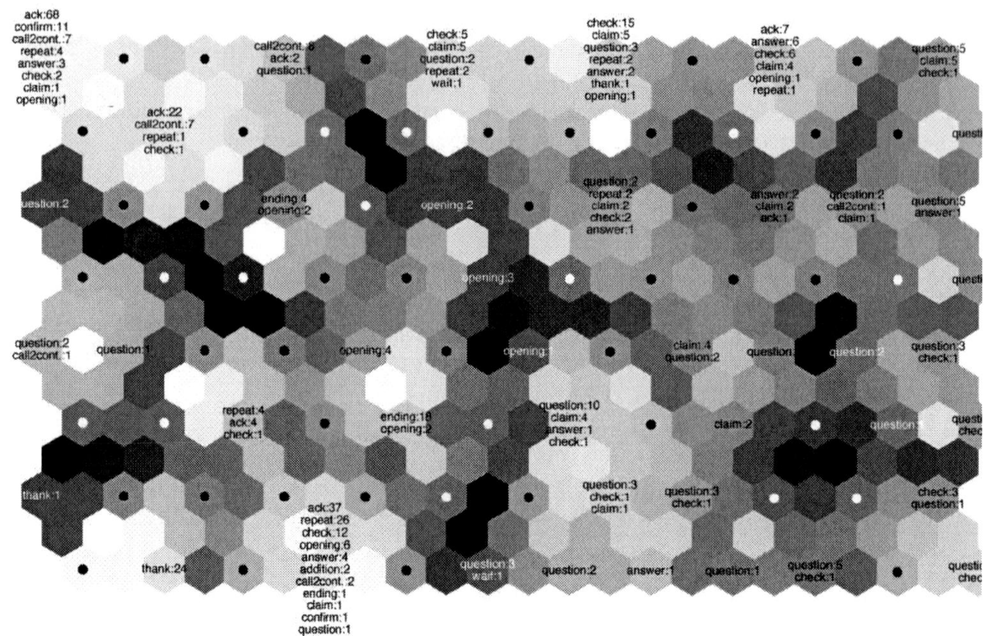

Fig. 1. The distribution of the dialogue acts with respect to each of the 12 features is shown in Figure 2. Labels on the map correspond to names of vectors, given manually in the

As can be seen from Figure 1, the map seems to distinguish rather clear clusters areas of the map for such metacommunication acts as opening and ending (in the middle of the map), and thanking (in   the lower left corner of the map),   but there is overlap among questions, answers, and claims. Acknowledgements also seem to cluster neatly, although the method found two different clusters, one together with call_to_continue (upper left corner of the map) and the other with repeats and checks (lower leftish of the map). The two separate clusters for acknowledgements suggest that the category under that name is not uniform in the feature space. There is also a cluster of checks (upper middle part o   f the map), although they are also dispersed around the map, and especially with acknowledgements.

In order to see the distinguishing power of each feature, we also studied their distribution among the data points, as is given in Figure 2. Each of the lit tle maps shows the clusters where the influence of the feature is at its most. (The map in Figure 1 is a map that is achieved by combining the effect of the individual features, Figure 2 pulls the features apart.)

Fig. 2. The response fields corresponding to individual features, numbered as map_p1, map_p2 etc., respective to features listed in Table 1.

As was expected, the main distinction between the various clusters seem to be due to the help of the features 'question word' (map_p2) and 'verb' (map_p9), i.e. checking whether the utterance contains a wh -word and whether it has a verb. The metacommunication acts like openings, endings, thanks, call_to_continue and acknowledgements seem to cluster mainly with the feature 'no -verb', and form clear clusters. The characteristic features of the two acknowledgement classes also seem to show a clear tendency for the division: the first cluster deals with the utterance having no verb (map_p9) but containing feedback words (map_p11), whereas the other cluster has no verb and no special feedback words either. The latter cluster also contains several repeats and checks, and the feature distribution seems to explain why this is so: these utterances are the ones that also lack of feedback words. On the other hand, the presence of feedback words seem to be the reason why the first acknowledgement cluster includes the act call_to_continue: both are expressed by the same kind of words. These overlapping clusters point to the fact that with   the current feature set we cannot distinguish   well enough between the different feedba ck-types, and obviously more features, possibly derived from the utterance prosody should be taken into account.

An interesting result is that can be seen from the map is that most check acts contain a verb. The checks without a verb get clustered together with acknowledgements and repeats.

7. Discussion and future work

The results show that with the simple feature set used, it is easy to distinguish metacommunication acts but there were no clear clustering separating   questions, answers, and claims. This is an area where we expect a longer sequential context to add distinctiveness. For example, questions and answers form adjacency pairs and one might expect that the previous dialogue act strongly suggests the next act t   ype Since there is no general solution to this within the self -organizing paradigm, we are currently developing a recurrent variant of the SOM, based on the ROSOM (Kaipainen & Karhu 2000) which includes the activity history of the whole network in the past in the current input.

The study reported here was carried through with a preliminary data that was not large enough to support any final conclusions but which served as a valuable guide to refine the elementary description as well as the methodology. Sign   ificant improvement in the distinctive power is to be expected with larger data. Clearer clusters can also be achieved by refining the elementary feature description.

Acknowledgements

The research is ca rried out in the context of the USIX -Interact project, a collaboration project between four Finnish universities, and funded by the National Technology Agency (TEKES), Sonera Oyj, ICL Invia Oyj, Lingsoft Oy , Gurusoft Oy, Tampere Technology Center Oy, the Arla Institute, and the Finnish Association of the Deaf.

Bibliography

Carletta, J., N. Dahlbäck, N. Reithinger, and M.A. Walker (eds.) 1997. *Standards for Dialogue Coding in Natural Language Processing*. Dagstuhl-Seminar-Report 167.

Jokinen, K. (2000). Learning Dialogue Systems. Proceedings of the LREC workshop 'From Spoken Dialogue to Full Natural Interactive Dialogue. P.13-17.

Kaipainen, M.; Karhu, P. (2000).   *Bringing Knowing -When and Knowing -What Together. Periodically Tuned Catego rization and Category -Based Timing Modeled with the Recurrent Oscillatory Self-Organizing Map (ROSOM)*, Minds and Machines 10: 203-229, 2000.

Kohonen, T. (1982). *Self -organized formation of topologically correct feature maps*   , Biological Cybernetics 43:59-69.

Koskenniemi, K. (1983).   *Two-Level Morphology: A General Computational Model for Word   - Form Recognition and Production* . Publications of the Department of General Linguistics, University of Helsinki.

Ritter, H.; Kohonen, T. (1989). *Self-Organizing Semantic Maps*, Berlin: Springer. Biological Cybernetics 61, 241-254.

Wall, J. T. (1988). *Variable organization in cortical maps of the skin as an indication of the lifelong adaptive capabilities of circuits in the mammalian brain*, TINS, Vol. 11, N0. 12.

Zadeh, L. A. (1965). *Fuzzy sets*, Information and Control, 8, 338-353.

Swedish SENSEVAL, a Developer's Perspective

Dimitrios Kokkinakis, Jerker Järborg and Yvonne Cederholm
Språkdata, Göteborg University
Box 200, SE-405 30, Sweden
{First.Last}@svenska.gu.se

Abstract

There are, hopefully, many computer programs for automatically determining which sense of a word is being used in a given context, according to a variety of semantic, defining or other types of dictionaries. SENSe EVALuation (SENSEVAL) is an open, community-based evaluation exercise for Word Sense Disambiguation (WSD) programs, arranged for a second consecutive time. The purpose of the exercise is to be able to say which programs and methods perform better, which worse, which words, or varieties of language, present particular problems to which programs. Moreover, not only do we want to know which programs perform best, but also, the developers of a program want to know when modifications improve performance, and how much and what combinations of modifications are optimal.

1. Introduction

According to dictionaries, common words have more than one meaning. Usually, only one of these meanings apply in a given context, either written or spoken. This is no issue for people in their daily interaction with others, but it is a difficult task for computers. The task is of great importance in a number of Natural Language Processing (NLP) applications, such as Machine Translation (MT) or (Cross-Language) Information Retrieval ([CL]IR). Word sense ambiguity is a potential source for errors in such tasks and it is considered as *the* great open problem at the lexical level of NLP. There are, however, several computer programs for automatically determining which sense of a word is being used in a given context, according to a variety of semantic, or defining dictionaries. SENSe EVALuation (SENSEVAL), Kilgarriff (1998), Kilgarriff & Palmer (2000) is an open, community-based evaluation exercise for Word Sense Disambiguation (WSD) programs arranged for a second consecutive time.

The purpose of the exercise is to be able to say which programs and methods perform better, which worse, which words, or varieties of language, present particular problems to which programs. Moreover, not only do we want to know which programs perform best, but also, the developers of a program want to know when modifications improve performance, and how much and what combinations of modifications are optimal. Specifically for Swedish, we would also like to investigate to what extent WSD can be done, the potential resources available for the task and create a framework that can be shared both within SENSEVAL and for future evaluation exercises of similar kind, national and international. SENSEVAL is designed to meet all these needs.

This paper will present some of the experiences we gained by participating as developers and organisers in the SENSEVAL exercise for Swedish. Particularly, the choice of the lexical and textual material, the annotation process, the scoring scheme, and the motivations for choosing the "lexical-sample" branch of the exercise.

2. Short History

SENSEVAL-1 was the first open evaluation exercise for WSD programs. Three languages (English [18 systems], French [5 systems] and Italian [2 systems]) and a total of 23 research groups participated. SENSEVAL-1 was held in Sussex, UK in 1998. The exercise was conceived at the SIGLEX workshop: "Tagging Text with Lexical Semantics. Why, What and How?" held in 1997 in Washington. A range of Machine Learning algorithms and a variety of lexical resources were utilised. Two important points are worth to be mentioned w.r.t. SENSEVAL-1. One was the fact that by the end of the exercise the purity of the approach was less important than the robustness of the system performance; and second, the discussion created more awareness among the participants of how fundamental the lexicon is to the task.

3. Lexical Sample

Three tasks were identified for SENSEVAL-2, these are: *the lexical-sample, the all-words* and *the 'in a system'* tasks. In the lexical sample task, first, we sample the lexicon, then we find instances in context of the sample words and the evaluation is carried out on the sampled instances (SENSEVAL-1 was a lexical-sample exercise). In the all-word task a system will be evaluated on its disambiguation performance on every word in the test collection. Finally, in the third type of task, a WSD system is evaluated on how well it improves the performance of a NL system (MT, IR etc). The reasons we chose the lexical-sample task for Swedish are summarised below:

1. Cost-effectiveness of annotation: it is easier and quicker for the human annotators to sense-tag the evaluation material;
2. The lexical-sample reduces the work of preparing training data since only a subset of the sense inventory is used;
3. More systems can/could (eventually) participate;
4. The all-words task requires access to a full dictionary, which is problematic from the copyright point of view, since industrial partners were also allowed to participate;
5. Provided that the sample is well chosen, the lexical sample strategy would be more informative about the current strengths and failings of WSD research than the all-words task (Kilgarriff & Palmer (2000)).
1.

Table 1 gives brief information w.r.t. the different languages participating in the lexical-sample part of SENSEVAL-2.

Language	Amount of Words	Available Context	Lexicon	Format	Corpus	Sample/ words
Basque	40	5 sents around	Euskal Hiztegia	TEI-SGML	Newspaper	75+15n
Chinese	15	2-3 sents ???		???	Sinica Corpus	10-60+?
Danish	100 (50/25/25)	50 tokens	SIMPLE+Nudansk Ordbog	???	Newspaper	75+15n
English	???	???	WordNet 1.7	XML	BNC, web, PennTreebank	???
Italian	100 (50/25/25)	2 sents around	ItalWordNet	XML	Newspaper, Periodical	???
Swedish	40 (20/15/5)	2 sents around	GLDB/SDB	XML	SUC	843-77+148-13

Table 1. Lexical-sample participants in SENSEVAL-2

4. SENSEVAL-2: Development Process

In this section we will give a concise description of how the whole exercise (for Swedish) was set up, putting more emphasis on some of the main ingredients of the work, i.e. resources, sampling, annotation and scoring.

A number of likely participants were invited to express their interest and participate in the Swedish SENSEVAL (summer, 2000). A plan for selecting the evaluation material was agreed in Språkdata, and human annotators were set on the task of generating the training and testing material. The material was released to the participants by the end of April, 2001 and the state-of-affairs at this moment (May, 2001) is that the participants are working with the material. During the second week of June, 2001 the results will be available, a two-day workshop will be held in Toulouse, France, devoted to the SENSEVAL-2 exercise. The Swedish SENSEVAL material was divided into three parts and released in stages:

- **Trial data**: freezing and showing the data formatting conventions (lexicon & corpus);
- **Training data**: the finalised sense inventory and portion of the 'gold standard';
- **Evaluation data**: the rest of the 'gold standard', untagged.

4.1 Dictionary and Text
At least three lexical resources were candidates for the Swedish lexicon-sample task. These were the Swedish versions of S-WordNet (http://www.ling.lu.se/projects/Swordnet) and SIMPLE (http://spraakdata.gu.se/simple/), and the Gothenburg Lexical Data Base (GLDB/SDB) (http://spraakdata.gu.se/lb/gldb.html). The GLDB/SDB was chosen since the S-WordNet had (up to that point) limited coverage and is also an ongoing project; while SIMPLE, although available, has limited coverage (in principle it could be used since it is linked to GLDB/SDB). GLDB/SDB is a generic defining dictionary of 65,000 entries.

Creating a sense-annotated reference corpus is a laborious task. Therefore, we developed the majority of the test and reference material within an ongoing, highly relevant for our mission project, namely SemTag ('Lexikalisk betydelse och användningsbetydelse' - Lexical Sense and Sense in Context); see Järborg (1999). For the textual material the Stockholm-Umeå Corpus (SUC), Ejerhed *et al.* (1992), was chosen, basically for two reasons. One because it is available to the research community, and, second because it is the corpus utilised in SemTag.

Table 2 shows information on the sense inventory, the amount of corpus instances and the distribution of senses (lexemes) and sub-senses (cycles) in the material.

Word	POS	Corpus** Instances	Lexemes/ Cycles	Word	POS	Corpus** Instances	Lexemes/ Cycles
barn/1	noun	656/115	3/6	betyda/1	verb	198/35	4/4
betydelse/1	noun	295/52	2/1	flytta/1	verb	188/33	2/4
färg/1	noun	110/19	4/11	fylla/2	verb	96/17	4/11
konst/1	noun	77/13	3/6	följa/1	verb	345/61	5/19
kraft/1	noun	152/27	4/11	förklara/1	verb	169/30	2/9
kyrka/1	noun	154/27	2/3	gälla/1	verb	843/148	4/6
känsla/1	noun	142/25	2/4	handla/1	verb	250/44	4/5
ledning/1	noun	91/16	4/1	höra/1	verb	523/92	5/14
makt/1	noun	128/22	3/4	måla/1	verb	96/16	2/7
massa/1	noun	93/16	6/3	skjuta/1	verb	79/14	6/15
mening/1	noun	168/29	4/1	spela/1	verb	267/47	6/23
natur/1	noun	90/16	3/4	vänta/1	verb	248/43	3/15
program/1	noun	139/24	4/10	växa/1	verb	203/36	2/9
rad/1	noun	145/25	4/3	öka/1	verb	436/77	2/2
rum/1	noun	223/39	3/7	öppna/1	verb	147/25	4/16
scen/1	noun	101/17	4/7	bred/1	adj.	103/18	3/1
tillfälle/1	noun	117/20	2/4	klar/1	adj.	307/54	4/11
uppgift/1	noun	174/30	2/3	naturlig/1	adj.	139/24	4/5
vatten/1	noun	285/50	2/3	stark/1	adj.	352/62	5/11
ämne/1	noun	198/34	4/4	öppen	adj.	189/33	7/21

Table 2. Swedish lexical sample (**Training/Testing; total: 8716/1525*)

4.2 Sampling

There is no standard method for sampling the lexical data. However, certain features were considered. These were:

Frequency   Polysemy   Part-of-speech   Distribution of senses

Words were chosen based not so much on intuition, but rather on their frequency and polysemy. Still, it is hard to find a balance between these two features since high frequency words tend to be monosemous in a corpus, while high polysemous words tend to have few senses in a corpus. In the case that a word was frequent and polysemous we tried to provide more data (context), than words that were less frequent. Part-of-speech information was accounted for choosing more nouns in the sample (highest portion in the GLDB/SDB), than verbs (less than nouns, but more than adjectives in the GLDB/SDB) and adjectives (which are less than nouns and verbs in GLDB/SDB). We chose a sample of words where the amount of senses was evenly distributed, i.e. lemmas with 2-7 senses and 1-23 subsenses.

4.3 Annotation Process

The annotation was carried out interactively using a concordance-based interface, Figure 1. Due to our limited financial resources only two professional lexicographers and a trained phd student were involved in the tagging process, which was preferred to (untrained) students doing the annotation. The replicability between those were on the 95% level.

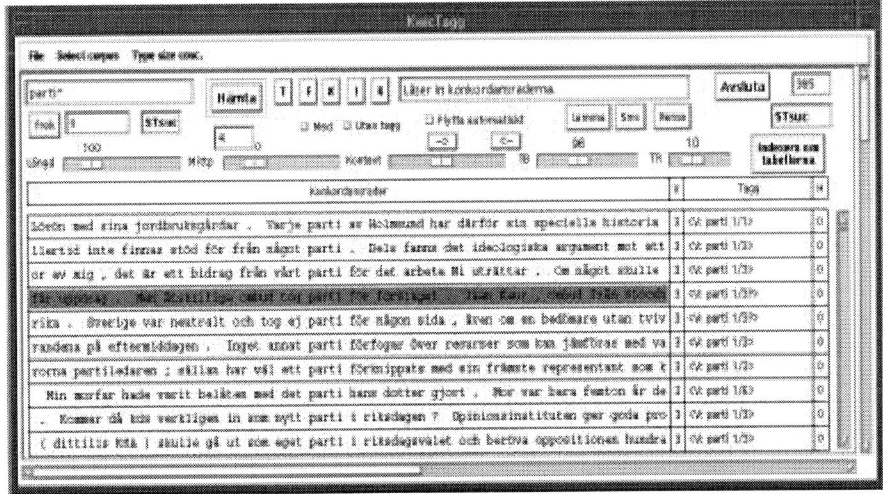

Figure 1. Annotation interface

Since some of the aims with SemTag is to improve the lexicographic descriptions in the GLDB/SDB and test in practice the validity of the lemma-lexeme model implemented, the development of the annotated instances for SENSEVAL-2 gave us a chance to revise our sense inventory and make adjustments and improvements to the descriptions found in the database; i.e. in the form of adding new sub-senses or modifying definitions of senses.

4.4 Interchange and Result Format

The corpus instances and dictionary format was in XML with DTDs provided. An example of a corpus instance (SUC file:AD04_BRV) for the 5th sense of the verb höra here: 'belong' is:

```
<instance id="höra.301"><answer instance="höra.301" senseid="höra_1_5"/>
  <context>Den ämnesdidaktiska forskningen kom igång i Sverige först på 70-talet.
    Geografiundervisningen diskuterades dock redan på 50-talet. Sverige <head>hörde
    </head> till de ledande nationerna när det gällde den" nya  geografin". Utbytet mellan
    Lund och USA var livligt och Gösta Wennberg som bodde och arbetade i Lund på den
    tiden tog starka intryck. 1964 kom han till Uppsala och blev metodiklektor på lärarhögskolan.
  </context>
</instance>
```

The systems required to return, for scoring, a one-line-per-answer for each unique corpus reference for the token being tagged and for which they were returning a result. One or more sense-identifiers, optionally associated with a probability measure (see also Section 5), could be attached. The BNF for scoring is:

```
<lexical_sample_answer>    ::= lexical-element instance-id <sense-tag-list>
<sense-tag-list>           ::= <weighted-list> | <unweighted-list>
<weighted-list>            ::= sense-id[/weight] {sense-id[/weight]}
<unweighted-list>          ::= sense-id {sense-id}
<weight>                   ::= INTEGER | positive REAL NUMBER
```

5. Scoring

Prior to SENSEVAL evaluating WSD performance was based on the exact match criterion given by the formula:

$$\%correct = 100 \times (\#exactly\ matched\ sense\ tags/\#assigned\ sense\ tags)$$

which is not consider a "fair" metric, and has a lot of drawbacks, such as that it does not account for the semantic distance between senses when assigning penalties for incorrect labels, and that it does not offer a mechanism to offer partial credit; *cf.* Resnik & Yarowsky (2000). Instead, in SENSEVAL-2 three scoring policies are adopted:

1. **Fine-grained**: answers must match exactly
2. **Coarse-grained**: answers are mapped to coarse-grained senses and compared to the gold standard tags, also mapped to coarse-grained ones (sense map is required; see below)
3. **Mixed-grained**: if a sense subsumption hierarchy is available, then the mixed-grained scoring gives some credit to choosing a more coarse-grained sense than the gold standard tag, but not full credit (also using a sense map; see below).

A "sense map" contains a complete list of all sense-ids involved in the evaluation and is necessary for performing the two last types of scoring policies. Each line in the sense map includes sense subsumption information and contains a list of the subsumer senses and branching factors.

6. Participants

Three groups showed interest on participating in the Swedish task:

Group	Method	Contact Person(s)
Uppsala University,	*TBL-tränade Prolog Word*	*Torbjörn Lager*
Linguistics	*Experts; (Peewees)*	*Natalia Zinovjeva*
Linköping University,	Multilevel Decision List Approach	Lars Ahrenberg, Magnus Merkel
Computer & Info. Science		Mikael Andersson
Göteborg University, Språkdata	*Machine Learning*	*Dimitrios Kokkinakis ***

Table 3. Swedish participants in SENSEVAL-2 (***also in the developer's group*)

7. Conclusions

The process of Word Sense Disambiguation is a complex, controversial matter, but relevant for a number of Natural Language Processing applications. Our contribution to the exercise will eventually sharpen the focus of WSD in Sweden; the material developed in SENSEVAL-2(Swedish) can be used as benchmark for other researchers that need to measure their system's WSD performance against a concrete reference point (although the number of words is rather small). We think that WSD opens up exciting opportunities for linguistic analysis, contributing with very important information for the assignment of lexical semantic knowledge to polysemous and homonymous content words. The existence of sense ambiguity (polysemy and homonymy) is one of the major problems affecting the usefulness of basic corpus exploration tools. In this respect, we regard WSD as a very important process and component when it is seen in the context of a wider and deeper NL processing system.

References

Ejerhed E., Källgren G., Wennstedt G. and Åström M. (1992), *The Linguistic Annotation of the Stockholm-Umeå Corpus project*. Technical Report No. 33, Univ. of Umeå

Järborg J. (1999), *Lexikon i konfrontation*. Research Reports from the Department of Swedish, Språkdata, GU-ISS-99-6, In Swedish

Kilgarriff A. (1998), *SENSEVAL: An Exercise in Evaluating Word Sense Disambiguation Programs*. In Proceedings if the 1st LREC, Granada, Spain pp 581-588

Kilgarriff A. and Palmer M. (2000), Introduction to the Special Issue on SENSEVAL. *Computer and the Humanities*, 00:1-13, Kluwer Acad. Publishers

Resnik P. and Yarowsky D. (2000), Distinguishing Systems and Distinguishing Senses: New Evaluation Methods for Word Sense Disambiguation. *Natural Language Engineering*, 5(2):113-133, Cambridge

Corpus-Based Extension of Semantic Lexicons in Large Scale

Dimitrios Kokkinakis, Maria Toporowska Gronostaj and Karin Warmenius
Språkdata, Göteborg University
Box 200, SE-405 30, Sweden
{First.Last}@svenska.gu.se

Abstract

During recent years there has been an increased interest to acquire or extend, on a large-scale, high-quality semantic lexicons. The methodology is usually corpus-driven. It is based on the (re-)use of machine readable resources of various types, and the application of cost effective ways to eliminate the acquistion bottleneck, i.e. derivational morphology, customization of off-the-shelf resources, statistical techniques and shallow parsing. This paper investigates how, and to what extent the flexibility and robustness of a partial parser can be utilized to fully automatically achieve this goal. Our work is based on the observation that members of a semantic group are often surrounded by other members of the same group in text. Given a few category members we use parsed corpora to collect surrounding contexts and try to identify other words that also belong to the same group.

1. Introduction

During recent years there has been an increased interest to use corpus-driven approaches to acquire high quality semantic lexicons on large scale: (Grefenstette (1994); Dorr & Jones (1996); Hearst and Schütze (1996); Takunaga *et al.* (1998); Lin (1998)). This paper investigates the use of a cost-effective way to eliminate the acquisition bottleneck by exploiting the flexibility and robustness of a system based on a partial parser. The parser uses fine-grained syntactic contexts for identifying similarities between words and acquire large quantities of high quality general purpose semantic knowledge. Given a few category members of a semantic group, we investigate whether it is possible to collect appropriate surrounding contexts and identify other words, on a large scale, that also belong to the same semantic group.

Our point of departure is not to acquire the semantic lexicons from scratch, rather, to build on what we have already at our disposal. That is, lexical resources of high quality, manually produced and verified but quantitatively *insufficient* for realistic large-scale tasks. Therefore, we focus our attention to explore and exploit inexpensive methods to progressively enrich the resources with several thousands of new, classified lexical units.

Our work is based on the observation that members of a semantic group are often surrounded by other members of the same group throughout a corpus. By a semantic group, we understand here for instance enumerative and conjunctive phrases of the form: *xa, xb, ..., xc* or *xa and xb, ..., and xc*, where *x* can be any content-poor item, such as determiners and numerals, and *a b c* nouns or names. We further slightly constrain this general observation by searching for particular types of phrases, of particular length and of particular semantic content provided by the available, limited semantic resources. These resources, then, are progressively enriched and applied in a bootstrapping manner back to the phrases extracted from the corpora in order to classify as many as possible of the words that are members of the retrieved phrases. The level of the fine-grained syntactic analysis is made possible through the use of a robust parser developed by Abney (1997) in which Kokkinakis & Johansson Kokkinakis (1999) have developed a large coverage grammar for written Swedish. The semantic lexicons we refer to are the Swedish SIMPLE lexicon (*Semantic Information for Multifunctional Plurilingual Lexica*) and gazeteers of person, location and organization names. Previous experiments in a small scale for Swedish (Kokkinakis *et al.* (2000)) have demonstrated that the task of enriching semantic resources using syntactic information is feasible. Therefore we wanted to investigate to what magnitude this can be done and evaluate, at least for some of the semantic groups, the quality of the acquired semantic units.

2. Related Research

Context similarity plays and important role in word acquisition. The use of syntax for generating semantic knowledge and ways of measuring semantic similarity based on distributional evidence and syntagmatic relations have been put forward in the literature by many researchers. A common characteristic of almost all approaches is the computation of the semantic similarity between two words on the basis of the extent to which words' average contexts of use overlap.

Our method has similarities to the work by Hearst (1992), who uses lexico-syntactic patterns of the form: 'NP {, NP}* {,} and other NP' for the extraction of hyponymic relations, such as: '...*temples, treasuries, and other important civic buildings'*. However, more influential source of inspiration has been the work described by Grefenstette (1994). He examined an approach to extract corpus-specific semantics using a system, SEXTANT, which processes a text by tagging, partially parsing and creating dependencies between words in phrases extracted. The dependency relations are considered as attributes of the SEXTANT, and they are compared using a weighted Jaccard similarity measure (i.e. Count(attributes shared by x and y)/Count(attributes processed by x or y)) in order to discover words used in a similar manner. A result from this process was a list of similar words for each word in the corpus.

When it comes to the acquisition and extension of name lists, for the benefits of tasks such as named entity recognition, similar approaches are applicable. Stevenson and Gaizauskas (2000), for instance, build categorised lists of names from manually annotated training data, combining various types of filters. The authors claim that a performance measure of 87% f-score on a standard data set is achieved using these corpus-derived lists.

3. Resources

We apply a method, described in a more detail in the next section, uniformally onto two semantic lexicons. The first is the Swedish SIMPLE lexicon, developed within the EU-financed project with the same name. The content and design of the SIMPLE model, applied in 12 European languages, is documented in Lenci *et al.* (1998). The notion of semantic type is central for the SIMPLE model and its ontology. Information on semantic class, domain, argument structure of predicative expressions etc., constitute a relevant part of the semantic type specification.

The Swedish lexicon provides descriptions for 10,000 semantic units (roughly 6,000 words), comprising 7,000 nouns, 2,000 verbs and 1,000 adjectives; this paper will elaborate on the noun part of the lexicon. As a vital part of the different entries' semantic unit is the notion of semantic class whose value is an element in a semantic class list (95 classes) hierarchically structured, e.g. ANIMAL and BUILDING. Ambiguous entries are also denoted as such. For instance, *glas* 'glass' is marked with the classes: AMOUNT, CONTAINER, MATERIAL and UNIT-OF-MEASUREMENT. The second lexicon is a list of frequent proper names: PERSON (4900), LOCATION (4300) and ORGANIZATION (1300). These originate from a previous work in the framework of creating an information extraction system for Swedish (in the EU-financed project AVENTINUS).

4. Methodology

We have experimented with a corpus-driven approach, using a cascaded finite-state syntactic parser (CASS-SWE), based on work done by Kokkinakis & Johansson Kokkinakis (1999), which seems a plausible way of progressively enriching the semantic resources. An advantage of CASS-SWE is its ability to identify, with high accuracy, arbitrarily complex nominal and other types of phrases, a property that we consider here as crucial for aiding the identification of new semantic entries. The method rests on the assumption that words entering into the same syntagmatic relation with other words are perceived as semantically similar. Essentially the approach is as follows:
1. Gather, part-of-speech annotate and parse large corpora (in our case using CASS-SWE, a parser that uses part-of-speech annotated input);
2. From the resulted analyzed forest of chunks, filter out long noun phrases;
3. Filter out knowledge-poor elements, such as determiners and punctuation; and use the lemmatised and normalised content of the extracted phrases;
4. First Pass:
    Measure the overlap between the members of the phrases extracted and the entries in the SIMPLE lexicon and the gazeteers;

If conditions apply, add new categorised entries in the database;
Repeat the previous two steps, until very few or nothing can be matched;
5. Second Pass:
Apply compound segmentation on the members of the phrases left;
Check whether they are lexicalised using a defining dictionary, do not use them if they are;
Repeat the process from step (4) by matching this time the heads with the content of the database;

The bootstrapping mechanism dynamically grows the original lists, so that each iteration produced a larger semantic dictionary.

4.1 Corpora and Part-of-Speech Annotation

The corpora we used consisted of over 42 million tokens. Most of the material was provided by the Swedish Language Bank[1]. We part-of-speech tagged the corpora using Brill's tagger (Brill (1992)) trained on Swedish material, using a very fine-grained tagset[2]. For instance, the noun *jurister* 'lawyers' receives by the tagger the description NCUPNI, which is interpreted as a *common noun, non-neuter, in plural form, nominative case* and *indefinite form*. Note also that a pre-tagger filter recognises a large number of multi-word expressions and compound names of the form 'Los Angeles' and 'Dow Jones'.

4.2 Parsing and Grammar Rules

The parsing process is using CASS-SWE, a flexible parser for Swedish, in which *levels* or *bundles* of rules of very special characteristics and content can be rapidly created. From the already encoded rules in CASS-SWE we extracted two subsets. One, having common nouns (63) and one proper nouns (45) respectively in their Right-Hand-Side. The only requirement we posed was that each extracted phrase should contain at least three members of each respective phrasal group. Knowledge-poor items such as conjunctions and determiners, which are not specific to any category and are common across all phrases, were removed. Phrases containing adjectives such as *andra/annan* 'other' were excluded, since the noun following (oftenly) signalls a higher in the hierarchy concept. As in the example: *skor, tröjor och andra produkter* 'shoes, blouses and other products'. Normalization was performed by using the base form of every common noun in the phrases. The rule subsets were then applied on the corpus. From the large forest of chunks produced, a large number of phrases for each category was extracted. The amount of unique retrieved phrases for the first group were 35,955 and for the second 71,636. Examples of the rules are given below. For clarity, the names of the tags on the RHS have been edited for readability:
Example of Common Noun Rule (F stands for punctuation):
  'Rule-CN --> DETERMINER? COM-NOUN (COM-NOUN F)* COM-NOUN CONJ COM-NOUN'
e.g.: *färger, penslar, papper och matsäckar* 'colours, brushes, paper(s) and lunch-boxes'
Example of Proper Noun Rule:
  'Rule-NP --> APPOSITION-NOUN? PROP-NOUN+ (F PROP-NOUN)+ CONJ PROP-NOUN+'
e.g.: *Venezuela, Trinidad och Island*
The retrieved phrases could be easily recognised since each level of rules can be indexed with a unique identifier. There is also the possibility to generate the results in a linear format having as content only the part of the phrases we are interested to retrieve and ignore other syntactic, irrelevant in this case, annotations produced by the parser.

4.3 First Pass Overlap

The way we measure the overlap between the members of the phrases extracted and the entries in the SIMPLE and the gazeteers is simply by matching a database with the content of the resources against the content of the phrases. We assume that if at least two of the members of a phrase (a figure arbitrarily taken) are also entries in the lexicon, with the *same* semantic class, and the rest of the phrase members *have not* received a semantic annotation, then there is a strong indication that the

---

1. The material consists of four are newspaper collections (*press95, press96, press97, press98*) and a collection of contemporary novels (*romii*). For more information on the material visit: http://spraakdata.gu.se/lb.
2. A slightly simplified variant of the tagset can be found in: http://spraakdata.gu.se/lb/parole/.

rest of the members are co-hyponyms, and thus semantically similar with the two already encoded in the lexicon. Accordingly, we annotate them with the same semantic class. For instance the common nouns: *jurist* 'lawyer', *optiker* 'optician' and *läkare* '(medical) doctor' have being manually coded in the (original) SIMPLE lexicon, with the OCCUPATION-AGENT semantic class (*individuals or groups of humans identified according to a role in professional, social or religious disciplines*). Thus, in the extracted noun phrase: *jurister, läkare, optiker, psykologer och sjukgymnaster* (after lemmatisation and removal of the knowledge poor items, the conjunction *och* 'and' and punctuation) the three first nouns will get the OCCUPATION-AGENT label, while the two last, namely 'psychologist' and 'physiotherapist' will also get the same label by the system. This is because they satisfy the condition stated earlier, namely that they have not received a semantic class annotation and the rest of the members of the phrase (at least two) have been assigned the same semantic class.

In case where original members of the lexicon are ambiguous in the same way, that is, they receive same labels, then a new word matched will also receive the ambiguous labelling. For instance, in the phrase: *flaskor, tallrikar, vinglas* 'bottles, plates, wine glasses' the last word is not matched by the lexicon, however the first two are assigned the classes CONTAINER and AMOUNT. Accordingly, the word *vinglas* will be assigned the two semantic classes.

The new items are inserted in the database and the process is repeated from step (4) until nothing else can be matched in the remaining phrases, or ambiguity, multiple, different classes for the members of a phrase, prohibits the continuation of the process. For example in the case of a phrase such as *barn, kvinnor, husdjur och möbler* 'children, women, pets and furniture' nothing will be entered in the database. Since, according to the SIMPLE, *barn* and *kvinnor* will be assigned the class BIO (*classification of human beings according to biological charactersitics, like age, sex, etc.*) and *möbler* the class FURNITURE. Therefore, the unknown to the lexicon word *husdjur* is prohibited from obtaining a semantic class, since two different classes appear within a single phrase.

4.4 Second Pass Overlap
After we tested the method outlined so far, we discovered that a large number of phrases were not used by the system since none or only one of the members of the phrases was covered by the lexicons, either the original or the enriched version. Therefore, we found it compelling to devise a way to deal with these cases by taking account the compounding characteristic of the Swedish language (proper nouns were not treated on the second pass). Over 27,000 common noun phrases were not matched while in 35% of these all content was annotated but no match could be obtained.

The fact now that over 70%, or approximately 80,000, of all the entries in the SAOL (1998) are compound forms casts light onto the need to design effective tools for compound segmentation, as new, casual compounds are created constantly in Swedish. We assume that a considerable number of casual or on the fly created compounds can inherit relevant parts of semantic information provided on their heads by the SIMPLE lexicon and thus, can be easily incorporated in it. In order to restrain automatic incorporation of lexicalised compounds with idiomatic, metaphoric or metonymic meaning, we check whether a compound is included as a separate entry in a defining dictionary (lexicalised). For this purpose we used the GLDB/SO (http://spraakdata.gu.se/lb/gldb.html). If this is the case, the compound is not subjected to automatic inheritance.

Compound segmentation involves identifying grapheme combinations that are not-permitted in non-compound forms in the language, which carry information of potential token boundaries. The heuristic principle for the segmentation is based on producing short *n-gram* character sequences from hundreds of non-compound lemmas, and then generating n-grams that are not part of the lists produced. After manual adjustments and iterative refinement a list of such graphemes has been produced and used for segmentation. Ambiguities are unavoidable, although the heuristic segmentation has been evaluated for high precision; we do not force the system to overgenerate spurious decomposition points.

Examples of n-gram sequences include: ivb, iv|b, e.g. *skriv|bord* 'writing desk' and ngss, ngs|s, e.g. *forsknings|skola* 'research school'; '|' denotes where the segmentation should take place, while *bord* and *skola* are heads on the previous compounds. We apply heuristic decomposition on the members of the phrases left, and run the process from step (4) once again. This time by matching the content of the enriched database with the compounds' heads of the segmented strings (if any) in the remaining phrases. For instance, in the phrase: *färjor, kryssnings|fartyg, tankers och ro-ro-|fartyg* 'ferries, cruise liners, tankers and ro-ro-vessels' no classes are assignd during the first pass, while during segmentation the second and fourth words' heads get the label VEHICLE since they match the entry *fartyg* 'vessel', and the rest two are matched with the same class since they satisfy the condition stated earlier (no other classes involved and at least two belong to the same one).

5. Evaluation

We will discuss now the results we obtained by applying the previously outlined method on large corpora, both in terms of quantity and quality. Table 1 summarizes the results with respect to the quantity aspects. The first pass was repeated six times. During the second pass the material in the remaining phrases was segmented and the enriched content of the database was matched against the heads of the segmented members of the phrases. This time resulting in fewer entries in the database. This can be explained by the fact that we are rather restrictive during segmentation.

	Original	Pass-1	Pass-2	Total
Common Nouns	2,921	5,110	1,100	9,131
Proper Nouns	10,550	25,700	---	36,250

Table 1. Quantitative acquisition results

Class	Original	New	Wrong/Spurious	Precision
FLOWER	19	26	3	88,5%
PHENOMEN.	36	29	9	69%
ORGANISAT.[NE]	1,300	395	22	94,4%
BIO	46	107	12	88,8%
IDEO	17	74	9	87,8%
VEHICLE	33	118	17	85,6%
APPARATUS	22	27	2	92,6%
GARMENT	25	184	19	89,7%
ILLNESS	38	66	8	87,9%

Table 2. Qualitative acquisition results

The most obvious way to evaluate the results of our technique is by using a gold standard (a human-compiled collection of related words). Since general-purpose thesauristic resources for Swedish are non-existent (there is a current effort to develop a Swedish WordNet at the university of Lund) and we do not have access to machine-readable versions of synonym dictionaries, we carried out two evaluations in another manner. First, we performed a manually qualitative evaluation for a number of semantic groups, based solely on our common sense and judgement, table (2). Precision was simply calculated as the ratio of valid entries to the total produced. Second, we tested a number of words based on the information found in synonym dictionaries for Swedish (Walter (1991); Strömberg (1998)). Two such words were *bil* 'car' and *rederi* 'shipping company', which according to the two dictionaries had 7+8=11 unique and 3+4=6 unique synonyms respectively. We then looked at the classes these words belonged to (according to SIMPLE), namely VEHICLE and AGENCY, to see whether the synonyms in the paper dictionaries occurred in that semantic class. For the word *bil* 8 of the synonyms occurred and 3 did not (*vagn, kärra, åk*); while for *rederi* 1 occurred and 5 did not (*fartygsbolag, linje, skeppsägare, båtbolag, sjöfartsbolag*). Varying figures, from no matches at all, to all matches, were found for a number of other words. Both methods have drawbacks, but seemed to be the closest we can come with respect to quality evaluation, this way, of course, we can (presumably) only evaluate precision. The general conclusion, that we can only partly stipulate on, is that existing synonym dictionaries cover a number of infrequent, sometimes "old-fashioned", terms and seemed not to be up-dated with the contemporary language style. Something that can only be achieved by processing large electronic corpora, which does not seem to be the case for the dictionaries consulted.

5.1 Error Analysis

There were four basic sources of erroneous entries identified. Part-of-speech and lemmatisation errors; a number of long, enumerative noun phrases with many unknown to the lexicon entries, where two or three (happened) to correctly get the same semantic label, but few the wrong one. This caused the undesired effect of introducing new entries with wrong labels. For instance, in the phrase: *tröja halsduk strumpa underkläder skiva album* 'sweater scarf sock underwear record album' the entries *tröja* and *strumpa* received the label GARMENT the rest no labels, and consequently *halsduk* and *underkläder* achieved the correct label (GARMENT) while *skiva* and *album* the wrong one. A final source of error was polysemy, which also exhibited similar effect as the previous one, and also prohibiting the incorporation of new entries. For instance, in the phrase: *depression ångest spänning* 'depression anxiety excitement' after the first iteration the two first words received by the lexicon the label EMOTION. The third one was also labelled EMOTION (according the discussion in Section 4.3), which is correct according to the specific subsense of that word in that context. Once received that label, later processing of phrases, where *spänning* has another sense, such as: *tryck#ATTRIBUTE spänning#EMOTION? vibration tyngdkraft#ATTRIBUTE* 'pressure tension vibration gravitation', the already received annotation for *spänning* causes a phrase as this one to be rejected for further processing since two different labels are involved in the phrase and *vibration* cannot get a correct label (*spänning* ought to have the ATTRIBUTE class in this context).

6. Contribution and Further Work

We have presented a simple, quite efficient method to acquire general-purpose semantic knowledge from large corpora. Our main contributions of this paper are: the use of partially parsed corpora for extending semantic lexicons, the application of a unified way to process compounds, while infrequent words are not a major headache as in other (statistically-based) approaches. Both parsing and compounding are of equal importance; through parsing we allow the incorporation of new, mainly non-compound words, through compounding we allow new compounds of existing words. Regarding further work, we have to devise a better way to evaluate the results and decrease the amount of spurious generated entries. Actually, most of them originate from part-of-speech errors and not so much from the competence of the grammar. We will also continue the work in augmenting the rest of the SIMPLE's vocabulary. Lack of semantic resources in electronic form, such as large ontologies for Swedish, prohibits us to make more solid evaluation. The future release of the Swedish WordNet will be considered for such evaluation.

References

Abney S. 1997. Part-of-Speech Tagging and Partial Parsing. *Corpus-Based Methods in Language and Speech Processing*, Young S. and Bloothooft G., eds, Chap. 4, pp. 118 136, Kluwer AP

Brill E. 1992. A Simple Rule-Based Part of Speech Tagger. *3rd Conference on Applied Natural Language Processing (ANLP)*, Trento, Italy

Dorr B. and Jones D. 1996. Acquisition of Semantic Lexicons: Using Word Sense Disambiguation to Improve Precision. *SIGLEX Workshop: "Breadth and Depth of Semantic Lexicons"*, pp. 42-50, Santa Cruz, USA

Grefenstette G. 1994. *Explorations in Automatic Thesaurus Discovery*. Kluwer AP

Hearst M.A. 1992. Automatic Acquisition of Hyponyms from Large Text Copora. *14th COLING*, pp. 539-545, Nantes, France

Hearst M.A. and Schütze H. 1996. Customizing a Lexicon to Better Suit a Computational Task. *Corpus Processing for Lexical Acquistion*, pp. 77-94, Boguraev B. and Pustejovsky J. (eds.). MIT Press

Kokkinakis D. and Johansson Kokkinakis S. 1999. A Cascaded Finite-State Parser for Syntactic Analysis of Swedish. *9th EACL*, pp. 245-248, Bergen, Norway

Kokkinakis D., Toporowska-Gronostaj M. and Warmenius K. 2000. Annotating, Disambiguating \& Automatically Extending the Coverage of the Swedish SIMPLE Lexicon. *2nd Language Resources and Evaluation Conference (LREC)*. Athens, Hellas

Lenci A. *et al.* 1998. *SIMPLE WP2, Linguistics Specifications*. Deliverable 2.1, Pisa

Lin D. 1998. Automatic Retrieval and Clustering of Similar Words. *COLING-ACL98*, Montreal, Canada

Sanfilippo A. *et al.* 1999. *Preliminary Recommendations on Lexical Semantic Encoding*. EAGLES LE3-4244, Draft version

SAOL 1998. *Svenska Akademiens Ordlista över Svenska Språket* (The Swedish Academy Word-List). Norstedts & Svenska Akademien

Stevenson M. and Gaizauskas R. 2000. Using Corpus-derived Name Lists for Named Entity Recognition. *6th Conference on Applied Natural Language Processing and First Conference of the North American Chap-*

ter of the Association for Computational Linguistics, pp. 290-296. Seattle

Strömberg A. 1998. *Stora synonymordboken*. Strömbergs Bokförlag AB, Falköping

Takunaga T., Fujii A., Iwayama M., Sakurai N. and Tanaka H. 1997. Extending a Thesaurus by Classifying Words. *"Automatic Information Extraction and Building of Lexical Semantic Resources" Workshop*, Vossen P. (*et al.*) (eds), pp. 16-21, Spain

Walter G. 1991. *Bonniers synonymordbok*. Bonniers

Transformation-Based Learning of Rules
for Constraint Grammar Tagging

Torbjörn Lager
Department of Linguistics
Uppsala University, SWEDEN
`Torbjorn.Lager@ling.uu.se`

Abstract

If we conceive of a Constraint Grammar as an ordered sequence of transformation rules of a particular kind – as reduction rules rather than replacement rules – the transformation-based learning method used to train Brill taggers can, with minor modifications, be used to train Constraint Grammar taggers as well. This paper makes a few observations based on this approach, and presents some initial and rather promising experimental results.

1 Introduction

Two kinds of rule based taggers – Brill taggers (Brill 1995) and Constraint Grammar taggers (Karlsson et al. 1995) – have, in terms of accuracy, efficiency, compactness and intelligibility, quite successfully stood up to the competition from the statistical camp. How these rule-based taggers work, and how they differ in the way they work, can be briefly explained as follows.

In a Brill tagger, a lexical lookup module assigns exactly *one* tag to each occurrence of a word (usually the most frequent tag for that word type), disregarding context. A rule application module then proceeds to *replace* some of the tags with other tags, on the basis of what appears in the local context.

In a Constraint Grammar tagger, a lexical lookup module assigns *sets* of alternative tags to occurrences of words, disregarding context. A rule application module then *removes* tags from such sets, on the basis of what appears in the local context. However, in order to guarantee that each word token is left with at least one tag, the rule application module adheres to the following principle: *don't remove the last remaining tag.*

Whereas Brill taggers came with a novel and effective learning method which made it possible to learn rules for new languages very quickly, Constraint Grammar taggers were from the outset developed by hand only. Since then, several

attempts have been made to induce Constraint Grammar rules – or 'Constraint Grammar'-like rules – from manually annotated corpora (Samuelsson et al. 1996; Cussens 1997; Eineborg & Lindberg 1998; Lindberg & Eineborg 1998; 1999).

In (Lager 1999) it was suggested that the transformation-based learning method used to train Brill taggers can, with minor modifications, be used to train Constraint Grammar taggers as well. This paper develops this suggestion further.

2 An Overview of the μ-TBL System

2.1 Background

The μ-TBL system – described in detail in (Lager 1999) – represents an attempt to use the search and database capabilities of the Prolog programming language to implement a generalized form of transformation-based learning.

The μ-TBL system is designed to be theoretically transparent, flexible and efficient. Transparency is achieved by performing a 'logical reconstruction' of transformation-based learning, and by deriving the system from there. Flexibility is achieved through the use of a compositional rule and template formalism, and 'pluggable' algorithms. As for the implementation, it turns out that transformation-based learning can be implemented very straightforwardly in a logic programming language such as Prolog. Efficient indexing of data, unification and backtracking search, as well as established Prolog programming techniques for building rule compilers and meta-interpreters, contribute to the making of a logically transparent, easily extendible, and fairly efficient system.

2.2 Transformation Rules

The object of TBL is to learn an ordered sequence of transformation rules. The μ-TBL system supports five kinds of transformation rules, but the relevant kind of rule in connection with learning Constraint Grammars is the *reduction rule*.

"

Reduction rules reduce the set of tags assigned to a word with a certain tag. An example would be "reduce a word's tag set with tag `vb` if the word immediately to the left is uniquely tagged as `dt`". Here is how this rule is represented in the μ-TBL system's formalism:

```
pos:red vb <- unique pos:dt@[-1]
```

This kind of rule will only remove a tag from a word if it is not the last tag for the word. If `vb` is the last value the above rule is not applicable and the reduction will not take place.

The use of the `unique/1` operator in a condition of a rule has the effect that the rule will trigger only if the assignments of tags to words in the relevant surroundings are non-ambiguous. (As Karlsson et al. (1995) put it, the rules are run in "careful application mode".)

Two or more rules may be connected into sequences – or *composed* – by means of the composition operator 'o', where `(R o Rs)` basically means that the output of applying the rule `R` forms the input to the application of the rules `Rs`.

2.3 Rule Templates

Rules that can be learned in TBL are instances of templates, such as "reduce with tag `A` if the word immediately to the left is uniquely tagged as `B`", where `A` and `B` are variables. Here is how we write this template in the μ-TBL system:

```
pos:red A <- unique pos:B@[-1] .
```

2.4 Rule Evaluation Measures

We now define two important rule evaluation measures. The *score* of a rule is the number of its positive instances minus the number of its negative instances:

$$score(R) = |positive(R)| - |negative(R)|$$

The *accuracy* of a rule is its number of positive instances divided by the total number of instances of the rule:

$$accuracy(R) = \frac{|positive(R)|}{|positive(R)| + |negative(R)|}$$

Score is a standard measure in TBL. The notion of rule accuracy is well-known in rule induction and inductive logic programming, and in this paper we will see that it has a role to play in the context of transformation-based learning too.

Corresponding to these two measures are two *thresholds* that are used to control the behaviour of the system and influence the learning results. The *score threshold* and the *accuracy threshold* are the lowest score and the lowest accuracy, respectively, that the highest scoring rule must have in order to be considered.

2.5 Learning

Transformation-Based Learning is a matter of repeatedly instantiating rule templates in training data, scoring rules on the basis of counts of positive and negative evidence of them, selecting the highest scoring rule on the basis of this ranking, and applying it to the training data. When the highest scoring rule does not meet the thresholds, the learning algorithm is terminated.

3 Learning Constraint Grammars

Using transformation-based learning to train Brill taggers is a well-established practice, and since (Lager 1999) contains examples of how to do this with the μ-TBL system, no more will be said on this issue here. However, (Lager 1999) also reports on a small experiment on the learning of Constraint Grammar rules from tagged corpora, and this will be further elaborated in the present paper.

In particular, the following aspects of transformation-based learning of Constraint Grammars will be investigated. How do the use of the uniqueness condition, the setting of the accuracy threshold, and the size of the training corpus, effect the result of training? How does the fact that rules are ordered matter?

Apart from the use of templates for reduction rules rather than templates for replacement rules, the learning of Constraint Grammars contrasts with the learning of Brill tagger rules only in how the accuracy threshold is set.

It is well known that replacement rules do not have to be very accurate: if a rule early in a sequence of replacement rules makes some errors, the errors can often be corrected by rules later in the sequence. By contrast, in a sequence of reduction rules there are no rules that can add tags once they have been (falsely) removed. Therefore, in order to maximize the accuracy of the whole sequence of rules, it must be induced under a validation bias which sees to it that each rule is as accurate as possible. In the μ-TBL system, this is taken care of by setting the accuracy threshold to a value of 1.0, or to a value close to 1.0.

3.1 Tagger Evaluation Measures

For all the experiments performed in the present paper, *recall* (R) and *precision* (P) will be calculated exactly as in (Karlsson et al. 1995:172), i.e. as follows.

$$R = \frac{\text{received appropriate tags}}{\text{intended appropriate tags}}$$

$$P = \frac{\text{received appropriate tags}}{\text{all received tags}}$$

The *F-score*, calculated as $F = (2RP)/(R+P)$ is used as a straightforward way of combining the measures of recall and precision. The *tags per word ratio* (T/W) is calculated as well.

3.2 Experiment 1

In the first experiment, each word token in a training corpus of 60,000 words was assigned the set of part of speech tags that it can have according to a lexicon. The data also indicated which member of this set was the correct one.

The score threshold and the accuracy threshold was set to 4 and 1.0, respectively, and the system was run with 26 templates which mixed in various ways conditions on part of speech tags with conditions on word forms. The uniqueness operator was not used in this experiment.

The system learned 902 rules, the first ten of which are shown below:

```
pos:red nn|dt <- pos:in@[-1,-2,-3] o
pos:ed rp <- wd:in@[0] & pos:nn@[-1] o
pos:ed rb <- wd:in@[0] & pos:nn@[-1] o
pos:ed nn|dt <- pos:nn@[1] o
pos:ed vb <- pos:dt@[-1] o
pos:ed vbn <- wd:said@[0] o
pos:ed vbp <- pos:to@[-1,-2] o
pos:ed vbp <- pos:md@[-1,-2,-3] o
pos:ed vbz <- wd:'s@[0] & pos:nn@[1] o
pos:ed rp <- wd:in@[0] & pos:nns@[-1] o
```

The graph in Figure 1 shows how recall and precision develops as the rules are applied to the test corpus.

As can be seen from the graph, precision increases with the number of rules that have been applied. It starts at 69.2% and reaches its maximum at 93.4%, when all rules have been applied. Recall decreases with the number of rules that are

applied. It starts from 100% and reaches its minimum of 98.9% when all rules have been applied.

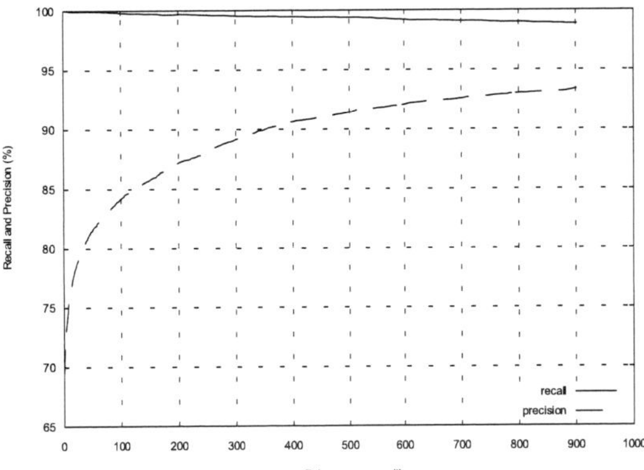

Figure 1: Recall and Precision as functions of the number of rules that have been applied

3.3 Experiment 2

In a second experiment, training was performed exactly as in Experiment 1, except that templates where the uniqueness condition was imposed on the context were used instead.

Training resulted in 1,030 rules. The effect when evaluating them on the test corpus is shown in the table and the graph in Figure 2.

Unique	#(Rs)	R	P	F	T/W
yes	1030	98.7	92.6	95.6	1.066
no	902	98.9	93.4	96.0	1.059

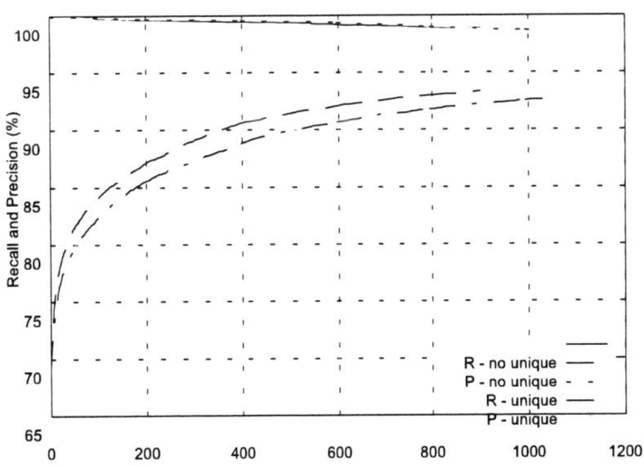

Figure 2: The effect of using the unique operator

Note that the tags per word ratio increases when the uniqueness operator is used. This is not hard to explain. The rules in the previous tagger were more 'daring', and therefore removed tags where the more careful tagger will not do so.

However, one would expect that there is something to be won by being careful, but surprisingly, the use of the uniqueness operator does not make any noticeable difference to recall. This is harder to explain, and we shall not attempt that here.

3.4 Experiment 3

In another experiment, the accuracy threshold (AT) was set to four different values: 1.0 (as before), 0.98, 0.95 and 0.90. Training was performed on the 60,000 word corpus, with templates and score threshold as before.

AT	#(Rs)	R	P	F	T/W
1.00	902	98.9	93.4	96.0	1.059
0.98	738	98.7	94.3	96.5	1.047
0.95	561	98.7	94.7	96.7	1.042
0.90	417	97.9	95.8	96.8	1.023

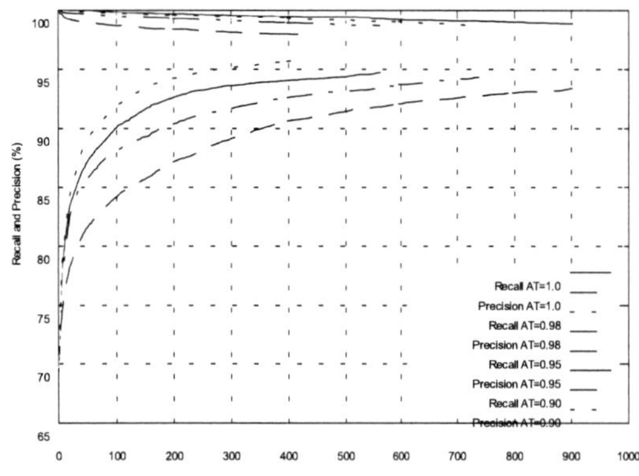

Figure 3: The effect of varying the accuracy threshold

The graph in Figure 3 illustrates nicely how the accuracy threshold can be used to control the recall-precision trade-off. Furthermore, it appears to be the case that an accuracy threshold slightly lower than 1.0 may have a beneficial effect on the overall result (in terms of F-score), perhaps by compensating for noise in the data.

4 Rule Order Dependency

Transformation rules are essentially ordered, with later transformations being dependent upon the outcome of applying earlier transformation rules.

Earlier reduction rule applications can affect what rules might later apply at a particular position P by removing a part of speech tag from the set of tags assigned to P. For example, given the (sketchy) 'text'

```
... question/{nn,vb} ...
```

and the (sketchy) rules

```
pos:red nn <- ... o
pos:red vb <- ...
```

it is clear that if the first rule is applicable to the word "question", the second is not, since that would have removed the last remaining tag.

The use of unique conditions introduces another kind of order dependency. Earlier reduction rule applications can also affect what rules might later apply at a particular position P by removing elements from the sets of parts of speech assigned to words in positions *local* to P. For example, given the (sketchy) 'text'

```
... what/{dt,pn} gave/{nn,vb} him/{pn} ...
```

and the rules

```
pos:red nn <- unique pos:pn@[1] o
pos:red dt <- unique pos:vb@[1]
```

the second rule is applicable only because the first rule is.

4.1 Experiment 4

To establish how much the order means in practice for sequences of reduction rules, a simple experiment was performed, in which a sequence of learned rules was reordered randomly, and then applied to the test corpus.

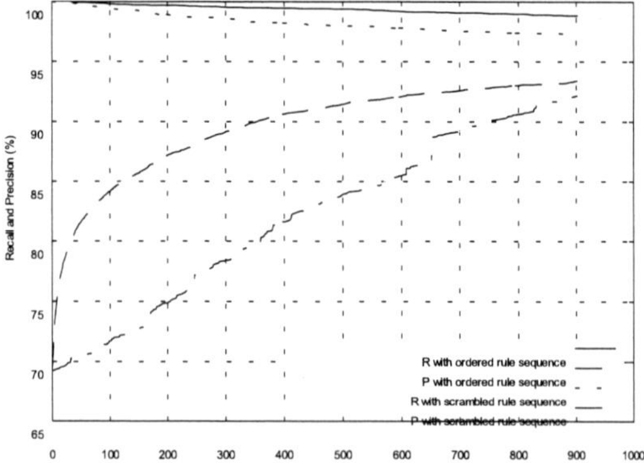

Figure 4: Comparing an ordered and a scrambled rule sequence

Recall decreased from 98.7% to 97.4% when the previous sequence of 902 rules was randomly reordered, and (as a consequence) precision dropped too (from 93.4% to 92.1%), but the number of tags per word stayed roughly the same.

Note that the precision curve corresponding to the randomly reordered rules sequence is flatter than the original curve. The explanation for this is that the really powerful rules are no longer applied first, but spread out randomly. This also accounts for the jaggedness of the curve.

How can the drop in recall be explained? Intuitively, if we change the order of rules, some rules apply too early, and others too late. For example, when a given CG rule is placed late in the sequence, the 'don't remove the last tag'-principle stops it from applying in (most) cases where it would have hurt, if it was placed earlier in the sequence. 'Being a bad rule' (or 'being a good rule') is not a property of a rule just by itself, but of a rule in a particular place in a sequence.

4.2 Discussion

Whereas order dependency is a well-known property of a sequence of Brill tagging rules, it may be argued that this is a point where our CG 'reconstruction' departs from the spirit of original Constraint Grammar. Whether this change of 'semantics' is for good or for bad, remains to be investigated further, but it does seem to be the case that the fact that a rule can leverage off the work performed by rules earlier in the sequence can boost the overall performance of a tagger.

Our Constraint Grammar rules – in contrast with rules in the original Constraint Grammar framework – share another interesting property with Brill tagging rules. The sequence of rules is optimized in the sense that it need only be applied once. This has been verified empirically by applying the sequence of rules twice on the same data, and the second pass has always turned out to have no effect at all.

5 Scaling Up

In an attempt to see how well transformation-based learning of Constraint Grammars works for a larger training corpus, 240,000 words of Swedish data was used. The tag set was also much larger: 156 tags instead of the 42 tags used before.

Training with 15 templates – which took three weeks to complete (*sic!*) – resulted in a sequence of 4,866 rules. These rules were applied to a 30,000 word test corpus. This resulted in 393 errors, which corresponds to a recall of 98.7%. The initial number of tags per word was 1.46 (which corresponds to a precision of 68.4%). After

applying the rules there were only 1.10 tags per word left, corresponding to a precision of 89.8%.

6 Summary and Conclusions

This paper has shown that if we conceive of a Constraint Grammar as an ordered sequence of transformation rules of a particular kind – as reduction rules rather than as replacement rules – the transformation-based learning method used to train Brill taggers can, with minor modifications, be used to train Constraint Grammar taggers as well.

The performance of the taggers – around 99% recall and 90% precision – is probably good enough to warrant further research. First and foremost, TBL algorithms which are more efficient for the particular task of learning reduction rules should be sought for. Secondly, an attempt to make better use of complex morphological features should be made, so that more general rules can be learned. Finally, work has already begun to develop ways to learn other kinds of Constraint Grammar rules (e.g. *selection rules)*, and this may eventually improve the performance further.

References

Brill, E., 1995, Transformation-Based Error-Driven Learning and Natural Language Processing: A Case Study in Part of Speech Tagging. *Computational Linguistics*, December 1995.

Cussens, J., 1997, Part of speech tagging using Progol, In *Proceedings of the 7th International Workshop on Inductive Logic Programming* (ILP-97), Prague.

Karlsson, F., Voutilainen, A., Heikkilä, J., Anttila, A. (eds.), 1995, *Constraint Grammar. A Language-Independent System for Parsing Unrestricted Text*. Mouton de Gruyter.

Lager, T., 1999, The μ-TBL System: Logic Programming Tools for Transformation-Based Learning, Paper presented at the *Third International Workshop on Computational Natural Language Learning* (CoNLL-99), Bergen, 1999.

Lindberg, N. and Eineborg M., 1998, Learning Constraint Grammar-style disambiguation rules using Inductive Logic Programming. In *Proceedings of COLING/ACL'98*.

Samuelsson, C., Tapanainen, P. and Voutilainen, A., 1996, Inducing Constraint Grammars, In: Laurent, M. and de la Higuera, C. (eds.) *Grammatical Inference: Learning Syntax from Sentences*, Springer Verlag.

Data-Driven Methods for PoS Tagging and Chunking of Swedish

Beáta Megyesi
Centre for Speech Technology
Royal Institute of Technology
SE-100 44, Stockholm, Sweden
bea@speech.kth.se

Abstract

In this paper well-known state-of-the-art data-driven algorithms are applied to part-of-speech tagging and shallow parsing of Swedish texts.

1 Introduction

In recent years, machine learning has become very popular for natural language processing (NLP) tasks, such as part of speech (PoS) tagging and shallow parsing, because the algorithms automatically and efficiently can learn from natural language data given a correctly annotated training corpus. There is a vast number of algorithms that have been developed and applied with good results to analyze natural languages on different linguistic levels. For example, Hidden Markov Modeling (Brants, 2000), Maximum Entropy (Ratnaparkhi, 1996), Memory-Based Learning (Zavrel & Daelemans, 1999) and Transformation-Based Learning (Brill, 1994) have been successfully applied to PoS tagging of English with an average accuracy of between 95% and 97%. Recently some attempts also have been made to build data-driven shallow parsers for English by finding syntactically related non-overlapping group of words, so called chunks (Abney, 1991)[1].

In this study, data-driven algorithms are applied to PoS tagging and chunking of Swedish. Common to these algorithms is that they have implementation for PoS tagging, are claimed to be language- and tag set-independent, and easily applicable to new languages given a set of correctly annotated training data.

First, each algorithm will be briefly described. Second, the evaluation and comparison of the data-driven PoS taggers is presented. Lastly, the method used for building shallow parsers and the results are given.

2 Data-Driven learning algorithms

Four well-known data-driven algorithms are used to analyze Swedish texts on different linguistic levels. Each algorithm is briefly described below.

MEMORY-BASED LEARNING (MB), described by Daelemans et al. (1996), is a case-based approach where new items are classified on the basis of similarities to the earlier examples stored in memory during learning. In this study, decision tree induction, called IG-TREE, was re-implemented for Swedish by Harald Berthelsen, based on the description given in Zavrel & Daelemans (1999)[2]. Here, an instance is represented by a vector where the elements are the different features of the instance. The system contains information about the focus word, the preceding and following word forms, the two preceding tags and the one following tag for known words. For unknown words, information about capitalization, the presence of a hyphen or a numeral feature, the preceding tag, the focus word, the ambiguous right tag and the last three letters occurring in the word is used.

The MAXIMUM ENTROPY (ME) framework, called MXPOST, is described by Ratnaparkhi (1996). It is a probabilistic classification-based approach based on a Maximum Entropy model where contextual information is represented as binary features that are used simultaneously in order to predict the PoS tag. The default binary features include the current word, the following and preceding two words and the preceding

---

[1] For a sample of individual research efforts in the field of data-driven chunking, see the Proceedings of the 4th Conference on Computational Natural Language Learning, 2000.

[2] The re-implementation of the Swedish tagger was necessary because it was not available on the ILK web page (http://ilk.kub.nl/software.html).

two tags. For rare and unknown words the first and last four characters are included in the features, as well as information about whether the word contains uppercase characters, hyphens or numbers. The tagger uses a beam search in order to find the most probable sequence of tags. For known words it generates the possible tags, and for unknown words it generates all tags in the tag set. The tag sequence with the highest probability is chosen.

TRANSFORMATION-BASED LEARNING (TBL), developed by Brill (1995), is a rule-based approach that learns by detecting errors. It begins with an unannotated text that is labeled by an initial-state annotator in a heuristic fashion. Then, an ordered list of rules learned during training is applied deterministically to change the tags of the words according to their contexts. TBL uses a context of three preceding and following words and/or tags of the focus word. Unknown words are first assumed to be nouns and handled by prefix and suffix analysis by looking at the first/last one to four letters, capitalization feature and adjacent word co-occurrence.

TRIGRAMS'N'TAGS (TNT) is a statistical approach, developed by Brants (2000). The tagger is a trigram Hidden Markov Model and uses the Viterbi algorithm with beam search for fast processing. The states represent tags and the transition probabilities depend on pairs of tags. The system uses maximum likelihood probabilities derived from the relative frequencies. The main smoothing technique implemented by default is linear interpolation. Unknown words are handled by suffix analysis, i.e. up to the last ten letters of the word. Additionally, information about capitalization is included as default.

3 Data-driven PoS taggers

The algorithms applied to annotate Swedish texts with PoS and morphological features are the Maximum Entropy approach (ME) (Ratnaparkhi, 1996), Memory-Based Learning (MB) (Daelemans, et al., 1996), Transformation-Based Learning (TBL) (Brill, 1994), and Trigrams'n'Tags, (TNT) (Brants, 2000). The aim is to find out how well the algorithms are able to annotate Swedish with PoS and morphological features, to find out the advantages and drawbacks of the methods and to describe the type of

Table 1: The tagging accuracy for all the words, and the accuracy of known and unknown words are given for each classifier. Training and test set are disjoint, consisting of 100k tokens, respectively. Tag set includes 139 tags.

ACCURACY	MB	ME	TBL	TNT
TOTAL %	89.28	91.20	89.06	**93.55**
KNOWN %	92.85	93.34	94.35	**95.50**
UNKNOWN %	68.65	78.85	58.52	**82.29**

errors they make, the effects of the tag set size, and the effect of the size of training material.

All experiments were run on the second version of Stockholm-Umeå Corpus (SUC), annotated with Parole tags (Ejerhed, et al., 1992). The SUC corpus was randomly divided into ten approximately equal parts in order to get subsets containing different genres. For a fair comparison of the methods, each algorithm was trained in each experiment on the same part of the SUC corpus to build four classifiers. Then, each classifier was evaluated on the same test set (117685 tokens) of which 85.23% are known and 14.77% are unknown words. The training and the test set were disjoint. The classifiers were allowed to assign exactly one tag to each token in the test. The baseline performance is 77.37% and is obtained on the test data by selecting the PoS tag that is most frequently associated with the current word. The systems were evaluated from three different aspects.

First, the average accuracy was counted for each classifier, trained on 10% of SUC (115862 tokens) with the entire tag set consisting of 139 tags. The results, given in Table 1, show that all systems outperformed the baseline, but the performance of the taggers is significantly lower than is reported for English.

TnT has the highest overall accuracy and also succeeds best in the annotations of known and unknown words. The ME tagger shows high performance because of the high precision of the annotation of unknown words. TBL manage to disambiguate known words but succeeds poorly on unknown words. MB is slightly better than TBL because of its better success in the annotation of unknown words. Furthermore, TBL and MB more often make mistakes in the mor-

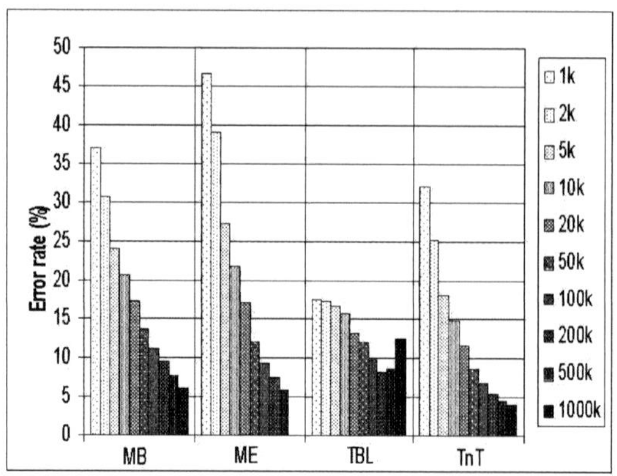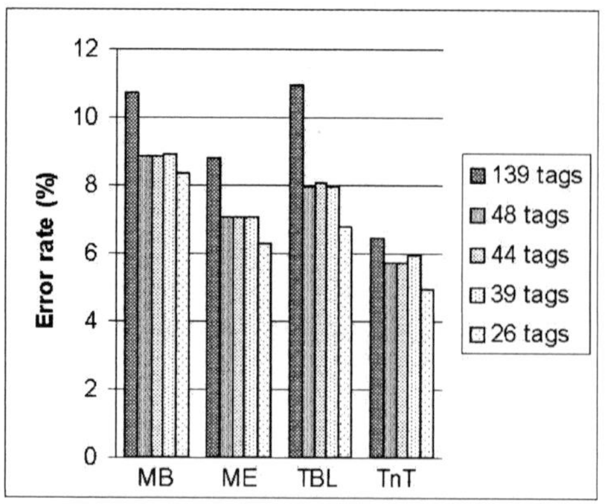

Figure 1: Error rates when training on 1000 to 1 million tokens, totally ten training corpora of various sizes, seen as ten columns for each classifier.

Figure 2: The error rate for each classifier when training on 139, 48, 44, 39 and 26 tags.

phological analysis of categories while ME and TNT more frequently confuse ambiguity classes among PoS categories.

Secondly, each algorithm was trained ten times on the same data set of various size from one thousand to one million tokens. Then, the same test set was annotated by each classifier. The results (see Figure 1) show that larger training data improves the overall accuracy greatly for MB, ME and TnT, but not for TBL. The reason for the low error rate of TBL is the possibility to use a large lexicon which decreases the amount of unknown words and increases the amount of possible categories for each token.

Lastly, each algorithm was trained on different size of tag sets: 139 tags, 48, 44, 39 and 26 tags. The results are shown in Figure 2. By decreasing the size of the tag set from 139 to 26 tags, the error rate decreases by 38% for TBL, 29% for ME, and 23% for MB and TNT. Thus, TBL and ME seem to be more sensitive to the size of tag set than MB and TNT. Furthermore, training on between 39 and 48 tags, the system performances show rather similar results. Thus, the size of the tag set as well as the type of information are crucial facts for system performance.

Concluding the results, TNT has the highest overall accuracy, succeeds best in the annotation of known as well as unknown words, and also fastest in both training and tagging. TBL has high performance on small training corpora, hence it can be used as an aid when building large corpora by applying a boot-strapping procedure. ME has high error rate of the annotation of known tokens when training on small corpora. MB is fast in both training and test and succeeds better in the morphological disambiguation than ME.

4 Data-driven chunkers/parsers

The purpose of this part of the study is to build data-driven shallow parsers by using the chunktag technique, i.e. divide the text into syntactically related non-overlapping groups of words, phrases. Thus, the aim is not the disambiguation of words according to their context since disambiguation takes place on the level of PoS annotation instead with the help of some background knowledge implemented in the PoS taggers containing information about contextual environment of the current word or tag.

The facts that the data-driven PoS taggers have knowledge about the contextual environment and are language- and tag set-independent lead to the thought that they can be assumed to be useful to parse texts, given a correctly annotated training data.

Since correctly chunked/parsed texts are not available for Swedish, a tree-bank was built to serve as training data and bench-mark corpus. For this purpose, an Earley Parser, SPARK (Aycock, 1998) together with a context-free grammar for Swedish developed by the author, was used.

The second version of the Stockholm-Umeå

corpus annotated with PAROLE tags served as input to the parser. The PoS tagged texts were parsed by SPARK for Swedish to serve as training data and bench-mark corpus.

Nine types of phrases were included: adverb phrase (ADVP), minimal adjective phrase (AP-MIN), maximal adjective phrase (APMAX), noun phrase (NP), preposition phrase (PP), maximal projection of NP (NPMAX), verb clusters (VC), infinitive phrase (INFP) and numeral expression (NUMP).

Additionally, each chunk was represented as three types of tags in a similar way as it was proposed by Ramshaw (1995) and used in the CoNLL-2000 competition:
- XB - the first word of the chunk X
- XI - non-initial word inside the chunk X
- O - word outside of any chunk.

Each word and punctuation mark in a sentence is accompanied by a tag which indicates the phrase structure the word belongs to in the parse tree together with the position information. Thus, a word may belong to several phrases as illustrated in the example below for the sentence 'The review of papers should be blind', represented first by parenthesis, and second by tags.

[NPMAX [NP Granskningen NP] [PP av [NP artiklar NP] PP] NPMAX] [VC borde vara VC] [AP anonym AP].
Granskningen/NPB_NPMAXB
av/PPB_NPMAXI
artiklar/NPB_PPI_NPMAXI
borde/VCB
vara/VCI
anonym/APMINB
./O

Thus, the label for a word forms a hierarchical grouping of the parts of the sentence into constituents where lower nodes are situated nearest the word and higher nodes are farthest out. The advantage of the hierarchical annotation on phrase level is that the user can choose the level of the analysis by skipping phrase categories on lower, or higher nodes. For example, the user may only want to use noun phrase extraction without any information on the constituents inside the noun phrase, or to get full analysis of every large phrase in the sentence. This type of annotation can be used in many different applications.

Three data-driven algorithms that have implementations for the PoS tagging approach are applied to build data-driven chunkers: MXPOST, based on the Maximum Entropy framework, Transformation-Based Learning (TBL), and Tri-grams'n'Tags (TNT) based on Hidden Markov Model. The goal is to find out how well the data-driven PoS taggers can learn the hierarchical phrasal structure.

Three types of tests were carried out for each PoS tagger based on the type of linguistic information included in the training data. First, the training corpus contained information about both the word, its PoS tag and the phrase tags. Second, only the word and its phrase tags were included in the training corpus. Third, the words were removed from the training data, only the PoS tags were kept with phrase labels.

In each experiment, the training corpus contained 92109 tokens and the test corpus 23744 tokens. Training and test sets were disjoint and the sentences were randomly chosen from the entire corpus.

The results are shown in the first three raws in Table 2. All systems in all three experiments improved the baseline performance of 59.66%, which was obtained by selecting the phrase tag that is most frequently associated with the current PoS tag.

Large differences can be found in the results depending on the type of information used in training. The systems have lowest performance when the words are annotated with both PoS information and phrase structure information. The low accuracy is not surprising since the tag set consists of a large amount of tags, totally 1033 different combinations of PoS and phrase tags trained on 20946 token (i.e. word) types. When training on both PoS and phrase structure information, the classifiers can be treated as both PoS taggers and parsers.

When PoS information is not present in the training data, the tag set includes 407 different phrase tag combinations. The smaller tag set makes the classification task easier and system performance increases.

Highest accuracy can be obtained when training is done on the basis of PoS and phrase tags only, without the presence of the words. TBL has highest accuracy, followed by ME and TnT. Here, the tag set consists of 407 different phrase tags – the same tag set that was used in the second experiment but the input (i.e. the PoS tags) to the systems contains only 139 different types. Thus, by decreasing the amount of the type of input data, higher performance can be obtained.

Due to the small size of training and test corpus in the earlier experiments and due to the promising results in the third experiment, the PoS taggers were trained on a larger training corpus using PoS tags and their phrase labels without the inclusion of words, and tested on a larger test set. Totally 139 different PoS tags including morphological features were trained with 570 different types of phrase labels. The training set consisting of 244094 tokens, totally 15640 sentences, and a test set containing 105536 tokens, totally 6698 sentences were used.

As is shown in the last raw of Table 2, accuracy can be further improved by increasing the size of the training corpus, hence increasing the amount of the different contextual environments in which the PoS tag can appear. TBL achieves the highest accuracy, 94.44%, followed by ME and TnT.

Table 2: Accuracy (%) is given for each classifier when training on 92109 tokens and testing on 23744 tokens in three different ways: first the word is annotated with both PoS and phrase tag(s), second, the word is annotated with phrase tag(s) only, and third the PoS served as input and labeled with phrase tags. The last raw shows the accuracy (%) for each classifier when training on 244094 tokens and testing on 105536 tokens using PoS categories labeled with phrase tags.

TYPE OF INFORMATION		ME	TBL	TNT
WORD	POS_PHRASETAGS	**73.78**	68.87	65.36
WORD	PHRASE TAGS	**80.72**	75.47	70.94
POS	PHRASE TAGS	91.58	**92.32**	90.40
POS	PHRASE TAGS	92.47	**94.44**	92.42

5 Conclusions

In this study, state-of-the-art data-driven learning algorithms have been applied to PoS tagging and shallow parsing of Swedish texts.

The first part presented a systematic evaluation and comparison of four data-driven algorithms successfully applied to PoS tagging of Swedish texts with an accuracy up to 97%. The effects of the size of the tag set and the size of the training data have been carefully examined.

The second part presented three state-of-the-art data-driven PoS taggers applied to shallow parse Swedish text. Phrase structure for each token is represented in a hierarchical structure containing tags for every constituent type the token belongs to. The results show that best performance (94.4%) can be obtained by training on the basis of PoS tags with constituent labels without considering the words themselves.

6 References

Abney, S. 1991. Parsing by Chunks. In *Principle-Based Parsing*. Kluwer Academic Publ.

Aycock, J. 1998. Compiling Little Languages in Python. In *Proceedings of 7th International Python Conference*.

Brants, T. 2000. TnT - A Statistical Part-of-Speech Tagger. In *Proceedings of the 6th Applied Natural Language Processing Conference*. Seattle, Washington, USA.

Brill, E. 1994. Some Advances in Rule-Based Part of Speech Tagging. In *Proceedings of the 12th National Conference on Artificial Intelligence (AAAI-94)*. Seattle, Washington.

Daelemans, W., Zavrel, J., Berck, P., and Gillis, S.E. 1996. MBT: a Memory-Based Part of Speech Tagger-Generator. In *Proceedings of Fourth Workshop on Very Large Corpora (VLC-96)*. pp. 14-27. Copenhagen, Denmark.

Ejerhed, E., Källgren, G., Wennstedt, O., & Åström, M. 1992. *The Linguistic Annotation System of the Stockholm-Umeå Project*. Dept. of General Linguistics, University of Umeå.

Ramshaw, L. A. and Marcus, M. P. 1995. Text Chunking Using Transformation-Based Learning. In *Proceedings of the Third ACL Workshop on Very Large Corpora*. ACL.

Ratnaparkhi, A. 1996. A Maximum Entropy Model for Part-of-Speech Tagging. In *Proceedings of the Conference on Empirical Methods in Natural Language Processing (EMNLP-96)*. Philadelphia, PA, USA.

J. Zavrel, and W. Daelemans. 1999. Recent Advances in Memory-Based Part-of-Speech Tagging. In *Proceedings of the VI Simposio Internacional de Comunicacion Social*. Cuba.

Comparing source and target texts in a translation corpus

Magnus Merkel
Department of Computer and Information Science
Linköping University
magme@ida.liu.se

1 Introduction

In this paper the Linköping Translation Corpus (LTC) is used as an example on how simple methods and tools can be applied to investigate the relationships between source and target texts in a translation corpus.

The Linköping Translation Corpus consists of English source texts linked to Swedish target texts. The text material comes from two major text types: user's guides to computer programs and fiction. There is also a shorter machine-translated text consisting of dialogue included in the corpus. LTC consists of 805,277 words in the source text and 732,628 words in the target texts, making the total word size of just over 1,500,000 words.

Table 1 below shows an overview of the translation corpus:

Table 1. The Linköping Translation Corpus - an overview

Text type	Title	No. of source words	No. of target words	Transl. method
User's Guide	Microsoft Access UG	179,631	157,302	Human
User's Guide	Microsoft Excel UG	141,381	127,436	Human
User's Guide	IBM OS2 UG	127,499	99,853	TM
User's Guide	IBM InfoWindows UG	69,428	53,619	TM
User's Guide	IBM Client Access UG	21,321	16,752	TM
Novel	Gordimer: A Guest of Honour	197,078	210,350	Human
Novel	Bellow: To Jerusalem and Back	66,760	65,268	Human
Dialog	ATIS dialogues	2,179	2,048	MT
Total		**805,277**	**732,628**	

Three of the translations were translated with the aid of IBM's translation memory tool (TM), which gave an extra dimension to the corpus.

Given a translation corpus such as LTC, one task is to uncover the characteristics of the translation as a whole, or to see whether the translations could be characterised as source-oriented or target-oriented translations (Newmark 1988). The analysis of translation corpus can be made in several steps, going from the simplest case, namely just to compare surface data from the source and target texts independently to a full-blown analysis of how the translator(s) have chosen to render the target text given lexical, syntactic and semantic constraints. In this paper, the first steps of such an analysis and later are shown as well as a sketch on how these analyses correspond with a thorough linguistic analysis of the relationships between the source and target texts.

2 Step 1: Source and target texts independently

The majority of the translation analyses comes from using the DAVE toolbox, developed at Linköping University. With the DAVE tools we extracted data on the Linköping Translation Corpus first as separate texts, i.e. the source texts and target texts independently, including data for

- Word type/token ratio
- Sentence type/token ratio
- Average number of words per sentence
- Number of repeated sentences
- Recurrent sentence rate

These data for the source and target texts, respectively, are listed in Table 2 and 3 below.

There is nothing strikingly unexpected in the source text data in Table 2, although it should be noted that the two novels (Gord and Bellow) contain the largest number of word types, longest sentences and lowest recurrent sentence rates. The fact that there are 184 sentences which are repeated in the Gordimer novel, may even seem somewhat high as repetitiveness is not a common characteristic for fiction, but at closer scrutiny, it turns out that almost all the repeated sentences is contained in the dialogue part of the novel. For example, utterances like "I know.", "Yes." and "All right." occur several times in the novel and constitute to a large extent these 184 repetitive sentences. Furthermore, it is worth mentioning the relative similarites between the two Microsoft texts (Access and Excel); the number of words per sentence is comparable as well as the recurrence rates. Of the IBM texts, the InfoWin text has a considerably higher recurrence rate than the others (31.1 per cent).

Table 2. Source texts – general data

	Access	Excel	OS2	InfoWin	Client	Gord	Bellow	ATIS
Word tokens	179631	141381	127499	69428	21321	197078	66760	2179
Word types	4370	4483	7537	3276	1680	17539	10139	245
Word type/ token	41.11	31.54	16.92	21.19	12.69	11.24	6.58	8.89
Sentences	14829	12610	12242	7834	2427	12310	4215	263
Words/ sentence	12.11	11.21	10.41	8.86	8.78	16.01	15.84	8.29
Repeated sentences	5361	3807	3333	4116	904	184	4	0
Recurrent sentence rate	14.7%	13.62%	13.93%	31.10%	17.55%	0.18%	0.01%	0.00%

Table 3. Target texts – general data

	Access	Excel	OS2	InfoWin	Client	Gord	Bellow	ATIS
Word tokens	157302	127436	99853	53619	16752	210350	65268	2048
Word types	6703	7246	10152	4308	2266	23599	13026	255
Word type/ token	23.47	17.59	9.84	12.45	7.39	8.91	5.01	8.03
Sentences	15079	13020	11943	7735	2457	13427	4285	263
Words/ sentence	10.43	9.79	8.36	6.93	6.82	15.67	15.23	7.79
Repeated sentences	5040	3853	3066	4351	933	291	8	0
Recurrent sentence rate	11.37%	13.06%	9.84	39.26%	18.70%	0.31%	0.02%	0.00%

Although the figures vary slightly, the same pattern is discernible for the target texts as for the source texts, namely that the novels contain the highest numbers of word types, longest sentences and lowest recurrent sentence rates. The Microsoft texts and IBM texts also seem to be relatively similar.

The next step is then to compare the general data from the source and target texts and see if we can conclude something about the translations. We do this by comparing the relative proportions of number of sentences, number of word tokens and recurrent sentence rates, by using the following simple measures (the figures summarized in Table 4 below):

- ST-Sentence = the number of source sentences/number of target sentences

- ST-Word ratio = number of source words/number of target words,

- ST-Recurrent sentence ratio = Recurrent sentence rate(Source text)/Recurrent sentence rate(Target text).

The figures tells us that only two of the texts have more source sentences than target sentences (namely OS2 and InfoWin). This could indicate that most of the texts contain more deletions or that the sentence pairs have a high degree of n-1 sentence correspondences, but at this point this is mere speculation. Only one text, the Gordimer novel, contain more running words in the translation than in the original text. Due to fact that Swedish contain more compounds (written as single words) than English, and that at a large proportion of the definite article "the" and the verb "do" do not have Swedish counterparts, it would be reasonable to expect that the number of words be smaller in the Swedish text. But, again we can only speculate that the text type, in this case fiction, seems to give rise to a relatively higher number of target words.

Table 4. Relative comparisons between source texts and target texts

	Acc.	Excel	OS2	Info	Client	Gord	Bellow	ATIS
ST-Sentence ratio	0.98	0.97	1.02	1.01	0.99.	0.92	0.98	1.00
ST-Word ratio	1.14	1.11	1,28	1.29	1,27	0.94	1.02	1,06
ST-Recurrent sentence ratio	1.29	1.04	1.09	0.79	0.94	0.58	0.50	N/A

82

This is apparent if we also look at the word ratio for the other novel by Bellow which contain fewer words in the translation compared to the original, but the figure (1.02) is still considerably lower than for the translations of the computer manuals.

The English-Swedish Parallel Corpus (ESPC) from Lund contain comparable ST-word ratios for the translations of fiction from English to Swedish (0.98). Looking at the total material (English to Swedish) including non-fiction, gives a ST-word ratio of 1.003 in ESPC.[1] This means that the non-fiction part of the ESPC corpus contain more source words than target words (ST-word ratio 1.028). The computer manuals in the Linköping Translation Corpus do seem to be different in this respect as the ST-word ratios range from 1.11 to 1.29. In relative terms it is reasonable to expect that more information is preserved or added in the fiction translations compared to the translations of manuals.

When we compare the values for sentence recurrence in the texts, we can see that two of the IBM texts (InfoWin and Client) actually have higher sentence recurrence rates in the target than in the source, which is in line with the first hypothesis as these texts were translated with the aid of translation memories.

The two Microsoft texts have higher recurrence rates for the source text than the target text which is in accordance with the second hypothesis, namely that consistency on the sentence level would be more difficult in traditional translation.

The text that does not fit the pattern then is the OS2 text, which has a higher recurrence rate in the source text than in the target text even though the translation was produced with translation memory.

3 Step 2: Source and target texts jointly (as an aligned corpus)

To be able to make more detailed observations on the relationships between the source and the arget text, it is necessary to investigate the source text and target text as a whole, that is, as parallel texts and this is done by using the DAVE tool box (see Merkel 1999).The DAVE toolbox contains some bitext-tailored tools, for example, a module for analysing discrepancies (or inconsistencies) in the translation as well as a module for bilingual concordancing.

The Discrepancy analysis provides information on how consistent or inconsistent the translations of the recurrent sentences are. The Bilingual concordance module lets the user browse and search the parallel text for any combination of source and target words and multi-word units and collect data for the co-occurrence of certain items.

In particular, the focus is on whether there are any observable differences in the translations as far as text type and method of translation are concerned, especially for the distinctions of source- vs. target-orientation, consistency and correspondence. The following types of extracted data from the Linköping Translation Corpus (LTC) are in focus: (i) sentence mappings, (ii) consistency and variation and (iii) co-occurrence data for a sample of lexical items.

2.1 Sentence mapping

The majority of the translations in the Linköping translation corpus contain 1-1 sentence mappings to the degree of a 96-98.35 per cent interval, as can be seen in Table 5. The OS2 text has a strikingly high proportion of deletions (1-0) and insertions (0-1) which indicate that the translation is not particularly close to the original, but is rather a kind of communicative, more target-oriented translation, cf. Newmark (1988). However, the translation of this text has been made with the aid of a translation memory tool, which contradicts a target-oriented translation as translation memories should actually steer translators towards source-oriented translation. For the time being we can only note that there seems to be something strange about the OS2 translation, given the use of translation tools and the fact that data from the sentence mappings give us another message.

The second translation that sticks out is the Gordimer text. Here there is only one aspect that seems peculiar, and that is the relatively high proportion of 1-2 mappings. Over 8 per cent of the pairs are instances of when one English sentence has been translated with two Swedish sentences.

Table 5. Sentence mappings from the parallel texts (excluding ATIS)

	Access		Excel		OS2		InfoWin		Client		Gord		Bellow	
	No.	%	No.	%	No.	%	No.	%	No.	%	No.	%	No.	%
Pairs	14704		12589		11932		7771		2426		12254		4209	
1-1	14169	96.36	12107	96.17	10444	87.53	7519	96.76	2386	98.35	11112	90.68	4122	97.93
1-0	21	0.14	15	0.12	408	3.42	107	1.38	4	0.16	4	0.03	2	0.05
0-1	4	0.03	6	0.05	253	2.12	7	0.09	0	0.00	0	0.00	0	0.00
2-1	121	0.82	26	0.21	390	3.27	66	0.85	1	0.04	41	0.33	6	0.14
1-2	376	2.56	426	3.38	308	2.58	70	0.90	35	1.44	999	8.15	77	1.83
Rest	14	0.09	9	0.08	129	1.08	2	0.02	0	0.00	98	0.8	2	0.05

---

[1] Data from ESPC was kindly provided to me by Bengt Altenberg (personal communication October, 7 1999). The fiction ST-word ratio is based on 276,591 source words/281,127 target words and the total ST-word-ratio on 494,374 source words/492,885 target words.

The explanation for this has to do with at least two different uses of punctuation characters in English and Swedish. First, in English the semicolon is used more often than in Swedish as a delimiter between main clauses, which means that perhaps we should have classified the semicolon as a possible sentence delimiter during the alignment process. Secondly, in English a comma may precede an utterance (within quotation characters) whereas in Swedish the line will commonly be indicated with a colon. The two different uses of semicolons and commas are shown in the two examples from the Gordimer novel in Table 6. The actual positions that were discussed above are underlined in the source and target texts.

Table 6. Different uses of the semicolon and the comma in English and Swedish

Source	Target
It was she who had given her glass to him that night at the Independence <u>party; the</u> Pole who had danced the gazatska became the man with ...	Det var hon som hade låtit honom överta sitt glas under <u>självständighetsfesten. Polacken,</u> som hade dansat en gazatska, blev den han....
A youthful black official at passport control said <u>uncertainly, "Just</u> a minute.	En ungdomlig, svart tjänsteman i passkontrollen svarade <u>litet osäkert: "Ett</u> ögonblick.

If we regard semicolons as sentence delimiters as well as commas in sequences of *<comma-space-quotation mark-uppercase letter>*, and then recalculate the proportions, it turns out that the proportion of 1-1 mappings increases to 95.94 per cent, which takes the Gordimer text up to roughly the same relative proportions as the other texts (except the OS2 text). A flexible method to handle "unusual" sentence boundaries has been suggested by Palmer and Hearst (1994) which may help to improve sentence alignment.

2.2 Discrepancy Analysis

By using discrepancy analysis it can be shown that all translated texts are more or less inconsistent. For manually translated texts the variations are what can be expected, but we discovered an unexpected high degree of inconsistency in the translation memory translated manuals and found that this was due to a clash between an established translation culture and new technology (see Merkel 1996). The discrepancy analysis also revealed relative differences between the manuals which showed how the Client translation actually was a more consistent translation and therefore probably more source-oriented translations than the other user's guides.

2.3 Bilingual concordancing

Co-occurrence data could be useful in several applications. In contrastive linguistics, it could form the basis for extracting exactly those sentence pairs that contain the word(s) that are of interest to the scholar. Altenberg (1998) has developed a measure, *mutual correspondence*, that aims to capture the degree of correspondence in parallel corpora between pairs of words in English-to-Swedish translations and Swedish–to-English translations jointly. For example, if the English word "however" is always translated into the Swedish "emellertid" and "emellertid" is always translated by "however" in English translations then the Mutual Correspondence (MC) between "however" and "emellertid" is 100 per cent.

As the Linköping translation corpus only contains translations in one direction, namely into Swedish, mutual correspondence cannot be calculated, but it is possible to investigate the relative word co-occurrence rate (WCR) for a source and a target word, as follows:

$$WCR = \frac{2 \times (cooccur(A, B) \times 100)}{freq(A) + freq(B)}$$

If a word A occurs 10 times in the source text, a target word B occurs 15 times in the target text and A and B co-occur 8 times, the WCR for A and B is 64 per cent (16/25). The measure actually takes into account the number of times a token of one of the words occurs in a co-occurrence relation in the corpus.

The MC measure will capture the extent to which two words are mutual translations of each other, while the WCR measure will measure the proportion of co-occurrence between one source and one target word given a corpus containing only one translation direction.

Altenberg measures the *translation bias* as the ratio of how many target tokens that are realised from the source word. The formula for translation bias (TB) can be expressed as follows:

$$TB(A, B) = \frac{cooccur(B, A)}{freq(A)}$$

which means a simple ratio between the number of times a target item, B, co-occurs with the source item, A, in relation to the total number of source items A.

Different hypotheses could be tested by investigating co-occurrence data and translation bias; for example, is it possible to conclude how source-oriented a target text is given only co-occurrence data of word pairs from different translations? Text-type specific translation corpora could provide information about what the standard co-occurrence rates would be for a core of word pairs. These pairs and their co-occurrence rates could then be tested on translations from the same text type and perhaps give an indication of how source-oriented the translations are.

Furthermore, co-occurrence rates could be used to investigate what word pairs that are most suitable to use as anchor words (Johansson and Hofland 1994), cognates (Simard et al. 1992) or cue words Wu (1994) in hybrid approaches to sentence.

The use of the bilingual concordance component from DAVE and the application of word co-occurrence rates to the corpus was applied to word pairs from the Linköping translation corpus. The word pairs belong to four different categories:

conjunctions, subjunctions, numerals and proper names/technical terms.

The brief analysis on word correspondences confirms the view that the best candidates for anchoring words can be found among cognates (numbers and proper names) an, to a certain extent, technical terms. Conjunctions and subjunctions can also function as potentially good candidates for most texts. It also shows that the texts that were considered to be more source-oriented in their translation style also exhibit more consistent translations on the word level.

The Bilingual concordance component is a useful tool for the contrastive linguist, the translation scholar and the language engineer. The contrastive linguist can compile statistical data on co-occurrence and extract sentence pairs from parallel corpora that are specifically interesting for a certain contrastive study. The translation scholar may be more inclined to study translation bias; that is, given a certain source object, what are the preferred choices of the translators as they appear in the text. The translation scholar will focus on the translation direction of the text, whereas the contrastive linguist will be more interested in the relationship between two language systems.

3 Step 3: Structural and Semantic Correspondence

In Ahrenberg & Merkel (2000), a descriptive model for measuring the salient traits and tendencies of a translation as compared with the source text were applied to the LTC. Here samples from each translation from the corpus were analyzed in detail to uncover structural and semantic changes in the translation. Many of the traits that we have seen in steps 1 and 2 were verified in this study. In Figure 1, below it is shown graphically how four of the translations are located as regards structural and semantic changes. The Gordimer translation contains more information than its orignal, but exhibits structural changes on the same level as the Access and Client translations. The MT-produced ATIS translation is, not surprisingly, shown to be equal in both structure and specification degree compared to its original. These data correlate with ST-Word ratio presented for these texts in step 2 earlier.

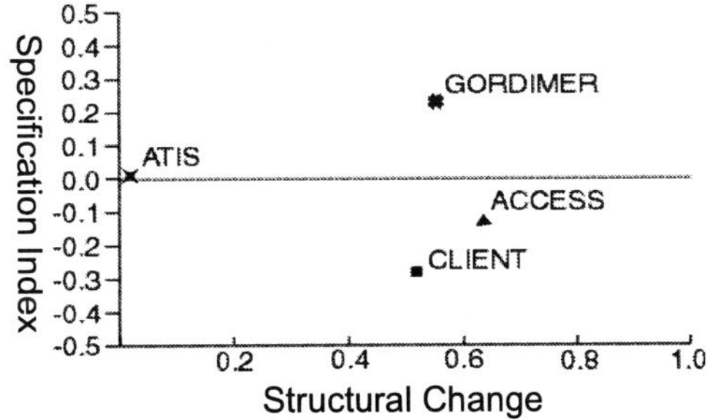

Figure 1. Four different translations displayed according to their tendency for structural and semantic change.

4 Current work: Step 4 - TransMap

At present, the project TransMap, conducted at Linköping University, is developing the analysis methods further by extracting and specifying correspondence data in translation corpora where word and phrase linking is done in combination with a word aligner and a user. The idea is to classify as correspondences on several levels including correspondences of base forms parts-of-speech, syntactic function, and type (such as pronominalization, deletion, addition, convergence and divergence). A shift in direction has here been made compared to the group's earlier work in that the present approach includes using available linguistic resources in the word alignment and phrase extraction tools, such as POS taggers and lemmatizers, and not just string data.

5 Conclusion

By comparing string level data in translation corpora, a great deal of information can be extracted, as have been shown in steps 1 and 2. Many characteristics that were uncovered with these simple methods were actually confirmed when a more thorough linguistic investigation was made on samples from each translation. It remains to be seen if these also holds when the more elaborate techniques of interactive linking and classification of translation units have been finished.

6 References

L. Ahrenberg & M. Merkel. Correspondence measures for MT evaluation. *Proceedings of the LREC 2000 Workshop on Evaluation of Machine Translation*, Athens, Greece 29th May, 2000, pp. 41-46, 2000.

B. Altenberg. Adverbial connectors in English and Swedish. *Out of corpora. Studies in honour of Stig Johansson*. H. Hasselgård & S. Oksefjell (eds.), Rodopi, Amsterdam: 249-268, 1998.

S. Johansson & K. Hofland. Towards an English Norwegian Parallel Corpus. *Creating and Using English Language Corpora*. U Fries, G. Tottie and P. Scheider. Zürich. Rodopi:25:37, 1994.

M. Merkel. Checking Translations for Inconsistency - a Tool for the Editor. In *Proceedings from AMTA-96*, Montreal:157-167, 1996.

M. Merkel. Understanding and Enhancing Translation by Parallel Text Processing. Ph.D. Thesis No. 607. Department of Computer and Information Science, Linköping University, 1999.

P. Newmark, *A Textbook of Translation*, Prentice Hall, London, 1988.

D.D. Palmer & M.A.Hearst. Adaptive Senence Boundary Disambiguation. *Proceedings of the Fourth Conference on Applied Natural Language Processing (ANLP-94)*, Stuttgart:78-83, 1994.

M. Simard, G.F. Foster, & P. Isabelle. Using Cognates to Align Sentences in Bilingual Corpora. *Proceedings of the Fourth International Conference on Theoretical and Methodological Issues in Machine Translation*, Montreal,1992.

D. Wu. Aligning a Parallell English-Chinese Corpus Statistically with Lexical Criteria. Proceedings of the 32n^d Annual Meeting of the ACL: 80-87, 1994.

Towards multimodal public information systems

Magnus Merkel & Arne Jönsson
Department of Computer and Information Science
Linköping University

1. Introduction

In the future e-Home, information from various sources, located both globally and locally, are at hand for a wide range of tasks. Many of these tasks involve finding out about public authorities' rules and regulations. The Public Tax authorities, for instance, provide hundreds of documents on their web site (forms, FAQ's, tax rules, etc.). Currently, the user is restricted to navigating and searching these information sources by clicking hyperlinks or typing in keywords in a search box.

Suppose a citizen needs to know what the local tax in his area is. By providing the keywords "kommunalskatt" (local tax) and "Linköping" to the search engine five documents are retrieved and the user can continue clicking on the provided links to see if the answer is provided in the documents found. On the other hand, supposing that the user had the ability to state the information problem in natural language, and the background system was something more than just a document retrieval system, this interaction could look like the following:

> Citizen: Hi, how much do I pay in local taxes in Linköping?
>
> System: Are you a member of the Swedish Church?
>
> Citizen: Yes, I think so.
>
> System: What parish do you belong to?
>
> Citizen: Slaka.
>
> System: You pay 31,55 per cent in local taxes.

Figure 1. Sample dialogue

In order to allow for such interaction a number of research issues must be addressed. From a language technology perspective we foresee a fruitful, and necessary, co-operation between two main application areas:

- **Multimodal interaction**. This means that the user and system can utilise various types of modalities in order to present information, not only natural language (spoken or written) but also graphics, images, videos, and tables. In this paper we will, however, only consider natural language processing aspects, and especially dialogue and domain knowledge management. In the scenario in Figure 1, above, the use of dialogue allows formulation of the information needs in a fragmented fashion. The system had to collect further information before it could present something useful and this also often involves clarification sub-dialogues. When such a request has been completed, it can be used to retrieve the required information.

- **Information processing of documents.** In this paper we use *information processing* to mean interpretation and adaptation of information stored as natural language documents. Dialogue systems need structured information in order to support advanced information retrieval and problem solving. Such structured knowledge bases are often hand crafted. For the vast amount of public information available on the Internet it is not feasible to manually create structured knowledge sources. Instead, we must be able to find the relevant information stored in unstructured formats and in a systematic way convert it to a suitable form. The problem is not only to bring structure to the information, a prerequisite for doing that is also to locate the relevant information, which, as the information is unstructured is a complex task.

In a newly-started project at Linköping University we are investigating and developing multimodal interaction systems which utilise knowledge and methods from these two areas of language technology, see Figure 2. The long-term vision is to integrate such systems within a common e-home framework, but we believe that a fruitful research strategy will start from specific examples, and work towards a common framework, instead of trying to develop such a framework in a top-down fashion.

We will work iteratively based on a method that unifies issues of conceptual design with a clear correspondence to the components of the customisation of a generic framework (Degerstedt & Jönsson, 2001). The method advocates that coding and design go together and that a dialogue system is implemented iteratively with cumulatively added capabilities. Coding should be carried out as soon as possible, before all details of the system's design are ready. A prototype is developed from the start and is gradually refined based on evaluations of its behaviour. Furthermore, dialogue systems are knowledge intensive and much knowledge is acquired during the development of the system. The evolutionary development, thus, mainly involves refining the knowledge sources.

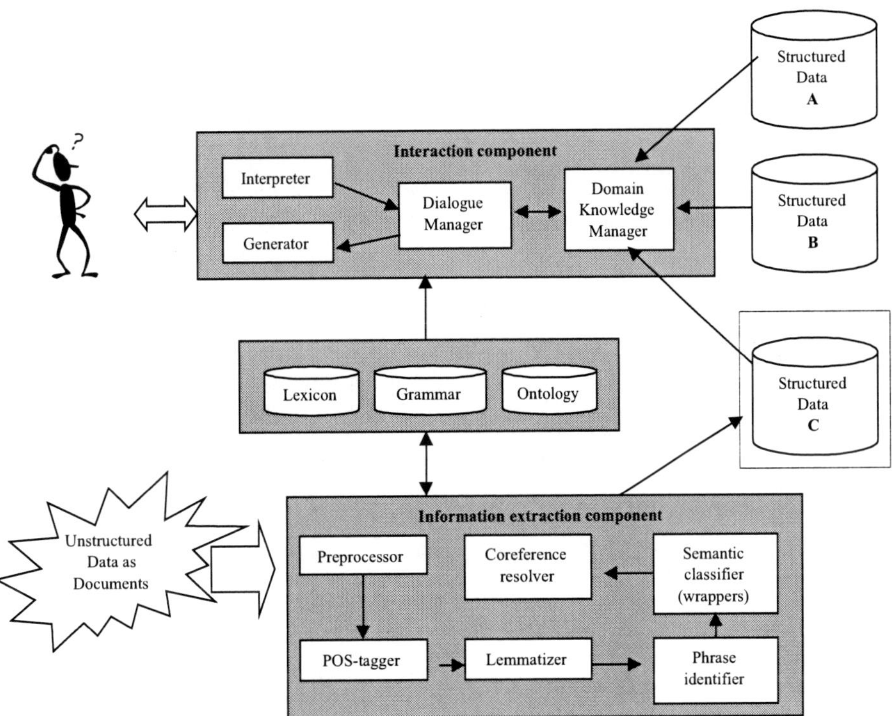

Figure 2. Interaction and information extraction combined

2. Interaction component

The interaction component interprets user utterances in context, access the background information system[1], integrate that with the interpreted utterance and generate a response. In this project the interaction will be handled by the MALIN dialogue system framework (Degerstedt & Jönsson, 2001). Dialogue systems often have a modular architecture with processing modules for interpretation, dialogue management, background system access, and generation, see Figure 2. The processing modules utilise a number of knowledge sources, such as, grammars, lexicons, a dialogue model, a domain model, and task models.

2.1 The Interpreter

The parser is an incremental chart parser that is modified to handle a grammar with rules that allow a partial and shallow parsing (Jönsson & Strömbäck, 1998) The interpretation is driven by the information needed by the background system and guided by expectations from the dialogue

---

[1] In Figure 2 the background information system is depicted by the three knowledge sources to the right termed Structured Data A, B and C. This reflects the distributed nature of background information sources that is typical for many of the information systems addressed in this work.

manager. The analysis is done by parsing as small parts of the utterance as possible.

Partial interpretation is particularly well-suited for dialogue systems, as we can utilise information from a dialogue manager on what is expected and use this to guide the analysis. Dialogue management also involves focus tracking as well as handling clarification subdialogues to further improve the interaction.

The lexicon is the main knowledge source for the parser. Fortunately, much information included in the lexicon can be acquired automatically from the information extraction component. Furthermore, as the grammar is based on partial information, many auxiliary words are not needed, which also makes automatic extraction and lexicon development easier.

2.2 The Dialogue Manager

The role of a dialogue manager differs slightly between different dialogue system architectures, but its primary responsibility is to control the flow of the dialogue by deciding how the system should respond to a user utterance. This is done by inspecting and contextually specifying the information structure produced by the interpretation module. If some information is missing or a request is ambiguous, clarification questions are specified by the Dialogue Manager and posed to the user. Should a request be fully specified and unambiguous the background system can be accessed and an answer is produced. As a basis for these tasks the Dialogue Manager can utilise a dialogue model, a system task model, and a dialogue history.

The Dialogue model holds a generic description of how the dialogue is to be constructed, i.e. to decide what action to take in a certain situation. It is used to control the interaction, which involves determining: 1) what the system should do next (and what module is responsible for carrying out the task) and 2) deciding what communicative action is appropriate at a given dialogue state.

The Dialogue model utilised in MALIN is the LINLIN model (Jönsson, 1997), which is a structurally based model that uses a dialogue grammar for dialogue control. The dialogue is structured in terms of discourse segments, and a discourse segment in terms of moves and embedded segments. Utterances are analysed as linguistic objects, which function as vehicles for atomic move segments. An initiative-response IR structure determines the compound discourse segments, where an initiative opens the IR-segment by introducing a new goal and the response closes the IR-segment. The LINLIN dialogue model classifies the discourse segments by general speech act categories, such as "question" (Q) and "answer" (A), rather than specialised (cf. Hagen 1999), or domain related (Alexandersson and Reithinger, 1995).

The dialogue segments form a dialogue tree. The nodes in the tree, termed dialogue objects, hold information such as the current objects and properties, the user request in focus, information on speaker, hearer, type of general speech act, etc. The dialogue tree is naturally specified in terms of a grammar.

The model assumes that decisions as to what to do next are made on the basis of focus information (cf. Leceuche et al. 2000), i.e. depending on how the focal parameters have been specified. Focus information can be copied between nodes in the dialogue tree, either horizontally by "focus inheritance", from one IR-segment to the next, or vertically by "answer integration" to handle sub-dialogues.

To develop a Dialogue Manager that easily can be customised to new domains and in which different dialogue strategies can be explored, the Dialogue Manager should only be concerned with phenomena related to the dialogue with the user. It should not be involved in the process of accessing the background system or performing domain reasoning. These tasks should instead be carried out by a separate module, a Domain Knowledge Manager.

2.3 The Domain Knowledge Manager

One novel feature of our architecture is the Doamin Knowledge Manager (Flycht-Eriksson, 2000). This module makes the MALIN framework especially suitable for unstructured domains.

The primary responsibility of the Domain Knowledge Manager is to provide domain- and application-specific information when the Dialogue Manager has produced a fully specified request. The Dialogue Manager can deliver a request to the Domain Knowledge Manager and in return expect to get the requested information or a motivation of why the information could not be retrieved. The Domain Knowledge Manager retrieves and integrates information from application information sources utilising the domain ontology. If the Domain Knowledge Manager encounters a problem it cannot solve by using its knowledge about the domain, a specification of the problem and the needed clarifying information is returned to the Dialogue Manager.

Access of application information sources can be problematic in two ways: no answer to the request can be produced, or too many answers are found. The first situation can occur if a request is inconsistent or if no object meets all the restrictions of the request. Two different approaches to dealing with this are for the system to try and fix it itself, or for the system to help the user to handle the situation. The first approach includes relaxing some of the constraints or resolving the inconsistency, both of which require reasoning about the domain. If the system fails or does not try to solve the problem itself, it can give the user as much help as possible when dealing with the problem, for example by stating the cause of the problem and suggesting how the request should be modified. The MALIN framework supports both approaches.

The second problematic situation, in which a request has resulted in too many answers from the background system, can arise from requests that are not specific enough. The solution chosen in the MALIN framework is to use the domain knowledge, manifested in the domain ontology, and decide which constraints should be asked for in order to specify the request, thus helping the user to formulate a more specific request.

3. Information Extraction component

The purpose of the information extraction component is to transform information from unstructured or semistructured document collections into structured information, in the form of a *document warehouse* where information from multiple document types and from multiple sources are stored (Sullivan 2001). The document collection for specific domains from a public agency, for instance, are most often found in various formats (html, pdf, xml and different office program formats) and they come from various sources such as multiple network servers, intranets and the Internet. The solution to the conversion from unstructured to structured information is to be found among techniques from the field of information extraction (Cowie & Lehnert 1996), basically a mix of string-based information retrieval and shallow linguistic approaches. The shallow linguistic analysis, such as generating wrappers (or agents) are used to identify entities such as names of people, prices, countries, etc, which provides a way of extracting certain sets of simple facts from the documents. Mattox et al. (1999) argue that many IE approaches based on shallow parsing will yield insufficient structure if the extracted information is to serve as a database to answer more elaborate and "important" queries. By important queries, they mean, for instance, questions about something that is not explicitly expressed in the document. If a document contains information about the national debts of all countries in absolute figures, then a more elaborate system should be able to answer queries about which countries that have a debt that *exceeds* X billion dollars.

There are several ways of identifying concepts and relations between objects in unstructured documents in a step-by-step manner:

1. Pre-processing (unveiling document formats such as headings, table structure, lists, etc).

2. Parts of speech tagging

3. Lemmatization

4. Phrase clustering

5. Semantic classification

6. Discourse reference identification

7. Identification of relationships between concepts

8. Output generation

Step 1 involves non-linguistic information and is done to normalise the documents into a common format that the rest of the machinery can build on. Step 2 through 4 requires syntactic and morphological taggers that can provide syntactic information for the domain(s) at hand. Step 4 can also be enhanced by statistically-based phrase extractors such Frasse-II (Merkel & Andersson 2000). Step 5 requires some knowledge about the domain and application at hand, usually expressed as a domain specific ontology. In the Message Understanding Conferences (MUC, e.g. described in Grishman & Sundheim, 1996), there has been strong encouragement to measure aspects of the internal processing of extraction systems and how

well they solved problems of coreference, word sense disambiguation and providing predicate-argument structure for a particular segment of text and sentence. The latter aspects all have bearing on steps 5 to 7 in that they pinpoint the need for a deeper understanding of content and relationships.

4. Pilot study

In this project we intend to develop wrappers that identify concepts from the domain documents in the tax domain. Initial investigations on how such wrappers can be developed and used were carried out during the spring of 2001.

Four student groups in Linköping were assigned the task of building a questioning-answering system in the domain of Swedish birds. One of the subtasks was to analyse a set of documents that contained information about roughly 100 Swedish birds and to use various approaches to identify entities and relationships in these unstructured documents. The structured bird document base was then to be connected to a natural language interface which the students had to write from scratch together with a module that should provide an answer to the user's question; thus enabling the user to search for birds using natural language. Here are some examples of the questions that the Bird system were planned to handle:

1. What is the latin name for magpie?
   Answer: Pica Pica

2. A bird that is greyish brown, yellow and has yellow and black streaks on the head and seen in pine forests?
   Answer: Goldcrest

3. Is a raven larger than a crow?
   Answer: Yes.

Figure 3. Sample dialogue from the Bird system

Semantic information was extracted from the enriched documents based on the XML-tags and some of this information was then added to the lexicon which was used by both the question interpreter and the search module. Some semantic knowledge was definitely hand-coded and some of the wrappers were not very generic, but given the time and situation, the solutions provided were nevertheless very encouraging.

The experiences from the Bird task gave many insightful experiences to information extraction. First, it was shown that five-six people could actually build a system from scratch with a small set of resources in two weeks time. Secondly, given a pre-made package for handling the interaction part, a great deal of more work could have been put into the semantic classification (the wrapping module), which would have meant that a more generic solution could have been adopted from the start. None of the groups did for instance use any explicit domain ontologies.

In the future system, depicted in Figure 2, the Extraction component is sketched. Some of the linguistic resources are shared with the Interaction component, for example, the lexicon and the ontology. When new concepts are being identified during the extraction process, the lexicon will (automatically) be updated and thereby increase the interaction component's ability to correctly interpret the user's questions.

5. Summary and future work

In this paper we have briefly presented current work on the development of a system that utilise information extraction techniques in a dialogue system. A number of issues has not been elaborated upon in this short paper, such as how to utilise various modalities, how to generate usable responses and how to integrate and interpret multi-modal interaction, instead focus has been on issues related to how and where dialogue systems meet information processing.

One important feature of our dialogue system's architecture is the use of a domain knowledge manager. The domain knowledge manager acts as the intermediator between the two sub-areas: information processing and multi-modal interaction. We have previously discussed the advantages of a separate module for domain knowledge management (Flycht-Eriksson and Jönsson, 2000). One such advantage is that the dialogue manager need not be aware of how the domain is structured and need not consider such issues as part of the contextual interpretation of a user request. A separate domain knowledge manager also means that the information processing components need not consider aspects of dialogue.

Common knowledge sources need to be developed, the properties of which have to be established. This also includes issues on the parts that are shared among the dialogue system and the information processing modules. Presumably, the ontology is a common resource, and so is the lexicon, whereas the grammars probably differ.

The development of a multi-modal information system that integrates a dialogue system with techniques from information extraction will, as stated above, be carried out iteratively from simple prototypes towards more complex dialogue systems. Thus, we will always have a working system whose capabilities can be incrementally augmented as the system evolves, e.g. while the ontology for the whole domain is being expanded.

References

Jan Alexandersson and Norbert Reithinger, "Designing the Dialogue Component in a Speech Translation System", Proceedings of the Ninth Twente Workshop on Language Technology (TWLT-9), pp 35-43, 1995.

Jim Cowie & Wendy G. Lehnert. Information extraction. *Communications of the ACM,* 39(1):80-91.

Lars Degerstedt and Arne Jönsson, "A Method for Iterative Implementation of Dialogue Management", 2nd IJCAI Workshop on Knowledge and Reasoning in Practical Dialogue Systems, August 5, 2001, Seattle

Annika Flycht-Eriksson, "A Domain Knowledge Manager for Dialogue Systems", Proceedings of the 14th European Conference on Artificial Intelligence (ECAI), IOS Press, Amsterdam, 2000.

Ralph Grishman & Beth Sundheim. Message Understanding Conference - 6: A Brief History. In *Proc. of the 16th Int'l Conf. on Computational Linguistics, Copenhagen,* 1996.

Eli Hagen, "An approach to Mixed Initiative Spoken Information Retrieval Dialogue", User modeling and User-Adapted Interaction, Vol. 9, No. 1-2, pp 167-213, 1999

Arne Jönsson, A model for habitable and efficient dialogue management for natural language interaction, Natural Language Engineering 3(2/3), pp 103-122, Cambridge University Press, 1997.

Arne Jönsson & Lena Strömbäck Robust Interaction through Partial Interpretation and Dialogue Management, Proceedings of Coling-ACL'98, Montrèal, Canada, 1998.

Renaud Leceuche, Dave Robertson, Catherine Barry and Chris Mellish, "Evaluating focus theories for dialogue management", International Journal on Human-Computer Studies, Vol. 52, pp 23-76, 2000.

David Mattox, L. Seligman & K. Smith. Rapper: A Wrapper Generator with Linguistic Knowledge. In *2nd Proceedings from the Workshop on Web Information and Data Management,* Kansas City, Missouri, pp. 6-11, 1999.

Magnus Merkel & Mikael Andersson. Knowledge-lite extraction of multi-word units with language filters and entropy thresholds. In *Proceedings of RIAO'2000,* Collége de France, Paris, France, April 12-14, 2000, Volume1, pp. 737-746, 2000.

Dan Sullivan. *Document Warehousing and Text Mining,* John Wiley & Sons, 2001.

PARSING ESTONIAN WITH CONSTRAINT GRAMMAR

Kaili Müürisep
Institute of Cybernetics at Tallinn Technical University
Estonia
kaili@phon.ioc.ee

Abstract

This paper describes the current state of syntactic analysis of Estonian using Constraint Grammar, focusing mainly on the determination of syntactic functions. Constraint Grammar of Estonian was written in 1996-2000 at the University of Tartu. The author has developed its syntactic part.

1. Introduction

The work with syntactic analyser of Estonian started five years ago at the University of Tartu. As a basis of the analyser we are using a formalism called Constraint Grammar, which is developed at the University of Helsinki by Fred Karlsson and co-workers (Karlsson et al, 1995).

The main idea of the Constraint Grammar is that it determines the surface-level syntactic analysis of the text, which has gone through prior morphological analysis. The process of syntactic analysis consists of three stages: morphological disambiguation, identification of clause boundaries, and identification of syntactic functions of words.

The underlying principle in determining both the morphological interpretation and the syntactic functions is the same: first all the possible labels are attached to words and then the ones that do not fit the context are removed by applying special rules called constraints. Constraint Grammar consists of hand written rules, which by checking the context decide whether an interpretation is correct or has to be removed.

2. Preceding steps

For morphological analysis of Estonian, we use the morphological analyser ESTMORF (Kaalep, 1997) that assigns adequate morphological descriptions to about 99% of tokens in a text. In Estonian fiction texts about 45% of morphologically analysed word-forms have more than one reading.

Morphologically analysed text is disambiguated by Constraint Grammar disambiguator (Puolakainen, 1998). The development of the disambiguator is in process but 85-90% of words become morphologically unambiguous and the error rate of this disambiguator is less than 2%. The disambiguating grammar consists of more than 1200 hand written rules, almost half of them treat concrete word forms (e.g. '*on*' - verb *be* in simple present 3rd person singular or plural), the others cover broader ambiguity classes. The difficult problem is the choice between the readings of a noun in nominative, genitive, partitive or short illative (aditive) case. The other sources of errors and ambiguities are participles and readings of adposition, adverb and noun of some word-forms.

3. Determination of syntactic functions

27 syntactic tags of ESTCG represent syntactic functions of traditional Estonian grammar (Erelt et al., 1993), although there are some modifications considering the specialities of Constraint Grammar: CG annotates every word with some syntactic label while linguistic grammar has a more general view treating multiple words as units. The syntax used in Constraint Grammar is word based, this means that no hierarchical phrase structure is constructed. The phrasal heads are labelled as subjects, objects, adverbials or predicatives. The modifiers have tags that indicate the direction where the head of phrase could be found but the modifiers and heads are not formally connected. The verb chain is marked by five labels: finite or infinite auxiliary or main verb and a label for negation.

Determination of syntactic functions is implemented in two modules. First, the parser adds all possible function tags to each morphological reading, and after that, syntactic constraints remove incorrect tags in the current context.

Syntactic tags are added to words by 180 morphosyntactic mapping rules. These rules describe which combination of syntactic tags should to be attached to the current morphological reading. For example, a noun in nominative case can be a subject, an object, a predicative, a premodifying or postmodifying attribute or an adverbial. In this stage of parsing at least one syntactic tag is assigned to every word but usually many more (approximately 3.8 tags per word in the case of Estonian).

After the mapping operation syntactic constraints are applied. ESTCG contains 1118 syntactic constraints. The rules were devised using training corpus of 20,000 words. Most of these rules have linguistic background, this means that they are generated using grammar books and author's personal linguistic intuition. Only some of them are compiled using statistical information about word order tendencies. As known, any natural language tends to have somehow irregular nature - it is very difficult (if not impossible) to describe a language with fixed rules. So ca 20% of syntactic constraints in ESTCG are heuristic rules - they are not 100% true but ease to solve some complicated ambiguity classes. ESTCG heuristic rules help to raise unambiguity rate from 79% to 91%, reducing correctness from 99.46% to 99.24% (results from training corpus). Attempts are made to devise rules, which will remove as few correct interpretations as possible and so result in as error-free analyses as feasible. The syntactic part of Estonian Constraint Grammar is fully documented in author's Ph.D. thesis (Müürisep, 2000).

A disambiguated and syntactically analysed sentence is shown in fig. 1. Morphological description is between "//"-symbols, syntactic tag begins with @-symbol. The direct translation is given after #-symbol. The last word in the sentence remains ambiguous between adverbial and postmodifying attribute. The phrase *koht infootsingul* (*'place on the information retrieval'*) has no meaning but the attribute tag can't be removed since the phrase with some other attribute in adessive case is quite usual, e.g. *koht laeval - 'place on the ship'*.

```
$LA$
   ####
Dokumenditöötluses                                    # in the document processing
   dokumendi_töötlus+s //_S_ com sg in #cap // **CLB @ADVL
on                                                    # is
   ole+0 //_V_ main indic pres ps3 sg ps af #FinV #Intr // @+FMV
oluline                                               # important
   olu=line+0 //_A_ pos sg nom  #line //  @AN>
koht                                                  # place
   koht+0 //_S_ com sg nom  //  @SUBJ
infootsingul                                          # on the information retrieval
   info_otsing+l //_S_ com sg ad  //  @ADVL @<NN
$.
   . //_Z_ Fst //
$LL$
   ####
```

Figure 1. Syntactically analysed sentence - *'Information retrieval has an important place (role) in the document processing'.*

ESTCG parser is based on original Constraint Grammar framework but has been re-implemented by us. It has some influence from CG-2 (Tapanainen, 1996), like possibilities for enhanced context addressing and doing morphological disambiguation after the phase of determination of syntactic functions. Our parser enables also rules for clause boundary detection and these rules are in use in ESTCG grammar.

4. Evaluation

Two types of texts were used to evaluate the performance of the syntactic analyser. If the morphological disambiguation has been made manually, i.e. the input text was unerroneous, the recall (the ratio of number of correct assigned syntactic tags to the number of all correct tags) was 98.5% and the precision (the ratio of number of correct assigned syntactic tags to the number of all assigned syntactic tags) was 87.5%.

If the prior analysis of the same text was made automatically (in this case the disambiguator made 2% errors and left 13% of words ambiguous, 1% of words were unknown for morphological analyser) the recall was 96.5% and precision 78%. In the first text 86-91% of words became syntactically unambiguous, and in the second one, the corresponding numbers were 81-84%. The benchmark corpus consists of 10,000 words and has not been used during the rule generation process.

The errors in manually disambiguated corpora are mostly caused by ellipsis, some errors occurred during determination of apposition and the third biggest group of error exists in sentences there one clause divides the other into two parts. There was only one error due to morphological ambiguity in the second test; all the other additional errors were caused by the faults from earlier steps of analysis.

In spite of all efforts some words still remain ambiguous. For example, it is very difficult to distinguish adverbial attributes from the adverbials (see example above). This is almost the same problem as PP-attachment in English, but additionally it is possible to use both premodifying and postmodifying adverbial attributes in Estonian. Of course the PP-attachment problem is also existent. The other complicated problem is the distinction of genitive attributes and objects, which are followed by any other noun, e.g.

(1)   Ta asetas mantli (gen @OBJ @NN>) tooli (gen @OBJ @NN>)
        seljatoele (@ADVL @<NN).

        He put coat-GEN chair-GEN back-ALLAT.

        'He put the coat onto the back of a chair.'

To make things even worse the morphological disambiguator often fails to solve the morphological ambiguities in the same position: noun in genitive case is frequently ambiguous between nominative or partitive case.

So the most difficult problem in the Estonian language appear to be determining the borders of noun phrases. It is often hard to decide which adjacent nouns belong to a common noun phrase, and which form separate noun phrases.

5. Further plans

Although the grammar is already effective enough to be used in practical applications, the authors of the grammar see the ways for further improvements.

We should increase the lexicon: in addition to valency information of verbs, the precise description of quantifiers and some type of adverbials is also needed. The presence of the lexicon of phrasal verbs is also essential.

We should increase the size of training and benchmark corpora and include new types of texts. This would enable experiments with statistical methods, which might be quite fruitful.

ESTCG parser is used as a part of the noun phrase parser and it is also included in experimental automatic summary generation software. We are looking for new application areas of the parser; the work of adjusting it for the needs of text-to-speech synthesiser is in progress.

6. Conclusion

This paper presents the application of the Constraint Grammar formalism to Estonian. Although this was the first attempt to write a computational grammar for Estonian, the achieved results show that the Constraint Grammar is flexible enough to use this framework for syntactic analysis of morphologically rich languages with relatively free word order like Estonian.

References

Erelt, Mati, R. Kasik, H. Metslang, H. Rajandi, K. Ross, H. Saari, K. Tael, S. Vare, 1993. *Eesti keele grammatika II.* Tallinn: ETA Eesti Keele Instituut

Kaalep, Heiki-Jaan, 1997. An Estonian Morphological Analyser and the Impact of a Corpus on its Development. *Computers and Humanities 31*: pp. 115-133.

Karlsson, Fred, Arto Anttila, Juha Heikkilä, Atro Voutilainen, 1995. *Constraint Grammar: a Language-Independent System for Parsing Unrestricted Text.* Mouton de Gruyter.

Müürisep, Kaili, 2000. *Eesti keele arvutigrammatika: süntaks.* Dissertationes Mathematicae Universitatis Tartuensis 22. Tartu.

Puolakainen, Tiina, 1998. Developing Constraint Grammar for Morphological Disambiguation of Estonian. *Proceedings of DIALOGUE '98*. Russia, Kazan. Vol. 2 pp. 626-630.

Tapanainen, Pasi, 1996. *The Constraint Grammar Parser CG-2*. Publications of the Department ofGeneral Linguistics, University of Helsinki, No. 27.

Identifying Situation Reference in Danish

Costanza Navarretta
Center for Sprogteknologi
Njalsgade 80
2300 Copenhagen S
costanza@cst.ku.dk

1 Introduction

This paper deals with the identification of anaphors whose antecedents are verbal phrases or discourse segments in Danish.[1]

These anaphors have been given different names in literature, such as discourse deictics (Levinson 1987, Webber 1991), anaphors to abstract objects (Asher 1993) and situation reference (Fraurud 1992). We follow Fraurud and call them situation anaphors. Situation reference is quite common especially in dialogues, but has seldom been dealt with in computational linguistics.

In this paper we first describe situation reference in Danish (section 2), then we shortly outline Eckert and Strube's algorithm for anaphora resolution a part of which we have modified and extended for identifying Danish situation anaphors (section 3). In section 4 we present our rules for identifying Danish situation reference and we present the results of the manual application of these rules on two dialogues. In section 5 we make some concluding remarks.

2 Danish Situation Reference

Situation anaphors in Danish are third-person neuter gender personal and demonstrative pronouns *det* (it/this/that), *dette* (this), *det her* (this) and *det der* (that). *Dette* is mostly used in written language, while *det her* and *det der* are common in conversations.

We have analysed the occurrences of situation anaphors in a number of dialogues from the collection "Samtale hos Lægen" ("The Talk at the Doctor's"), henceforth **SL**, collected from 1993 to 1995 in the field of psychology of language by researchers at the University of Copenhagen (Duncker & Hermann 1996, Hermann 2000). Furthermore we have analysed situation anaphors in some newspaper articles from **Berlingske Tidende**. As in English situation

---

[1]The research described has been done under the **Staging** project, funded by the Danish Research Councils.

anaphors can refer to an infinitive, one or more verbal phrases, one or more
clauses, a preceding discourse segment or something that can be vaguely inferred from the context. Danish deictics are also used in cases where elliptical
constructions are common in English. Some examples of situation reference are
the following:

- the anaphor co-refers with an infinitive:

  (1)   *At ryge er farligt og det er ogs å dyrt*
         (Smoking is dangerous and it is also expensive)

- the anaphor co-refers with a clause:

  (2)   **A:** *Du skal tage en blodprøve*
         (You have to take a blood test)
         B: *Hvorfor det?*
         (Why is that?)
         (**SL**)

- the anaphor is used as the subject complement of *være* (be) and *blive*
  (become) in answers (or in coordinated successive clauses):

  (3)   **A:** *Blev du færdig med opgaven?*
         (Did you finish the task?)
         B: *Ja, det blev jeg*
         (lit. Yes, that was I)
         (Yes, I did)

- the anaphor co-refers with a verb phrase when it is used as the object
  complement for the verb *have* (have), *gøre* (do) and modal verbs:

  (4)   *Alle faldt, men det gjorde jeg ikke*
         (lit. All fell, but that did I not)
         (All fell, but I did not)

- the anaphor co-refers with a clause in constructions with attitude verbs
  and other verbs which take clausal complements, such as *synes* (think),
  tro (believe) *vide* (know), *sige* (say), *håbe* (hope):

  (5)   **A:** *Han falder snart i søvn*
         (He will soon fall asleep)
         B *Det h åber jeg ikke*
         (lit. That hope I not)
         (I hope not)

3 Eckert and Strube's Algorithm

Although situation reference is very common, especially in dialogues, most of the algorithms for resolving pronominal anaphora do not deal with it. An exception is the algorithm proposed by Eckert and Strube (Eckert & Strube 1999*b*, Eckert & Strube 1999*a*), the ES-algorithm henceforth, which was defined for resolving anaphors with individual NP antecedents and with abstract object antecedents. The ES-algorithm is based on rules for discriminating among individual and situation anaphors based on the predicative contexts in which the anaphors occur. Individual anaphors are resolved by a centering-based algorithm (Strube 1998), while some types of situation anaphors are resolved with an algorithm proposed by Eckert and Strube. The athors manually test the approach on selected dialogues and obtain a precision of 63,6% for discourse deictics and 66,2% for individual anaphors.

The algorithm has been adapted to Danish with slightly better results in (Navarretta 2000), but it was found too simplistic for correctly classifying and resolving different types of situation reference. Although we agree, we believe that identifying uses of third-person neuter gender singular personal and demonstrative pronouns as situation anaphors is useful in NLP processing systems and that Eckert and Strube's approach to recognize them from their context is worth pursuing. Thus we have both modified the original rules in Eckert and Strube's algorithm, and added Danish specific rules. The rules are mainly based on the occurrences of situation anaphors in the Danish dialogue collection and corpus of written texts.

4 Identification Rules

In the following we present some of the defeasible preference rules for identifying situation anaphors which we have defined for Danish. We have marked with a star those rules which are simply translations of the rules proposed by Eckert and Strube. defeasible.

- * constructions where a pronoun is equated with an abstract object, e.g., *x er et forslag* (x is a suggestion)

- * copula constructions with adjectives which can only be applied to abstract entities, such as *x er sandt/usandt* (x is true/untrue), *x er rigtigt* (x is correct)

- * arguments of verbs which take S'-complements, e.g., *tro* (believe), *antage* (assume), *sige* (say)

- * anaphoric referent in constructions such as *x er fordi du er holdt op med at ryge* (x is because you have stopped smoking) and *x er p å grund af at du er gravid* (x is because you are pregnant)

- object of *gøre* (do)

- subject complement with *være* (be) and *blive* (become)

- object of *have* (have) if the verb was not used as a main verb in the previous clause

- object of modal verbs

- in copula constructions where the adjective can both refer to an individual NP and to an abstract object, such as *x er godt* (x is good), *x er dårligt* (x is bad), *elske x* (love x) the anaphor co-refers with an abstract object if the previous clause contains a raising adjective construction (or related constructions where an infinite is the subject)

The latter rule covers cases where the contexts of an anaphor can allow both an individual NP and an abstract object. Consider as illustration the examples (6-a) and (6-b).

(6)   a.   *Peter boede i et rødt hus. Det hadede han.*
           (Peter lived in a red house. He hated it.)
      b.   *Det er dødsygt at sidde p å et vaskeri. Det hader jeg.*
           (It is boring to be in a laundry. I hate it)

The identification rules we have proposed would identify the *det* in example (6-b) as a situation anaphor.

To test the identified rules we have manually marked situation anaphors in two randomly chosen dialogues from the **SL** collection and in a newspaper article. Then we have manually applied the identification rules to the two unmarked dialogues. We have compared the results from human marking and from marking according to the identification rules. In 83 % of the cases the same situation anaphors were identified. Failure cases were mainly anaphors occurring in constructions which allow for both individual and situation reference or anaphors occurring in constructions which we had not identified. The obtained results are encouraging, but it must be noted that we have tested the rules on the same type of dialogue which we also used for identifying the discriminating rules, thus more tests should be done on different dialogue and text types.

5   Concluding Remarks

We have proposed preference rules for identifying situation reference in Danish by modifying and extended the rules for recognizing situation anaphors proposed by Eckert and Strube. We have also presented the results of a first test of these rules, and these results were encouraging, but should be confirmed by more tests on different types of dialogue and text. Although the identified rules are general, they are not yet exhaustive. We believe that the rules can be used in different NLP applications, such as text understanding and dialogue systems to mark situation anaphors that cannot be resolved by common resolution algorithms which only deal with individual anaphors.

References

Asher, N. (1993), *Reference to Abstract Objects in Discourse*, Vol. 50 of *Studies in Linguistics and Philosophy*, Kluwer Academic Publishers, Dordrecht, the Netherlands.

Duncker, D. & Hermann, J. (1996), 'Patientord og lægeord - særord eller fællesord?', *Månedsskrift for Praktisk Lægegerning - Tidsskrift for Praktiserende Lægers Efteruddannelse* pp. 1019–1030.

Eckert, M. & Strube, M. (1999*a*), Dialogue Acts, Synchronising Units and Anaphora Resolution, *in* J. van Kuppevelt, N. van Leusen, R. van Rooy & H. Zeevat, eds, 'Amstelogue'99 Proceedings - Workshop on the Semantics and Pragmatics of Dialogue'.

Eckert, M. & Strube, M. (1999*b*), Resolving Discourse Deictic Anaphora in Dialogues, *in* 'Proceedings of the EACL-99', pp. 37–44.

Fraurud, K. (1992), *Processing Noun Phrases in Natural Discourse*, Department of Linguistics - Stockholm University.

Hermann, J. (2000), Understandings between doctors and patients - some methodological issues, *in* 'Proceedings ofm the Conference on Medical Interaction, Oct. 18-20', University of Southern Denmark, Odense.

Levinson, S. (1987), 'Pragmatics and the grammar of anaphora: a partial pragmatic reduction of Binding and Control Phenomena', *Journal of Linguistics* **23**(2), 379–434.

Navarretta, C. (2000), Abstract Anaphora Resolution in Danish, *in* L. Dybkjær, K. Hasida & D. Traum, eds, 'Proceedings of 1st SIGdial Workshop on Discourse and Dialogue - Held in conjunction with The 38th Annual Meeting of the ACL', Hong Kong, pp. 56–65.

Strube, M. (1998), Never Look Back: An Alternative to Centering, *in* 'Proceedings of the 36th Meeting of the ACL', Vol. II, Université de Montréal, Montreal, Quebec, Canada, pp. 1251–1257.

Webber, B. L. (1991), 'Structure and Ostension in the Interpretation of Discourse Deixis', *Natural Language and Cognitive Processes* **6**(2), 107–135.

On Statistical Methods in
Natural Language Processing

Joakim Nivre

1 Introduction

What is a statistical method and how can it be used in natural language processing (NLP)? In this paper, we will try to throw some light on this question by examining the different ways in which NLP methods deserve to be called "statistical", an exercise that will hopefully throw some light also on methods that do not deserve to be so called.

2 NLP: Problems, Models and Methods

NLP problems have to do with natural language input and output. Here are a few typical and uncontroversial examples of NLP problems:

- Part-of-speech tagging: Annotating natural language sentences or texts for parts-of-speech.

- Natural language generation: Producing natural language sentences or texts from non-linguistic representations.

- Machine translation: Translating sentences or texts in a source language to sentences or texts in a target language.

In part-of-speech tagging we have natural language input, in generation we have natural language output, and in translation we have both input and output in natural language.

If our aim is to build effective components for computational systems, then we must develop *algorithms* for solving these problems. However, this is not always possible, simply because the problems are not well-defined enough. The way out of this dilemma is the same as in most other branches of science. Instead of attacking real world problems directly with all their messy details, we build mathematical models of reality and solve abstract problems within the models instead. Provided that the models are worth their salt, these solutions will provide adequate approximations for the real problems. An abstract problem Q is a binary relation on a set I of problem *instances* and a set S of problem *solutions*. The abstract problems that are relevant to NLP are those where either I or S (or both) are linguistic entities or representations of linguistic entities. More precisely, an NLP problem P can be modeled by an abstract problem Q if the instance set I is a subset of the set of permissible inputs to P and the solution set S is a subset of the set of possible solutions to P.

2.1 Application Methods

A method for solving an NLP problem P typically consists of two elements:

1. A mathematical model M defining an abstract problem Q that can be used to model P.

2. An algorithm A that effectively computes Q.

We will say that M and A together constitutes an *application method* for problem P with Q as the *model problem*. For example, let G be a context-free grammar intended to model the syntax of a natural language NL and let Q be the parsing problem for G. Then G together with, say, Earley's algorithm is an application method for syntactic analysis of NL with Q as the model problem.

2.2 Acquisition Methods

The term *acquisition method* will be used to refer to any procedure for constructing a mathematical model that can be used in an application method. For example, any procedure for developing a context-free grammar modeling a natural language or a hidden Markov model for part-of-speech tagging is an acquisition method in this sense. In the following, we will concentrate almost exclusively on acquisition methods that make use of machine learning techniques in order to induce models (or model parameters) from empirical data, specifically *corpus* data. An empirical and algorithmic acquisition method typically consists of two elements:

1. A parameterized mathematical model M_θ such that providing values for the parameters θ will yield a mathematical model M that can be used in an application method for some NLP problem P.

2. An algorithm A that effectively computes values for the parameters θ when given a sample of data from P.

If the data sample must contain both inputs and (correct) outputs from P, then A is said to be a *supervised* learning algorithm. If it is sufficient with a sample of inputs, we have an *unsupervised* learning algorithm.

2.3 Evaluation Methods

If acquisition and application methods were infallible, no other methods would be needed. In practice, however, there are many factors which may cause an NLP system to perform less than optimally and we therefore need methods for evaluating NLP systems. We will use the term *evaluation method* to refer to any procedure for evaluating NLP systems. However, the discussion will focus on extrinsic evaluation of systems in terms of their accuracy. For example, let P be an NLP problem, and let (M_1, A_1) and (M_2, A_2) be two different application methods for P. A common way of evaluating and comparing the accuracy of these two methods is to apply them to a representative sample of inputs from P and measure the accuracy of the outputs produced by the respective methods. A special case of this evaluation scheme is where $A_1 = A_2$ and the models M_1 and M_2 are the results of applying two different acquisition methods to the same parameterized model M_θ and training corpus C. In this case, it is primarily the acquisition methods that are being evaluated.

3 Statistical Models and Methods

For the purpose of this paper, we will say that a model or method is *statistical* (or *stochastic*) if it involves the concept of probability (or related notions such as entropy and mutual information) or if it uses concepts of statistical theory (such as statistical estimation and hypothesis testing).

4 Statistical Methods in NLP

4.1 Application Methods

Most examples of statistical application methods in the literature are methods that make use of a stochastic model, but where the algorithm applied to this model is entirely deterministic. Typically, the abstract model problem computed by the algorithm is an *optimization problem* which consists in maximizing the probability of the output given the input. Here are some examples:

- Language modeling for automatic speech recognition using smoothed n-grams to find the most probable string of words $w_1, \ldots, w_n$ out of a set of candidate strings compatible with the acoustic data [Jelinek 1990].

- Part-of-speech tagging using hidden Markov models to find the most probable tag sequence $t_1, \ldots t_n$ given a word sequence $w_1, \ldots w_n$ [Merialdo 1994].

- Syntactic parsing using probabilistic grammars to find the most probable parse tree T given a word sequence $w_1, \ldots, w_n$ (or tag sequence $t_1, \ldots, t_n$) [Stolcke 1995].

- Word sense disambiguation using Bayesian classifiers to find the most probable sense s for word w in context C [Gale *et al* 1992].

- Machine translation using probabilistic models to find the most probable target language sentence T for a given source language sentence S [Brown *et al* 1990a].

4.2 Acquisition Methods

Statistical acquisition methods are methods that rely on *statistical inference* to induce models (or model parameters) from empirical data, in particular corpus data. The model induced may or may not be a stochastic model, which means that there are as many variations in this area as there are different NLP models. We will therefore limit ourselves to a few representative examples:

- Supervised learning of HMM taggers [Merialdo 1994].

- Unsupervised learning of HMM taggers [Cutting *et al* 1992]

- Transformation-based learning [Brill 1995].

- Decision tree parsing [Magerman 1995].

4.3 Evaluation Methods

Evaluation of NLP systems can have different purposes and consider many different dimensions of a system. Consequently, there are a wide variety of methods that can be used for evaluation. Many of these methods involve empirical experiments or quasi-experiments in which the system is applied to a representative sample of data in order to provide quantitative measures of aspects such as efficiency, accuracy and robustness. These evaluation methods can make use of statistics in at least three different ways:

- Descriptive statistics is often used to derive measures such as accuracy rate, recall and precision.

- Statistical estimation may be used to derive confidence intervals for descriptive measures.

- Hypothesis testing may be used to test the significance of any differences found when comparing alternative methods.

5 Conclusion

In this paper, we have discussed three different kinds of methods that are relevant in natural language processing:

- An *application method* is used to solve an NLP problem P, usually by applying an algorithm A to a mathematical model M in order to solve an abstract problem Q approximating P.

- An *acquisition method* for an NLP problem P is used to construct a model M that can be used in an application method for P. Of special interest here are empirical and algorithmic acquisition methods that allow us to construct M from a parameterized model M_θ by applying an algorithm A to a representative sample of P.

- An *evaluation method* for an NLP problem P is used to evaluate application methods for P. Of special interest here are experimental (or empirical) evaluation methods that allow us to evaluate application methods by applying them to a representative sample of P.

We have argued that statistics, in the wide sense including both stochastic models and statistical theory, can play a role in all three kinds of methods and we have supplied numerous examples to substantiate this claim.[1] We have also tried to show that there are many ways in which statistical methods can be combined with traditional linguistic rules and representation, both in application methods and in acquisition methods.

---

[1]More examples will be given in the full paper.

References

[Brill 1995] Brill, E. (1995) Transformation-Based Error-Driven Learning and Natural Language Processing: A Case Study in Part-of-Speech Tagging. *Computational Linguistics*, 21(4), 543–566.

[Brown *et al* 1990a] Brown, P., Cocke, J., Della Pietra, S., Della Pietra, V., Jelinek, F., Lafferty, J., Mercer, R. and Rossin, P. (1990) A Statistical Approach to Machine Translation. *Computational Linguistics* 16(2), 79–85.

[Cutting *et al* 1992] Cutting, D., Kupiec, J., Pedersen, J. and Sibun, P. (1992). A Practical Part-of-speech Tagger. In *Third Conference on Applied Natural Language Processing*, ACL, 133–140.

[Gale *et al* 1992] Gale, W. A., Church, K. W. and Yarowsky, D. (1992) A Method for Disambiguating Word Senses in a Large Corpus. *Computers and the Humanities* 26, 415–439.

[Jelinek 1990] Jelinek, F. (1990) Self-Organized Language Modeling for Speech Recognition. In Waibel, A. and Lee, K.-F. (eds) *Readings in Speech Recognition*, pp. 450–506. Los Altos, CA: Morgan Kaufman.

[Magerman 1995] Magerman, D. (1995) Statistical Decision-Tree Models for Parsing. In *Proceedings of the 33rd Annual Meeting of the Association for Computational Linguistics*, 276–283.

[Merialdo 1994] Merialdo, B. (1994) Tagging English Text with a Probabilistic Model. *Computational Linguistics* 20(2), 155–172.

[Stolcke 1995] Stolcke, A. (1995) An Efficient Probabilistic Context-Free Parsing Algorithm That Computes Prefix Probabilities. *Computational Linguistics* 21(2), 165–202.

Using Linguistic Information to Improve the Performance of Vector-Based Semantic Analysis

Magnus Sahlgren (mange@sics.se)
David Swanberg (davidswanberg@yahoo.com)
RWCP Theoretical Foundation SICS Laboratory
Swedish Institute of Computer Science (SICS), Box 1263, SE-164 29 Kista, Sweden

Abstract

In this paper, we will show that the performance of vector-based semantic analysis can be improved by considering basic linguistic structures in the data— e.g. morphology. For this purpose, we have used a new method for vector-based semantic analysis that computes semantic word vectors based on distributed representations by means of random labeling of words in narrow context windows. This form of representation is more natural than previously reported techniques, and, as we will show, equivalent or even superior in performance when subjected to a standardized synonym test.

Vector-Based Semantic Analysis

The use of vector-based models of information for the purpose of semantic analysis is an area of research that has gained substantial recognition over the last decade. Pioneering techniques such as Latent Semantic Analysis (LSA; Landauer & Dumais, 1997) and Hyperspace Analogue to Language (HAL; Lund & Burgess, 1996) have demonstrated the viability of computing semantic word vectors from the co-occurrence statistics of words in large text data.

However, the prevailing techniques have been almost exclusively statistical, and consequently paid little or no attention to the linguistic structures of the data used in the experiments. This negligence regarding linguistics has, of course, been at least partly deliberate, as one of the primary goals of the techniques has been to develop representations of word meanings from text data "that was minimally preprocessed, not unlike human human-concept acquisition" (Burgess & Lund, 1998).

LSA and HAL are both purely statistical methods that treat the text data simply as a bag-of-words in which the only relevant piece of structural information is the words-by-contexts co-occurrence frequencies. What separates the two approaches is their treatment and conception of *context*. In LSA, the text data is represented as a words-by-documents co-occurrence matrix where each cell indicates the frequency of a given word in a given text sample of approximately 150 words. The frequencies are normalized, and the normalized matrix is transformed with Singular Value Decomposition (SVD) into a smaller matrix with reduced dimensionality. The purpose of using SVD to reduce the dimensions of the normalized frequency matrix is that this operation appears to accomplish inductive effects that capture latent semantic structures in the text data. Words are thus represented in the reduced matrix by semantic vectors of n dimensionality (300 proving to be optimal in Landauer & Dumais' (1997) experiments).

In HAL, the data is represented as a words-by-words co-occurrence matrix where each cell indicates the co-occurrence counts for a single word pair (a word pair being an asymmetrical relation so that "xy" and "yx" represent different entries in the matrix). Each word is thus represented in the matrix by both a row and a column, and these row/column pairs may be concatenated to produce a co-occurrence vector for each word. Assuming an $n \times n$ co-occurrence matrix, words are thus represented as semantic vectors of $2n$ dimensionality.

The point in all of this is that the word vectors capture relative meaning, thereby deserving the epithet "semantic". The semantic content is relative rather than absolute since it is only in relation to each other that the vectors *mean* anything, so semantic similarity between words can be established by comparing the vectors with each other. That the vectors in this way capture word meaning has been verified in a number of experiments where the high-dimensional vectors are used for executing different kinds of linguistic tasks pertaining to semantic knowledge, such as passing a standardized synonym test (Landauer & Dumais, 1997), comparing vector similarities with reaction times from lexical priming studies (Lund & Burgess, 1996), or evaluating the quality of content of student essays on given topics (Landauer, Laham, Rehder & Schreiner, 1997).

Random Indexing

We have studied the use of high-dimensional random distributed representations for accumulating a words-by-contexts co-occurrence matrix from which semantic word vectors can be extracted. In Kanerva, Kristofersson & Holst (2000), 1,800-dimensional semantic word vectors were computed using 1,800-dimensional sparse random *index vectors* representing documents of approximately 150 words each. The index vectors were accumulated into a words-by-contexts matrix by adding a document's index vector to the row for a given word every time the word appeared in that document. This Random Indexing method is comparable to LSA except that the resulting matrix is significantly smaller than the words-by-documents matrix of LSA, since the dimensionality of the index vectors is smaller than the number of documents. By comparison, assuming a vocabulary of 60,000 words divided into 30,000 text samples, LSA would represent the data in a 60,000 × 30,000 words-by-documents matrix, whereas the matrix in Random Indexing would be 60,000 × 1,800, when 1,800-dimensional index vectors are used. This seems to accomplish the same inductive effects as those attained in LSA by applying SVD to the matrix, but in a more efficient way.

In the present experiment, the high-dimensional random vectors of Random Indexing have been used to index words and to calculate semantic word vectors by means of *narrow* context windows consisting of only a few adjacent words on each side of the focus word. As an example, imagine that the number of adjacent words in the context window is set to two. This would imply a window size of five space-separated linguistic units, i.e. the focus word and the two words preceding and succeeding it—a what we may call a "2 + 2 sized" context window. Thus, the context for the word *is* in the sentence *This parrot is no more* would be "This parrot" and "no more," as denoted by:

$$[(\text{This parrot}) \text{ is } (\text{no more})]$$

The reason for using narrow context windows as opposed to whole documents is the assumption that the semantically most significant context is the immediate vicinity of a word. Computing semantic word vectors using random indexing of words in narrow context windows is done by first assigning an n-dimensional sparse random vector called a *random label* to each word type in the text data. These random labels have a small number k of randomly distributed −1s and +1s, with the rest set to 0. The present experiment has utilized 1,800-dimensional random labels with $k = 8.7$ (±2.9). Thus, a label might have, for example, four −1s and five +1s.

Next, every time a given word—the focus word f_n—occurs in the text data, the labels for the words in its context window are added to its *context vector*. For example, assuming a 2 + 2 sized context window as represented by:

$$[(w_{n-2}\ w_{n-1})\ f_n\ (w_{n+1}\ w_{n+2})]$$

the context vector of f_n would be updated with:

$$L(w_{n-2}) + L(w_{n-1}) + L(w_{n+1}) + L(w_{n+2})$$

where $L(x)$ is the random label of x. This summation has also been weighted to reflect the distance of the words to the focus word. The weights were distributed so that the words immediately preceding and succeeding the focus word would get more significance in the computation of the context vectors. For the four different window sizes used in these experiments, the window slots were given weights as follows:

$$1 + 1: [(1)\ 0\ (1)]$$
$$2 + 2: [(0.5, 1)\ 0\ (1, 0.5)]$$
$$3 + 3: [(0.25, 0.5, 1)\ 0\ (1, 0.5, 0.25)]$$
$$4 + 4: [(0.1, 0.1, 0.1, 1)\ 0\ (1, 0.1, 0.1, 0.1)]$$

where the 0 in the middle represents the focus word.

This method is comparable to HAL, except that we use *distributed* representations that are more "brainlike," efficient and scalable. By comparison, assuming a vocabulary of 60,000 words, the HAL vectors would be (2 × 60,000) 120,000-dimensional, whereas our vectors are only 1,800-dimensional, regardless of the size of the vocabulary. Also, we use somewhat smaller context windows to capture the meaning of words. For example, in Burgess & Lund (1998), a context window spanning 10 words were used, whereas we found in our experiments that the performance of the method degrades significantly when the window size exceeds an upper limit of 4 + 4 words.

Introducing Linguistic Information

Up to this point, the only structural relations of language that are utilized in the creation of the context vectors by the above-described techniques are the distributional patterns of linguistic entities. Since there are more complex structural features of language (like morphology and part-of-speech information, e.g.) that may very well be significant for uncovering semantic information, it seems unmotivated not to take these features into account. By introducing linguistic information to the system, we would have the opportunity to investigate whether or not this addition of structural information enhances the performance of vector-based semantic analysis.

First, a naïve form of morphological analysis was tested. By simply truncating the word tokens at a predefined number of letters one would hope to approximate word stems. Truncation lengths of 6, 8, 10 and 12 were investigated. A more reliable and linguistically established way of extracting the word stems of each word token is, of course, to use a parser. In our experiments, the Conexor FDG-parser was used. The point in using morphological analysis is to convert word tokens into word types, thus reducing the vocabulary and thereby compressing the words-by-context matrix. By comparison, the complete vocabulary when no preprocessing has occurred is, in our text data, 94,000 words, and when truncating the words after eight characters 79,000.

In an attempt to resolve problems due to ambiguity, the morphologically analyzed text was also marked with part-of-speech information. Since the system (without linguistic information) is insensitive to different semantic meaning with two or more identical word representations (e.g. the verb and the noun "roll"), it will create the exact same entry in the matrix for them both. By appending to the beginning of every word a part-of-speech tag consisting of one letter, this ambiguity will be remedied. In this way the verb "roll" would be "vroll" and the respective noun would be "nroll," allowing the system to produce different entries in the matrix for the originally same word representations depending on which part-of-speech the representation in question affiliates to.

Evaluation and Results

The technique was evaluated on a ten-million-word balanced corpus of unmarked English with the help of a vocabulary test, TOEFL (Test Of English as a Foreign Language). This is a standardized test employed by, for example, American universities to survey foreign applicants' knowledge of the English language. In the synonym finding part of the test, the test taker is asked to find the synonyms to certain given words. For each given word, a multiple-choice answering suggestion of four alternatives is provided, where one alternative is the intended synonym, and is supposed to be indicated by the test person. In the present experiment, 80 test items of this type have been used.

Table 1: Average results (±1.5) given in percent of correct answers to the TOEFL-test, where Tr. means truncation length, WS means word stems and PoS+WS means part-of-speech tagged word stems.

Linguistic Analysis	Context Window				Average (±0.73)
	1 + 1	2 + 2	3 + 3	4 + 4	
None	64.5	67	65.3	65.5	65.6
Tr. 6	55	57.5	57.3	55.3	56.3
Tr. 8	61.5	64.3	62	63.3	62.8
Tr. 10	66	68.5	66.3	66.3	66.8
Tr. 12	64.8	65.3	63.8	64.8	64.6
WS	63.5	70.8	72	66	68.1
PoS+WS	66	64.5	65	65.5	65.3
Average (±0.56)	63.0	65.4	64.5	63.8	

The numbers in the cells of Table 1 are the average results of five runs. The standard deviation for these results is 1.5. For the average result of each context window, the standard deviation is 0.56, and for the average of each "linguistic parameter" 0.73. All results are given in percent of correct answers to the TOEFL-test. By comparison, tests with LSA on the same text data, using the LSIBIN program from Telecordia Technologies, produced top scores at 600 factors of 58.75% using the unnormalized matrix, and 65% using a normalized one. The average result reported by Landauer & Dumais (1997) with LSA (using normalization and different text data) is 64.4%, and foreign (non-English speaking) applicants to U.S. colleges average 64.5%.

The results from our experiments show that by using high-dimensional random distributed representations to label words in narrow context windows, it is possible to reach a result on a standardized synonym test that is equivalent with the performance of previously reported techniques. Without using linguistic information, the system averages 65.6%. However, when supplying morphological information in the form of carefully applied truncation (using a truncation length of 10 characters), the system's average result increases to 66.8% correct answers. When using stemming of the words, the result is even better, with an average of 68.1% correct answers to the synonym part of TOEFL.

Adding part-of-speech information does not further improve the performance reached when using carefully applied truncation or proper word-stem analysis. The average result when adding part-of-speech information drops to 65.3%. This might be an effect of the increase in the number of unique words in the text data that is the consequence of supplying part-of-speech information for each word.

That the inclusion of morphology in the form of proper word-stem analysis or carefully applied truncation yields the best overall results indicates that taking advantage of other inherent structural relations in text, in addition to the distributional patterns of linguistic entities, really might be significant for uncovering semantic information. We thus conclude that the performance of vector-based semantic analysis benefits from the implementation of linguistic information.

Acknowledgements

We wish to thank Pentti Kanerva, Anders Holst and Jussi Karlgren. This research is funded by Japan's Ministry of International Trade and Industry (MITI) through Real World Computing Partnership (RWCP). The training corpus and 80 TOEFL-test items used in these experiments were provided by courtesy of Professor Thomas Landauer, University of Colorado.

References

Burgess, C. & Lund, K. (1998) The dynamics of meaning in memory. In Dietrich, E. & Markman, A. B. (Eds.), (2000) *Cognitive dynamics: Conceptual change in humans and machines.* Mahwah, NJ: Lawrence Erlbaum Associates.

Kanerva, P., Kristofersson, J. & Holst, A. (2000) Random Indexing of text samples for Latent Semantic Analysis. In Gleitman, L.R. & Josh, A.K. (Eds.), *Proceedings of the 22nd Annual Conference of the Cognitive Science Society* (p. 1036). Mahwah, New Jersey: Erlbaum.

Landauer, T. K. & Dumais, S. T. (1997) A solution to Plato's problem: The Latent Semantic Analysis theory of acquisition, induction and representation of knowledge. *Psychological Review*, 104 (2), pp. 211–240.

Landauer, T. K., Laham, D., Rehder, B., & Schreiner, M. E. (1997) How well can passage meaning be derived without using word order? A comparison of latent semantic analysis and humans. In Shafto, M. G. & Langley, P. (Eds.), *Proceedings of the 19th annual meeting of the Cognitive Science Society* (pp. 412–417). Mawhwah, NJ: Erlbaum.

Lund, K. & Burgess, C. (1996) Producing high-dimensional semantic spaces from lexical co-occurrence. *Behavior Research Methods, Instruments & Computers*, 28 (2), pp. 203–208.

Sylvana Sofkova Hashemi
Department of Linguistics, Göteborg University
sylvana@ling.gu.se

ABSTRACT

This paper reports on the development of a finite state system for finding grammar errors in Swedish text written by children. The writing problems are more frequent for this group and the distribution of the error types is different from texts written by adults. The detection approach involves subtraction of automata that represent two "positive" grammars with varying degree of detail. The difference between the automata corresponds to the search for writing problems that violate the grammars. The constituents of various fragments are identified by the use of lexical-prefix-first strategy and application of incremental parsing. While the grammatical coverage is still rather small, yielding rather large numbers of false alarms, the technique can be applied to agreement phenomena, verb selection phenomena and some word order phenomena. The aim is to include also detection of missing sentence boundaries.

Research and development of grammar checking techniques has been carried out since the 1980's, mainly for English and also for other languages, e. g. French (Chanod, 1993), Dutch (Vosse, 1994), Czech (Kirschner, 1994), Spanish and Greek (Bustamente and León, 1996). In the case of Swedish, the development of grammar checkers started not until the later half of the 1990's with several independent projects, resulting in the first product release in November 1998 - *Grammatifix* (Arppe, 2000; Birn, 2000), now part of the Swedish Microsoft Office 2000.

The work described here is a continuation of a project from this starting period, that explores the use of finite state techniques for grammar checking. The approach differs from the other Swedish projects not only in the choice of technique used, but also in that the grammatical errors are found without any description of the erroneous patterns. The detection process involves partial parsing as writing of "positive" grammars at different accuracy levels that as transducers can be subtracted from each other. The difference between the automata corresponds to the search for writing problems that violate the grammars. Karttunen et al (1996) use this technique to find instances of invalid dates.

The current system, using the *Xerox Finite-State Tool* (XFST) (Karttunen et al, 1997), is divided in four main modules: the lexicon lookup, the grammar, the parser and the error finder. A simple emacs environment is used both for testing and development of finite state grammars. The environment shows the results of an XFST process run on the current emacs buffer in a separate buffer. An XFST mode allows for menus to be used and recompile files in the system.

The analyses of writing problems is based on a corpus of 31 756 words (3 361 word types), composed of (mostly) computer written and hand written essays written by children between 9 to 13 year old. In general, the text structure of the compositions reveals clearly the influence of spoken language and performance difficulties in spelling, segmentation of words, the use of capitals and punctuation, varying both by individuals and age.

In total, 306 grammatical error instances were found in the 134 narratives. The most recurrent grammar problem concerns the omission of finite verb inflection (28%), i. e. when the main finite verb in a clause is in infinitive form and the appropriate present or past tense endings are dropped (a quite usual phenomena in spoken Swedish). Other more frequent grammar problems are wrong choice of a pronoun (15%), wrong pronoun case (8%), extra or missing words (11%), errors in verb chains (6%) and agreement in noun phrases (5 %).

Punctuation problems are also included in the analyses. In general, the use of punctuation varies from no usage at all (mostly among the youngest children) to rather sparse marking. The omission of end of sentence marking is quite obvious problem (35%), but the most frequent punctuation problem concerns the comma (81%).

The lexicon is built as a finite state transducer, using the Xerox tool *Finite-State Lexicon Compiler* (Karttunen, 1993). It takes a string and maps inflected surface form to a tag containing part-of-speech and feature information, e. g. applying the transducer to the string *kvinna* 'woman' will return *[nn utr sin ind nom]*. The word analyser is based on *LEXIN* (58 326 word forms; Skolverket, 1992) and the lexicon developed in Daniel Ridings' lexicon project in the Language Technology Programme, HSFR/NUTEK (100 000 word forms). The network does not handle unknown words. The size of the lexicon is rather small, but the LEXIN-part includes valuable information on valency (see further in Andersson et al, 1998 and 1999).

The system uses a simple lookup without any disambiguation. The reason for that is that the disambiguation heuristics of a tagger may fail with a text that contains errors, because the information needed for the detection of errors is (often) filtered out (see Cooper and Sofkova Hashemi, 1998). The strategy of a lexical lookup which leaves all lexical information present without attempting any disambiguation seems to be the most safe strategy in order to ensure that no information needed is lost.

The grammar module is further subdivided into a *broad grammar* and a *narrow grammar*, that include regular expressions reflecting truths about the grammatical structure of Swedish, differing in the level of detail. For example the simple regular expression in the *broad* grammar:

    define VC [Verb Adv* Verb (Verb)];

recognises potential verb clusters (both grammatical and ungrammatical), consisting of a sequence of two or three verbs in combination with some adverbs (zero or more). On the other hand, the following rules in the *narrow* grammar take into account the internal structure of a verb cluster, i. e. the rules define the grammar of (modal or temporal) auxiliary verbs followed by optional sentence adverb(s) and main verb:

define VC1	[Mod Adv* VerbInf];	*kan (inte) springa* "can (not) run "
define VC2	[Mod Adv* PerfInf VerbSup];	*skall (inte) ha sprungit* "will (not) have run[sup]"
define VC3	[Perf Adv* VerbSup];	*har (nog) sprungit* "have (not) run[sup]"
define VC4	[Perf Adv* ModSup VerbInf];	*har (inte) velat springa* "have (not) want[sup] run[sup]"

The various kinds of constituents are marked out in a text using the lexical-prefix-first method, i. e. parsing first from left margin of a phrase to the head and then extending the phrase by adding on complements.

The actual parsing (based on the broad grammar definitions) is incremental similarly to the methods described in Ait-Mokhtar and Chanod (1997). With this method, the parsing results vary depending on the order in which the various grammatical facts are applied. The system recognises the higher phrases in the first phase (e. g. vp, pp, np) and then applies the second phase in the reverse order (e. g. np, pp, vp). This method gives a greater efficiency and flexibility to the system by decreasing the size of the nets when compiling and that (some) false parses can be blocked.

The error finder is a separate module in the system which means that the grammar and parser could be used directly in a different application. The nets of this module correspond to the difference between the two grammars, broad and narrow. For example, the regular expression:

```
[ "<vc>" [VC - VCgram] "</vc>" ]
```

where VC is the part of the broad grammar describing broad structure of a verb cluster and VCgram is the part of the narrow grammar describing the grammar of auxiliary verbs, will find verb clusters that violate these constraints within the VC-boundaries that have been previously marked out by applying the broad grammar.

So far the technique was used to detect agreement errors in noun phrases, verb selection phenomena (in particular selection of finite and non-finite verb forms in main and subordinate clauses and infinitival complements) and local word order phenomena (e. g. placement of negation). Also some attempts were maid to detect missing sentence boundaries, starting with clause and verb subcategorisation and trying to make use of the valency information stored in the lexicon of the system.

Further, it is possible to use this method to perform error diagnostics. This is achieved by subtraction of small parts of the narrow grammar representing specific constraints that can be violated.

The grammatical coverage of the system is still rather small, yielding a large number of false alarms. There are in general two kinds of false alarms that occur: either because of the "smallness" of grammar for the particular constituents occurring in the phrase, or due a false parse depending either on the ambiguity of constituents or the "wideness" of the parse, i. e. too many constituents are included when applying the longest-match strategy. The following example shows an ambiguous parse:

Linda , brukade ofta vara i stallet.[1]
"Linda , used to be often in the stable."

```
<Error finite verb> <vp><vpHead><np>Linda </np></vpHead></vp>
</Error> , <vp><vpHead> <vc> brukade ofta <np>vara </np> </vc>
</vpHead><pp><ppHead>i </ppHead><np>stallet </np></pp></vp>.
```

---

[1] The example is authentic, including the comma after the proper name 'Linda', that also influence the parsing result, i. e. without the comma 'Linda' would be parsed as part of a verb cluster than a separate verb phrase.

where 'linda' is a proper name and parsed as a noun phrase, but it also is an (infinite) verb in infinitive (*to wrap*) and will then be marked as a verb phrase. Then the error finder marks this phrase as a finite verb error, due the violation of this constraint in the narrow grammar that does not allow any infinite verbs without the presence of a preceding (finite) auxiliary verb or infinitival marker 'att'. Next example shows the effect of the longest-match strategy:

I hålet som pojken hade hittat fanns en mullvad.
"In the hole that the boy had found was a mole."

<pp><ppHead>I </ppHead><np>hålet </np></pp> som <np>pojken </np><vp><vpHead> **<Error verb after Vaux>** <vc>**hade hittat fanns** </vc></Error> </vpHead><np>en mullvad </np></vp>.

where the verb cluster boundary is too wide, including both a verb cluster and a finite verb belonging to the next clause (here missing the appropriate punctuation marking).

Increasing the coverage of the positive grammar will solve some problems with false marking, but also some kind of filtering techniques (e. g. finite state intersection grammar; Tapanainen, 1997) should be involved in the solution of false parsing. However, involving filtering of any kind may also cause that the errors in the text may not be found.

The simple finite state technique of subtraction presented in this paper, has the advantage that the grammars one needs to write to find errors are always positive grammars rather than grammars written to find specific errors. This means that they will find a large class of errors without having to specify them individually. Although the grammatical coverage of the system is rather small, the technique can be applied to detect some kinds of grammar errors. Most of the false alarms depend on the smallness of the grammar, other occur due the ambiguity of the constituents resulting in false parses. Further expansion of the grammatical coverage and some other filtering techniques are needed in order to block the false alarms.

In conclusion, the robustness and modularity of this system makes it possible to perform both error detection and diagnostics and that the grammars can be reused for other applications that do not necessarily have anything to do with error detection, e. g. for educational purposes, speech recognition, and for other users such as dyslectics, aphasics, deaf and foreign speakers.

Ait-Mokhtar, S. and Chanod, J-P. (1997) Incremental Finite-State Parsing. In *Proceedings of ANLP'97*, Washington March 31st to April 3rd, pp. 72-79

Andersson, R., Cooper, R. and Sofkova Hashemi, S. (1998) Finite State Grammar for Finding Grammatical Errors in Swedish Text: a finite-state word analyser, Report-9808. Department of Linguistics, Göteborg University.

Andersson, R., Cooper, R. and Sofkova Hashemi, S. (1999) Finite State Grammar for Finding Grammatical Errors in Swedish Text: a system for finding ungrammatical noun phrases in Swedish text, Report-9903. Department of Linguistics, Göteborg University.

Arppe, A. (2000) Developing a grammar checker for Swedish. In *Proceedings of the 12th Nordic Conference in Computational Linguistics, Nodalida´99.* Department of Linguistics, Norwegian University of Science and Technology, Trondheim, pp. 13-27.

Birn, J. (2000) Detecting grammar errors with Lingsoft's Swedish grammar checker. In *Proceedings of the 12th Nordic Conference in Computational Linguistics, Nodalida´99.* Department of Linguistics, Norwegian University of Science and Technology, Trondheim, pp. 28-40.

Cooper, R. and Sofkova Hashemi, S. (1998) Finite State Grammar for Finding Grammatical Errors in Swedish Text: Report-9809. Department of Linguistics, Göteborg University.

Chanod, J-P. (1993) A Broad-Coverage French Grammar Checker: Some Underlying Principles. In *Proceedings of the Sixth International Conference on Symbolic and Logical Computing.* Dakota State University Madison, South Dakota.

Bustamente, F. R. and León, F. S. (1996) GramCheck: A Grammar and Style Checker. In *Proceedings of the 16th International Conference on Computational Linguistics,* Copenhagen, pp. 175-181.

Karttunen, L. (1993) Finite-State Lexicon Compiler. Technical Report ISTL-NLTT-1993-04-02, Xerox Palo Alto Research center, Palo Alto, California.

Karttunen, L., Chanod, J-P., Grefenstette, G. and Schiller, A. (1996) Regular Expressions for Language Engineering. In Natural Language Engineering 2 (4), pp. 305-328.

Karttunen, L., Gaál, T. and Kempe, A. (1997) Xerox Finite-State Tool. Technical Report Version 6.0.4, Xerox Research Centre Europe, Grenoble, Meylan, France.

Kirschner, Z. (1994) Czecker – a Maquette Grammar-Checker for Czech. In *The Prague Bulletin of Mathematical Linguistics 62*, Prague: Universita Karlova.

Skolverket (1992) Lexin: språklexikon för invandrare. Stockholm: Nordstedts Förlag.

Tapanainen, P. (1997) Applying a Finite-State Intersection Grammar. In Roche, E. and Schabes, Y. (eds.) *Finite-State Language Processing,* The MIT Press.

Vosse, T. (1994) *The Word Connection. Grammar-Based Spelling Error Correction in Dutch.* Doctoral Dissertation. Enschede: Neslia Paniculata.

UplugWeb - Corpus Tools on the Web

Jörg Tiedemann
Department of Linguistics
Uppsala University
Box 527
SE-75120 Uppsala
Sweden
Tel +46 (0)18-471 7007
Fax +46 (0)18-471 1416
joerg@stp.ling.uu.se

15th May 2001

1 Introduction

In this report UplugWeb, a collection of web-based corpus tools, is described. The system applies modules of the Uplug corpus tools that have been developed with a focus on word alignment of parallel texts. UplugWeb provides tools for monolingual texts and for parallel bilingual texts of limited size.

The Uplug system was developed within the co-operative project on parallel corpora PLUG [SH99]. It is a modular system designed for processing text corpora with a focus on parallel texts and word alignment [Tie99a]. Several modules that carry out various tasks of processing textual data have been developed and integrated in the Uplug environment. The main application is the Uppsala Word Aligner, UWA [Tie99b].

The UplugWeb interfaces give external users access to the Uplug corpus tools without a local installation of the system. It allows external users to run UWA processes on texts of limited size and the results of the process are returned to the user on the web, as well as by e-mail.

2 The System

The UplugWeb tools provide interfaces for running sub-systems of UWA, which might be of interest even as stand-alone tasks, such as phrase generation and morphological pattern recognition. UplugWeb also includes interfaces for running the complete word alignment process on small-size bitexts. A module for sentence alignment has been integrated in the Uplug environment as well. The results are sent to the user via e-mail on demand. Time-consuming tasks (such as word alignment) run as background processes. In such cases, the UplugWeb interface prints a message about the processing queue in which the tasks were scheduled and the results are sent by e-mail.

The following tools are included in UplugWeb:

Bilingual Sentence Alignment: The Uplug sentence aligner applies the approach proposed by Gale and Church ([GC93]) modified and adjusted to the requirements at Uppsala University [TKS96]. The sentence aligner takes two plain text files as its input and converts them to sentence aligned bitexts with SGML markup in conformity with the TEI standard [SMB94].

Bilingual Word Alignment: The UplugWeb word aligner applies the Uppsala word aligner (UWA). UWA produces two kinds of output: token links and type links. Token links include all word and phrase instances that have been aligned in the text, i.e. token pairs including information about the origin in the text in form of byte spans and segment identifiers. Type links are compiled from token links and comprise unique word or phrase pairs including their linking frequency.

Generation of Word Collocations: Phrase generation is one of the pre-processing tasks in word alignment by UWA (assuming static segmentation) [Tie00]. However, this task might also be interesting as a stand-alone process. The phrase generation module takes a monolingual plain text file as its input and generates significant word collocations. The process is iterative starting with bigrams. Significance is measured by means of co-occurrence metrics such as Mutual Information, Dice, or t-scores. The generation applies additionally a list of phrase boundary words in order to improve the result. The system will use automatically generated lists of stop word if necessary.

Generation of Morphological Pattern: The generation of morphological patterns is based on investigations of string similarity between wordforms in a monolingual corpus. Based on matching and non-matching parts, the system tries to compute common patterns for various word groups. Similarity measures and types of dissimilarity (suffix, prefix, and/or infix) can be adjusted according to the users needs. Similar words are clustered into (morphological) categories with the affix pattern attached.

Handling Web Processes: The system takes care of the processing queue in such a way that simultaneous tasks do not block each other and that the local web server is not overloaded by the UplugWeb system.

Handling Bilingual Corpora: UplugWeb includes tools for exploring bilingual texts and word alignment results. Submitted bitexts will be stored in the UplugWeb database and the user can search for bilingual concordances in the complete collection. Furthermore, it is possible to "hide" corpora from other users ("private" corpora). Word alignment results will be stored in a general link database that can be searched by the users. UplugWeb includes an interface for exploring word alignments related to their origin.

3   Results

Results of the tools as described above are not presented in this abstract. Texts of different types in several languages have been processed by the UplugWeb toolbox for small-scale tests and evaluation.

4 Conclusions

The UplugWeb interfaces are intended for demonstration purposes. They represent a small-scale version of the Uplug corpus tools. The web-processes are restricted to small-sized corpora and the performance depends on the load on the local web-server. Access to the web-interfaces is restricted by web-authorization as a means of controlling the number of users. The UplugWeb toolbox can be used for educational purposes and for small-size applications.

References

[GC93]   W. A. Gale and K. W. Church. A Program for Aligning Sentences in Bilingual Corpora. *Computational Linguistics*, 19:75–102, 1993.

[SH99]   Anna Sågvall Hein. The PLUG Project: Parallel corpora in Linköping, Uppsala, and Göteborg: Aims and achievements. Technical Report 16, Department of Linguistics, University of Uppsala, 1999.

[SMB94] C.M. Sperberg-McQueen and Lou Burnard.   Guidelines for Electronic text Encoding and Interchange.   Availabe from http://etext.virginia.edu/TEI.html, 1994.

[Tie99a] Jörg Tiedemann.   Automatic Construction of Weighted String Similarity Measures. In *Proceedings of the Joint SIGDAT Conference on Empirical Methods in Natural Language Processing and Very Large Corpora (EMNLP/VLC)*, Department of Linguistics, Uppsala University, Sweden, 1999.

[Tie99b] Jörg Tiedemann.   Uplug - a modular corpus tool for parallel corpora. Technical Report 17, Department of Linguistics, University of Uppsala, 1999.

[Tie00]   Jörg Tiedemann.   Exatracting Phrasal Terms using Bitexts. In *Proceedings of the Workshop on Terminology Resources and Computation, in connection with LREC-2000*, pages 57–63, Athens, Greece, 2000. European Language Resources Association.

[TKS96] Erik F. Tjong Kim Sang. Aligning the Scania Corpus. Technical report, Department of Linguistics, University of Uppsala, 1996.

A   URL's

Uplug Main Page

http://stp.ling.uu.se/~joerg/uplug

Links to Private Pages

http://stp.ling.uu.se/~joerg/uplug/PrivateHomeName.html

Sentence Alignment

http://stp.ling.uu.se/~joerg/uplug/SentAlign.html

Word Alignment

http://stp.ling.uu.se/~joerg/uplug/UwaWeb.html
http://stp.ling.uu.se/~joerg/uplug/UwaWeb_tei.html
http://stp.ling.uu.se/~joerg/uplug/UwaWebPro.html
http://stp.ling.uu.se/~joerg/uplug/UwaWebPro_tei.html

Phrase Generation

http://stp.ling.uu.se/~joerg/uplug/GenPhrases.html
http://stp.ling.uu.se/~joerg/uplug/GenPhrasesPro.html

Morphological Pattern Generation

http://stp.ling.uu.se/~joerg/uplug/GenMorph.html
http://stp.ling.uu.se/~joerg/uplug/GenMorphPro.html

Query Tools

http://stp.ling.uu.se/~joerg/uplug/SearchLinks.html
http://stp.ling.uu.se/cgi-bin/joerg/uplug/SearchLinkDB.pl
http://stp.ling.uu.se/cgi-bin/joerg/uplug/UserCorpora.pl

Parsing Swedish

Atro Voutilainen
Conexor oy
atro.voutilainen@conexor.fi

This paper presents two new systems for analysing Swedish texts: a light parser and a functional dependency grammar parser. Their design follows two Helsinki-based frameworks: Constraint Grammar CG (Karlsson & al 1995) and Functional Dependency Grammar FDG (Tapanainen and Järvinen 1997).

CG and FDG

CG is a reductionistic constraint rule formalism whose input is lexically analysed ambiguous text and whose output is disambiguated text. Disambiguation is carried out by constraints on lemmas and tags that discard alternative analyses on the basis of contextual information, typically coded by a linguist. The ENGCG morphosyntactic tagger was introduced in 1992 (Voutilainen & al.) and compared with a state-of-the-art statistical tagger in 1997 (Samuelsson & Voutilainen).

CG was successful in word-class tagging but not adequate for full-scale parsing. A considerable effort on finite-state parsing was made by Koskenniemi, Tapanainen and Voutilainen (see their articles in Roche & Schabes, eds., 1997). A more successful effort was made by Tapanainen and Järvinen, who extended CG into a functional dependency grammar formalism and interpreter/compiler capable of introducing explicit functional dependencies and of applying large grammars efficiently.

Earlier work on Swedish tagging and parsing

As discussed in Voutilainen (forthcoming 2001), most efforts at Swedish tagging and parsing have focused on wordclass tagging, mostly in the statistical paradigm. A somewhat more informative analysis is given by Lingsoft's SWECG (morphology + function tags) and shallow finite-state Abney-style parsers (Kokkinakis & Johansson 1999). The Swedish Core Language Engine (Gambäck 1997) produces full syntactic parses, but, as argued by Gambäck, it seems to work only for texts from very restricted domains.

Swedish Light Syntax

In design, SweLite follows Conexor's EngLite (see demo at www.conexor.fi). The first major component is the morphological analyser, based on a recent extension of Koskenniemi's Two-Level formalism. The analyser contains a large lexicon, morphology and guesser for unknown words. The morphological analyser produces analyses, many of them ambiguous. The parser uses mapping statements to introduce light syntactic ambiguity, so before any disambiguation is done, an ambiguous analysis looks like this:

```
"<tvingas>"
      "tvinga" <Pass> V INF &MV
      "tvinga" <Pass> V PRES &MV
      "tving#as" <Neu> <Indef> N SG/PL NOM &>N &NH
      "tv#in|gas" <Utr> <Indef> N SG NOM &>N &NH
```

Morphological alternatives are given on lines of their own; syntactic ambiguity is shown as the occurrence of several syntactic tags (here: *&MV* = main verb; *&NH* = nominal head; *&>N* = premodifier). Disambiguation is carried out with hand-coded contextual constraints. Here is a sample parse in tabular format:

```
Man          man          &NH PRON SG NOM
ställer       ställa        &MV V PRES
upp          upp          &AH ADV
verkligt      verkligt      &>A ADV
höga         hög          &>N A NOM
mål          mål          &NH N NOM

,            ,
som          som          &NH PRON NOM
tränarna      tränare       &NH N PL NOM
och          och          &CC CC
skidåkarna    skid#åkare     &NH N PL NOM
tvingas       tvinga        &MV V PRES
leva         leva         &MV V INF
med          med          &AH ADV     &AH PREP
.            .
```

On the basis of light syntactic tags and morphology, identification of basic linguistic entities, e.g. nominal phrases, is possible. Identifying relations between the entities requires more information.

Swedish FDG

Tapanainen and Järvinen (1997) give examples of indexing rules whereby functional dependencies between words can be introduced. In the best case, a successful grammar gives a complete dependency structure; in practice many sentences receive only partial dependencies (e.g. due to gaps in the grammar or structural peculiarities in the sentence).

A dependency grammar was written for Swedish. The goal of the present grammar is to show the main nominal arguments as well as relations between clauses. The functional description of adverb phrases and prepositional phrases (e.g. agent, source, goal, benefactive, time) remains to be described in a future version.

Here is a sample parse for a newspaper sentence (`One puts up really high goals that trainers and skiers are forced to live with.'):

```
1    Man          man          subj:>2        PRON SG NOM &NH
2    ställer       ställa        main:>0        V PRES &MV
3    upp          upp          advl:>2        ADV &AH
4    verkligt      verkligt      ad:>5          ADV &>A
5    höga         hög          attr:>6        A NOM &>N
6    mål          mål          obj:>2         N NOM &NH
7    ,            ,
8    som          som          pcomp:>14      PRON NOM &NH
9    tränarna      tränare       subj:>12       N PL NOM &NH
10   och          och          cc:>9          CC &CC
11   skidåkarna    skid#åkare     cc:>9          N PL NOM &NH
12   tvingas       tvinga        mod:>6         V PRES &MV
13   leva         leva         obj:>12        V INF &MV
```

14	med	med	advl:>13	PREP &AH
15	.	.		

Column 5 contains morphology and light syntax; column 4 shows functional dependencies. For instance, the pronoun *Man* acts as subject for word number 2, *ställer*. Functional dependencies are not given for every word; partial dependencies result in the analysis of sentences where the grammar or lexicon is incomplete or mispredictive. In practice, around 70% of `normal' nonfiction utterances get a complete dependency analysis (i.e. every word in the sentence gets a regent); the remaining sentences get partial dependencies to enable at least some level of usefulness for further processing e.g. in knowledge-intensive applications.

Let us look at a few other sentences. First, an example of coordination (`The old dog and the young cat eat breakfast and then sleep on the mat.'):

0				
1	Den	den	det:>3	DET SG NOM &>N
2	gamla	gammal	attr:>3	A NOM &>N
3	hunden	hund	subj:>8	N SG NOM &NH
4	och	och	cc:>3	CC &CC
5	den	den	det:>7	DET SG NOM &>N
6	unga	ung	attr:>7	A NOM &>N
7	katten	katt	cc:>3	N SG NOM &NH
8	äter	äta	main:>0	V PRES &MV
9	frukost	frukost	obj:>8	N SG NOM &NH
10	och	och	cc:>8	CC &CC
11	sedan	sedan	advl:>12	ADV &AH
12	sover	sova	cc:>8	V PRES &MV
13	på	på	advl:>12	PREP &AH
14	mattan	matta	pcomp:>13	N SG NOM &NH
15	.	.		

Two coordinations are involced: the subjects *Den gamla hunden och den unga katten* and the clauses (verbs) *äter frukost och sedan sover*. In both cases, the first coordinated element is treated as a regent: it bears the function of the coordination and enters a dependency relation with another word. So, for example, *hunden* is labelled as a dependent (subject) of word number 8, *äter*. The coordinating conjunction and non-initial coordinates are regarded as dependents (coordination) of the first coordinate, so for instance words number 4 and 7 are regarded as dependents of *hunden*. Likewise, word number 10 *och* and 12 *sover* are shown as dependents of word number 8 *äter*.

Next, let us look at a complex sentence (from the Finnish *Hufvudstadsbladet* newspaper), *En fransk regeringstalesman meddelade att rapporten nu skickas till tretton EU-länders regeringar, som diskuterar vad man skall göra beträffande sanktionerna.* (`A French government speaker told that the report will now be sent to governments of thirteen EU countries that will discuss what one will do concerning the sanctions.')

0				
1	En	en	det:>3	DET SG NOM &>N
2	fransk	fransk	attr:>3	A SG NOM &>N
3	regeringstalesman	regerings#talesman	subj:>4	N SG NOM &NH
4	meddelade	meddela	main:>0	V PAST &MV
5	att	att	pm:>8	CS &CS
6	rapporten	rapport	subj:>8	N SG NOM &NH

7	nu	nu	advl:>8	ADV &AH
8	skickas	skicka	obj:>4	V PRES &MV
9	till	till	advl:>8	PREP &AH
10	tretton	tretton	attr:>11	<Card> NUM PL NOM &>N
11	EU-länders	EU-#land	attr:>12	N PL GEN &>N
12	regeringar	regering	pcomp:>9	N PL NOM &NH
13	,	,		
14	som	som	subj:>15	PRON NOM &NH
15	diskuterar	diskutera	mod:>12	V PRES &MV
16	vad	vad	obj:>19	PRON NOM &NH
17	man	man	subj:>18	PRON SG NOM &NH
18	skall	skall	v-ch:>19	V PRES &AUX
19	göra	göra	obj:>15	V INF &MV
20	beträffande	beträffande	advl:>19	PREP &AH
21	sanktionerna	sanktion	pcomp:>20	N PL NOM &NH
22	.	.		

This sentence starts with a main clause *En fransk regeringstalesman meddelade* whose nucleus *meddelade* is linked to the axiom. One of the dependents of *meddelade* is the object clause *att rapporten nu skickas till tretton EU-länders regeringar..*; this object status is shown by the functional dependency of *skickas*. This object clause itself is a complex one: a modifier clause *som diskuterar..* is revealed as such by *mod:>12* for *diskuterar*. This verb governs the nominal clause *vad man skall göra beträffande sanktionerna*; this nominal clause is given the status of object, as shown by *obj:>15* for *göra*.

Note in passing that the topicalised object *vad* is described correctly as such; as shown by Tapanainen and Järvinen, the present formalism is suitable for the description of non-projective phenomena as well, which are problematic for several other frameworks (e.g. Link Grammar).

An informal evaluation

The Swedish FDG parser (a development version from 30. 4. 2001) was tested against newspaper articles (6149 words, 406 sentences, 2.-3. 5. 2001) from *Hufvudstadsbladet* and *Dagens Nyheter*. To allow some degree of comparison to another system (Tapanainen and Järvinen 1997), the parser's ability to identify the heads of subjects (S), objects (O) and subject complements (SC) and to link them to their proper regents (main verbs) was measured in terms of precision (the ratio **obtained desired analyses / all obtained analyses * 100**) and recall (the ratio **obtained desired analyses / all desired analyses * 100**).

This evaluation was carried out by examining the (visual) output of the parser, so some correct and incorrect or partial analyses may have remained undetected. I believe even this evaluation gives a reasonably realistic picture of the system's ability to identify these categories. Here are the results (Tapanainen and Järvinen's corresponding results are given in parentheses):

	precision	**recall**
S	98% (95%)	92% (83%)
O	95% (94%)	90% (88%)
SC	97% (92%)	95% (96%)

The Swedish parser seems to be less 'prudent' than the English one; there are more complete dependencies (i.e. every word gets a regent in the sentence) in the analyses. This probably shows in the higher recall of the Swedish system. Maybe contrary to expectations, also the precision of the Swedish system appears to be higher, though with a smaller margin (with the exception of SC).

Of course, one should interpret this comparison with a grain of salt: the evaluation methodology was somewhat informal in both experiments; the functional categories may contain some slight differences; and the texts and languages are not quite identical, either.

Another way of looking at the parser's ability to analyse these main nominal FDs is to compare the number of sentences with S/O/SC to sentences with completely correct S/O/SC analyses. In this data, there were 371 sentences with at least one S or O or SC; of these sentences, 291 (78%) received a faultless analysis as far as functional dependency analysis of S/O/SC goes; each of the remaining 80 sentences contained at least one incomplete or incorrect S/O/SC analysis.

Technical information

The Swedish FDG parser is fast: on a fast PC with Linux, it analyses well over a thousand words per second. The Swedish Lite parser is about 2.5 times faster than FDG.

Both systems, like Conexor's analysers for other languages (English, French, German, Spanish, Finnish) are available for Linux, Sun Solaris, WIN/NT (COM) and Java.

The Swedish parsers become testable on-line at http://www.conexor.fi during the summer of 2001.

References

Björn Gambäck. 1997. *Processing Swedish Sentences: A Unification-Based Grammar and some Applications*. The Royal Institute of Technology and Stockholm University.

Fred Karlsson, Atro Voutilainen, Juha Heikkilä and Atro Anttila (Eds.) 1995. *Constraint Grammar. A language-independent system for parsing unrestricted text*. Mouton de Gruyter.

Kokkinakis D. and Johansson Kokkinakis S. (1999), A Cascaded Finite-State Parser for Syntactic Analysis of Swedish, *EACL'99*.

Three articles (Koskenniemi, Tapanainen, Voutilainen) in Emmanuel Roche and Yves Schabes (Eds.), *Finite State Language Processing*. MIT Press.

Christer Samuelsson and Atro Voutilainen 1997. Comparing a Linguistic and a Stochastic Tagger. *EACL-ACL'97*.

Pasi Tapanainen and Timo Järvinen 1997. A non-projective dependency parser. *ANLP'97*.

Atro Voutilainen, Juha Heikkilä and Arto Anttila 1992. *English Constraint Grammar*. Dept. of General Linguistics, University of Helsinki. Publications 21.

Towards a Discourse-Oriented Representation of Information Structure in HPSG

Graham Wilcock
Dept of General Linguistics, University of Helsinki
00014 Helsinki, Finland
`gwilcock@ling.helsinki.fi`

1   A Syntax-Oriented Representation

A representation for information structure in HPSG was proposed by Engdahl
& Vallduví (1996). Arguing that information structure is a distinct dimension,
which should not be associated only with phonology, only with syntax, or only
with semantics, they propose that a feature INFO-STRUCT (which includes
FOCUS and GROUND, the latter including LINK and TAIL) should be located
within the CONTEXT feature in the HPSG framework.

However, the specific representation which they use is syntactic: LINK and
FOCUS are equated with the syntactic constituents (NPs and VPs) which re-
alize the topic concept and the focus information. As the primary concern of
Engdahl & Vallduví (1996) is with information *packaging*, this has the advantage of facilitating the description of the realization of information structure
(by intonation in English, by word order in Catalan), but it has the major disadvantage that the packaging is only indirectly tied to the information which
is packaged, which is itself part of the semantic content.[1]

This syntax-based representation of information structure enables the distinction between narrow focus and wide focus to be represented. Example (1)
can be interpreted either with narrow focus on the object noun phrase or with
wide focus on the whole verb phrase.

(1)   The president [F hates [F the Delft china set]].

To represent these alternatives, the value of FOCUS at higher nodes (S
and VP) is equated with the smaller syntactic constituent (the object NP) to
represent the narrow focus reading, or with the larger syntactic constituent (the
whole VP) to represent the wide focus reading, as shown by examples (17) and
(18) of Engdahl & Vallduví (1996).

This would be an elegant way to capture the narrow and wide focus readings.
However, there are a number of cases where informational partitioning does not
correspond to syntactic constituency. Among the examples given by Engdahl
& Vallduví are subject-verb focus (3) and complex focus (4):

---

[1] In a footnote, Engdahl and Vallduví themselves suggest that it would be more appropriate
for the value of INFO-STRUCT to be structure-shared with the CONTENT information.

(2)   What happened to the china set? [F The BUTLER BROKE] the set.

(3)   Who did your friends introduce to whom?
      John introduced BILL to SUE, and **Mike**...

To handle these examples, Engdahl & Vallduví change the representation so
that set values will be used: the value of FOCUS will not be a single syntactic
constituent which exactly spans the focus scope, but an otherwise arbitrary
set of syntactic constituents which together make up the relevant sequence of
words. The representation thereby loses its initial elegance. With this change,
examples (1) and (2) will have a singleton set value for FOCUS, and set values
will also be used for LINK and TAIL.

2   A Semantics-Oriented Representation

We now examine a different approach to information structure, based on the
practical requirements of dialogue modelling in robust dialogue system projects.
These requirements appear to support a closer link between the information
structure representation and the semantic representation. Dialogue responses
need to be generated from the semantic information. Old and new discourse
referents need to be distinguished, and referents are usually identified by indices
in the semantic representation. In addition, topic continuities and topic shifts
need to be tracked, and the topics are also identified by semantic indices, even
when a topic is some kind of event.

As an example of this approach we take the dialogue modelling framework
used in PLUS (Pragmatics-based Language Understanding System), described
by Jokinen (1994). In PLUS, the semantic representation consists of flat quasi-
logical forms with simple indices for discourse referents. The dialogue manager
component takes account of information structure and decides what semantic
representations to supply to the generator. Jokinen defines **Topic** as a distinguished discourse entity which is talked about, and which is an instantiated
World Model concept. **NewInfo** is a concept or property value which is *new*
with respect to some Topic. The representation for both is based directly on
the semantic representation. Jokinen gives an example from PLUS (Topics are
in italics, NewInfo bold-faced):

(4)   User: *I need a car.*
      System: Do you want to **buy or rent** *one?*
      User: **Rent**. (topic: *car*)
      System: **Where?** (topic: *rent*)
      User: In **Bolton**. (topic: *rent*)

      ...

Jokinen (1994) explains that in the first system contribution in (4), NewInfo
is the disjunction 'buy or rent', which has the representation:

(5)   Goal: know(s,[wantEvent(w,u,d),disj(d,b,r),
            buyEvent(b,u,c,_),hireEvent(r,u,c,_),car(c),user(u)])
      NewInfo: disj(d,b,r)

Compared with the syntax-oriented representation of information structure, this semantics-oriented representation appears to have the advantage of facilitating topic tracking and distinguishing old and new referents, due to the direct use of semantic indices (c = *car*, r = *rent*, etc.). Further examples of its use in practical dialogue modelling are described by Jokinen (1994).

Although many examples of narrow and wide focus could be elegantly represented in this approach, simply by NewInfo taking the appropriate index value, other examples cannot be represented by a single semantic index: if *hates* has semantic index h, the wide VP focus reading in (1) would need NewInfo to be both h and s. It is not possible to unify these indices, because the hating event (h) and the china set (s) are ontologically distinct items. The conclusion is that the value of NewInfo should be a *set* of indices, giving representations like those sketched in (6) (narrow NP focus) and (7) (wide VP focus):

(6)   Semantics: hateEvent(h,p,s),president(p),Delft(s),china(s),set(s)
       NewInfo: {s}

(7)   Semantics: hateEvent(h,p,s),president(p),Delft(s),china(s),set(s)
       NewInfo: {h,s}

The kind of flat quasi-logical form used in PLUS has the disadvantage that it lacks an adequate treatment of quantifier scope. An approach has been developed in Minimal Recursion Semantics (Copestake, Flickinger & Sag 1997) in the HPSG framework to provide a solution to this problem. Basically, MRS is a flat indexed quasi-logical form like the one used in PLUS, but MRS has typed feature structures as used throughout HPSG.

The representation for quantifier scoping in MRS is achieved by the use of *handles*, extra identifiers that are unified with the role arguments of other relations. This technique not only enables recursive embedding to be simulated, but also allows quantifier scope to be either fully resolved or underspecified. We give an example from Copestake et al. (1997) using their linear notation to save space. The unscoped representation of *every dog chased some cat* is:

(8)   1:every($x,3,n$), 3:dog(x), 7:cat(y), 5:some($y,7,m$), 4:chase(e,x,y)

       top handle: p

Here 1, 3, 4, 5, 7 are handles and m, n and p are variables over handles. This unscoped representation can be further instantiated to give scoped representations by unifying m, n and p with the appropriate handles:

(9)   1:every($x,3,4$), 3:dog(x), 7:cat(y), 5:some($y,7,1$), 4:chase(e,x,y)

       top handle: 5 (wide scope *some*)

(10)   1:every($x,3,5$), 3:dog(x), 7:cat(y), 5:some($y,7,4$), 4:chase(e,x,y)

       top handle: 1 (wide scope *every*)

The top handle allows the clause to be embedded in a longer sentence. In the scoped representations, it is unified with the widest scoped quantifier.

3 Towards a Discourse-Oriented Representation

We have described both a syntax-oriented approach and a semantics-oriented approach, but our aim is to move towards a discourse-oriented approach to information structure. If information structure is a distinct dimension, as argued by Engdahl & Vallduví (1996), its representation should not be too closely tied to either syntax or semantics. This has long been a fundamental assumption in functionally-oriented approaches such as Systemic Functional Grammar.

For example, Teich (1998) illustrates how focus scope is handled by SFG. In the *function structures* in (10) and (11) there is a syntax-oriented layer (Subject-Finite-Object), a semantics-oriented layer (Actor-Process-Goal), and **two** other layers of discourse-oriented information.

<table>
<tr><td>(11)</td><td>
<table>
<tr><td>Actor</td><td>Process</td><td>Goal</td></tr>
<tr><td>Theme</td><td colspan="2">Rheme</td></tr>
<tr><td>Given</td><td colspan="2">New</td></tr>
<tr><td>Subject</td><td>Finite</td><td>Object</td></tr>
<tr><td>*Fred*</td><td colspan="2">*ate the beans*</td></tr>
</table>
</td><td>(12)</td><td>
<table>
<tr><td>Actor</td><td>Process</td><td>Goal</td></tr>
<tr><td>Theme</td><td colspan="2">Rheme</td></tr>
<tr><td colspan="2">Given</td><td>New</td></tr>
<tr><td>Subject</td><td>Finite</td><td>Object</td></tr>
<tr><td colspan="2">*Fred ate*</td><td>*the beans*</td></tr>
</table>
</td></tr>
</table>

However, we noted that the semantics-oriented approach had advantages in topic-tracking and distinguishing old and new referents due to its direct use of semantic indices. A representation for use in practical dialogue systems, while not directly tied to either syntax or semantics, should nevertheless be relatively close to the semantic information. We therefore take the MRS representation as a starting point for a representation of information structure in HPSG, but follow Engdahl & Vallduví (1996) in locating INFO-STRUCT in CONTEXT.

To avoid confusion, we also follow Engdahl & Vallduvi's feature terminology: INFO-STRUCT includes FOCUS and GROUND, and GROUND includes LINK and TAIL. However, the values of FOCUS, LINK and TAIL will not be syntactic constituents, they will be variables over handles. These variables will be unified with particular handles in the semantics in order to represent specific focus scopings and topic interpretations. An advantage of handles is that they can be unified with each other without implying that semantic entities lose their distinct identities. However, we will follow the earlier approaches and use set values. In our representation, these will be sets of handles.

We start by adding information structure to the MRS quantifier example of Copestake et al. (1997), *every dog chased some cat*. If we assume a context (perhaps *what did every dog chase?*) in which *every dog* is interpreted as link, and *some cat* has narrow focus, we can use a representation such as:

(13) 1:every(x,3,4), 3:dog(x), 7:cat(y), 5:some(y,7,1), 4:chase(e,x,y)

     TOP-HANDLE:5, LINK:{1}, TAIL:{4}, FOCUS:{5}

By contrast, if we assume a context (perhaps *what did every dog do?*) in which there is wide focus across *chased some cat*, we need to include handles 4 and 5 in the value of FOCUS, giving:

(14) 1:every(x,3,5), 3:dog(x), 7:cat(y), 5:some(y,7,4), 4:chase(e,x,y)

     TOP-HANDLE:1, LINK:{1}, FOCUS:{4,5}

We now sketch new representations of some of the examples of Engdahl &
Vallduví (1996). The alternative focus scope readings of example (1) can be
represented by (15) (narrow focus) and (16) (wide focus):

(15) 1:the(x,2), 2:president(x), 3:the(y,4), 4:china(y), 4:set(y), 5:hate(e,x,y)

      TOP-HANDLE:5, LINK:{1}, TAIL:{5}, FOCUS:{3} (narrow focus)

(16) 1:the(x,2), 2:president(x), 3:the(y,4), 4:china(y), 4:set(y), 5:hate(e,x,y)

      TOP-HANDLE:5, LINK:{1}, FOCUS:{3,5} (wide focus)

Example (21) of Engdahl & Vallduví (1996), *The president* [F HATES] *the
Delft china set*, is of course:

(17) 1:the(x,2), 2:president(x), 3:the(y,4), 4:china(y), 4:set(y), 5:hate(e,x,y)

      TOP-HANDLE:5, LINK:{1}, TAIL:{3}, FOCUS:{5}

The problematic subject-verb focus in example (2), [F *The* BUTLER BROKE]
the set, can be represented by:

(18) 1:the(x,2), 2:butler(x), 3:the(y,4), 4:set(y), 5:break(e,x,y)

      TOP-HANDLE:5, TAIL:{3}, FOCUS:{1,5}

Using the NAME relation of Copestake et al. (1997), the complex focus in
example (3) can be represented by:

(19) 1:NAME(x,John), 2:NAME(y,Bill), 3:NAME(z,Sue), 5:introduce(e,x,y,z)

      TOP-HANDLE:5, LINK:{1}, TAIL:{5}, FOCUS:{2,3}

Finally, the PLUS example in (4), *Do you want to* **buy or rent** *one?* might
possibly be represented by:

(20) 1:want(w,u,2) 2:or(3,4) 3:buy(b,u,c) 4:rent(r,u,c) 5:car(c), 6:user(u)

      TOP-HANDLE:1, LINK:{1}, TAIL:{5}, FOCUS:{2}

References

Copestake, A., Flickinger, D. & Sag, I. A. (1997), Minimal Recursion Semantics:
An Introduction, Ms. Stanford University.

Engdahl, E. & Vallduví, E. (1996), Information packaging in HPSG, *in*
C. Grover & E. Vallduví, eds, *Edinburgh Working Papers in Cognitive
Science, Vol. 12: Studies in HPSG*, University of Edinburgh, pp. 1–32.

Jokinen, K. (1994), Response Planning in Information-Seeking Dialogues, PhD
thesis, University of Manchester Institute of Science and Technology.

Teich, E. (1998), Types of syntagmatic grammatical relations and their representation, *in Processing of Dependency-based Grammars: Proceedings of
the Workshop, COLING-ACL'98*, Montreal.

AUTHOR INDEX